THE
WEXFORD

917.132043 Car

Carroll, P.
The Wexford.

PRICE: $30.00 (3559/he   )

A classic photo of the Wexford, *showing the "romance" of the* Wexford *profile. The photo, originally from the late Dr. William "Bill" N. Watters, has been enhanced by Captain "Bud" Robinson.*

From the author's collection.

THE WEXFORD

Elusive Shipwreck of the Great Storm, 1913

PAUL CARROLL

NATURAL HERITAGE BOOKS
A MEMBER OF THE DUNDURN GROUP
TORONTO

Copyright © Paul Carroll, 2010

All rights reserved. No part of this publication may be reproduced, stored in a retrieval system, or transmitted in any form or by any means, electronic, mechanical, photocopying, recording, or otherwise (except for brief passages for purposes of review) without the prior permission of Dundurn Press. Permission to photocopy should be requested from Access Copyright.

Published by Natural Heritage Books
A Member of The Dundurn Group

Editor: Jane Gibson
Copy Editor: Allison Hirst
Design: Jennifer Scott
Printer: Transcontinental

Library and Archives Canada Cataloguing in Publication

Carroll, Paul, 1944-
        The Wexford : elusive shipwreck of the great storm, 1913 / by Paul Carroll.

Includes bibliographical references and index.
ISBN 978-1-55488-736-1

        1. Wexford (Ship). 2. Shipwrecks--Huron, Lake (Mich. and Ont.). I. Title.

G530.W49C37 2010   917.13'2043   C2009-907475-3

1   2   3   4   5   14   13   12   11   10

  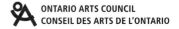

We acknowledge the support of the Canada Council for the Arts and the Ontario Arts Council for our publishing program. We also acknowledge the financial support of the Government of Canada through the Canada Book Fund and The Association for the Export of Canadian Books, and the Government of Ontario through the Ontario Book Publishers Tax Credit program, and the Ontario Media Development Corporation.

Care has been taken to trace the ownership of copyright material used in this book. The author and the publisher welcome any information enabling them to rectify any references or credits in subsequent editions.

J. Kirk Howard, President

Printed and bound in Canada.
www.dundurn.com

Front cover image: *The Last Sighting*, oil, 2000, artist Captain C. "Bud" Robinson.
Back cover image: *The Goderich Lighthouse, circa 1880*, watercolour, 2000, artist Paul Carroll.

Dundurn Press	Gazelle Book Services Limited	Dundurn Press
3 Church Street, Suite 500	White Cross Mills	2250 Military Road
Toronto, Ontario, Canada	High Town, Lancaster, England	Tonawanda, NY
M5E 1M2	LA1 4XS	U.S.A. 14150

This lamentable tale of the *Wexford* shipwreck is dedicated to the memory of thousands of mariners, especially those unknown sailors whose bodies have never been recovered and whose names have never been recorded, lost on the Great Lakes over the long history of plying these waters for commercial trade from the time of the European explorers to the present day.

My manuscript preparation is dedicated to my two sons, Karsten and Kalen, who know that persistence and determination can accomplish extraordinary goals.

Thou rulest the raging of the sea:
when the waves thereof rise, Thou stillest them.

— Psalm 89, Verse 9

TABLE OF CONTENTS

Colour Plates	11
Maps and Tables	15
Foreword by David L. Trotter	17
Acknowledgements	23
Prologue	31
Introduction	39
"*Wexford* Found Off Grand Bend" by Tim Cumming	45

Chapter 1	Historical Perspectives: Great Britain to the Great Lakes	53
Chapter 2	The Skipper's Log	75
Chapter 3	The Final Voyage	83
Chapter 4	The Crew List, November 1913	103
Chapter 5	A Memorial: November 16, 1913	115
Chapter 6	Weather Forecasting in 1913: Descriptions of the Storm	123
Chapter 7	The Carnage of the Storm	153
Chapter 8	The Aftermath: Consequences Abound	165
Chapter 9	The Goderich Inquest	175
Chapter 10	Searching for the *Wexford*	201
Chapter 11	The Wreck Today	211
Chapter 12	The Plunder of the *Wexford*	229
Epilogue	Remembering the *Wexford*, November 11, 2000	237

| Appendix A | "Discovery of the *Wexford*" by David Bannister | 243 |
| Appendix B | A Letter to the Minister of Culture, Province of Ontario | 249 |

Appendix C   Legislation Affecting Marine Archaeological Sites   255
Appendix D   Shipwrecks Along the Huron Shoreline   261
Appendix E   The Plimsoll Marks and Well-Deck Ships   267
Appendix F   Poetical Tributes to Mariners   271

Notes   275
Bibliography   309
Index   313
About the Artists   321
About the Author   323

Following page 144

Plate 1. *The Last Sighting*, oil, 2000, artist Captain C. "Bud" Robinson, showing the *Wexford* as she struggled with the heavy seas offshore from Goderich on the afternoon of Sunday November 9, 1913, just as the storm began to intensify to horrific proportions. The image of the Goderich Lighthouse, for which improvement plans had been designed but never enacted, is shown in the background on the right hand side. This striking painting is now owned by Mr. and Mrs. Keith Homan, The Ridge, Ridgewood Park, Goderich. In describing his painting, Bud cites the lines of the poem *The Dirge of the Lakelands* by Captain William Leonard:

> Where is the lea or shelter
> For we — of the nation's care.

Courtesy of Captain C. "Bud" Robinson.

Plate 2. *The Wexford*, watercolour, 2001, artist Robert McGreevy, perhaps as she steamed along in a lull between the beginning and the end of the storm, downbound on Lake Huron, early in the day, in a strong northwesterly breeze. The artist has completed hundreds of magnificent paintings to preserve and to celebrate our extensive marine heritage on both sides of the international border that runs through our Great Lakes. Mr. McGreevy went out of his way to make an accurate scan of this image available for use in this book. He drove for several hours to pick up the original painting from its current owner, remove it from its frame, transport it to a professional printer, reassemble it, and, then return it to the owner. *Courtesy of Robert McGreevy.*

Plate 3. *The Wexford,* acrylic, 2000, artist William Nieuwland, from an aerial perspective as she is whipped by the winds and lashed by heavy seas during her last voyage. The artist created his image at the time of the discovery of the *Wexford.* There was a sizeable group established, The Friends of the *Wexford,* which took pains to try to protect the vulnerable wreck site as well as to celebrate the significance of her discovery in the waters northwest of Grand Bend. *Courtesy of William Nieuwland.*

Plate 4. *The Goderich Lighthouse, circa 1900,* watercolour, 2000, by the author, showing the storm signals in place, as another late November gale intensified. The original photograph is from the collection of Duncan and Linda Jewell and is used in the text. Although most sources suggest that the lighthouse was improved on the basis of needs made apparent by the tragic events of the Great Storm of 1913, recent archival drawings show that certain upgrades were already on the drawing boards before this horrific maritime event.

Plate 5. *Vessels in Winter Storage at Goderich Harbour, circa* 1910, colourized postcard from a photograph by Reuben R. Sallows of one of the few occasions the *Wexford* wintered at Goderich. The vessels shown are as follows: The tug in the foreground might be the *W.L. Forrest.* Beginning on the left side closest to the elevator: the *Paliki,* the *J.A. McKee,* and our *Wexford.* The three in the background are the *Dundee,* the *Midland Queen,* and the *Neeping.* To the right of the tall chimney on the water and electric plant is the *Turret Chief* or possibly the *Turret Cape.* These ship names have been verified after additional research by Captain "Bud" Robinson. Colourized postcard published by James F.

Thompson, Goderich, colourized by The Valentine & Sons' Publishing Co. Ltd., Montreal and Toronto. Printed in Great Britain. *Courtesy of Glen I. Gardiner.*

Plate 6. *The Wexford in Harbour at Collingwood,* colourized postcard from the collection at the Collingwood Museum. The image shows the *Wexford* beside a smaller unidentified vessel in the Collingwood ship-yards of the Collingwood Shipbuilding & Engine Company Limited as she underwent repairs. Original postcard by the Valentine & Sons' Publishing Co. Ltd., Montreal and Toronto. Printed in Great Britain. *Courtesy of the Collingwood Museum, Access Number X969-549-1Harbour.*

Plate 7 *The Turret Chief.* Iced up at Goderich Elevators, *circa* 1907, another "floating hearse" lost on Lake Superior in the 1913 Great Storm, but recovered the following year. Ice from late season storms had a major effect on the viability of ships to weather intense conditions. In addi-tion to violent winds and tumultuous waves, ice encrustation must have played a major role in the foundering of some vessels lost in the Great Storm. This image is sometimes misidentified as the *Wexford. Courtesy of Bob Carey and Glen I. Gardiner.*

Plate 8(a) The R.M. Hudson Flag. This is the flag first carried by the *Wexford* at the time of her construction in 1883. Over her lifetime she carried the shipping flags of three different companies. Image as shown in the 1904 edition of *Lloyd's Book of House Flags and Funnels of the Principal Steamship Lines of the World and the House Flags of Various Lines of Sailing Vessels,* Lloyd's Registry, London. Image created by Captain "Bud" Robinson.

Plate 8(b) The Signal Flags of 1899. The signal flags are shown in a poster as produced for mariners by the Maryland Weather Service in 1899. The signal system was not the same as that used on the Canadian side of the Great Lakes. In a lighter moment, during one inquest following the Great Storm, it was reported that ships' masters hung their coats over their barometers so as not to be distracted by the "falling glass." *Courtesy of National Oceanographic and Atmospheric Administration Historical Collection, Image 01823; Maryland Weather Service.*

MAPS AND TABLES

Maps

Map 1   Sites Along the Lake Huron Shoreline.   38

Map 2   Location of Vessels Totally Lost on Lake Huron   190
         in the Great Storm of 1913.

Map 3   Proposed Improvements to Goderich Harbour,   196
         circa 1868–70.

Map 4   Various Locations Where the *Wexford*   203
         Has Been "Found!"

Map 5   Sunderland and the River Wear: 242
         "The Largest Shipbuilding Town in the World."

Tables

Table 1   *Wexford* Specifications.   57

Table 2   Ships and Lives Lost, 1812–1912.   116

Table 3   Losses from the *Lake Carriers' Report*, 1913.   157

FOREWORD

My first contact with Paul Carroll was about a decade ago, when the Port of Goderich Marine Heritage Committee was getting ready to conduct side-scan work in search of that elusive shipwreck that we all wanted so badly to find — the *Wexford*. After that initial project, I was a guest presenter, sharing my shipwreck hunting tales at the local Marine Heritage Festivals, where Paul was one of the chief planners. My wife, Mickey, and I enjoyed a number of weekends over a period of several years as the guests of Paul and his wife, Mary, at their log house, nestled in a woodland setting along Black's Point Road — ironically, the site where so many mariners believed the *Wexford* rested, well hidden, offshore.

Working closely with Jan Hawley and Bob Carey, in whose name the official survey licence was held, Paul and others could hardly contain their excitement about the possibility of confirming the long-held rumours that the *Wexford* was most surely lurking nearby. When she was truly found at last, she could tell her story, and would become the "anchor," so to speak, of a new diving industry in the Goderich area. She would also become the main point of attraction for divers, joining a number of other smaller, less significant wreck sites along the Lake Huron shoreline in that area, such as the so-called "Labour Day Wreck," just off the river mouth, which had appeared and disappeared for years but had never been definitively documented as to its age or even the name of the vessel. There was also the "boneyard" — the last resting place of derelict vessels towed out from Goderich Harbour in the early years, and often burned and sunk in the graveyard for old ships just at the south edge of the old waterfront town.

Paul seemed to be one of the key organizers with the group and was a keen historian, anxious to conduct the land-based research component of the wreck study, should she be found. A team of side-scan helpers was established, and a tug boat, the *Daniel Mac*, suitable for conducting the work at sea, was acquired, courtesy of the local marina operator, Dick Peever. And the work began.

Imagine our surprise, and our disappointment, when the target of our quest was actually discovered just a few miles south from our own survey area, and by a fisherman using a simple finder, at essentially the same time as we laboriously "mowed the lawn" in repetitive swaths along the shore in 50- to 90-foot depths with my sophisticated Klein scanner. Our efforts, not to be lessened or minified, moved south the next day, and we began the documentation survey while our divers conducted underwater confirmation dives to verify that what was found was, in fact, the elusive shipwreck that had foiled discovery efforts for more than eight decades. It was indeed the *Wexford*. And although she was not exactly where predicted, she was certainly close by — just far enough out of reach to have maintained her secret hiding place for a very long time.

And so the documentation began, with Paul taking a lead role in pulling the masses of information soon to be acquired together in some cohesive form. His quest to produce a book has resulted in this current endeavour. I understand that his intense two-year period of research was interrupted by several other publishing projects, which for some reason took priority, and the big *Wexford* project seemed to take a back seat for a while. If you can find a rare copy of the 2001 *Huron Historical Notes*, for example, you will be well served by reading his account of the intriguing maritime history along the Huron shores.

Anyway, here it is — the documentation of the *Wexford*, finally completed. This book will be a valuable addition to the collection of works already written about the Great Storm of 1913 and its casualties. Unlike most of the other material, this volume largely provides a single focus. It is primarily about one ship, and addresses every aspect — from its early history to the current status of the recently discovered wreck and the failed efforts to protect her fragile artifacts. Paul has tried to address the challenges that follow the discovery of a major shipwreck such as this. The resultant publicity, which in this case set off a veritable contagion of activity at the dive site, was continent-wide. There was no time to complete the underwater survey before eager, but not yet welcomed, visitors began to arrive and contaminate the site — and also, indeed, to relieve the wreck of some of her undocumented treasures. What is wrong? What is right? My own experience verifies that it is better to maintain strict confidence about such discoveries until all the documentation has been completed.

Shipwreck hunting is the first phase of a large effort to preserve and to celebrate our underwater heritage. My own experience as a shipwreck hunter goes back to the 1960s and 70s, when my own passion for marine history and my love for scuba diving led me to conduct more formal searches to discover what lay beneath these Great Lakes waters. I have been riding the technology curve since the late 70s — over 30 years of discovery and exploration of our "Inland Seas." In the early 1970s there was no Loran C (an early position-finding system based on the cross-referencing of land-based radio direction signals) or Global Positioning System (GPS) to mark a shipwreck discovery or to record areas searched on the Great Lakes. However, technology was about to have a major impact on divers, historians, and shipwreck hunters. In 1978, I had the fourth Loran C in use on the Great Lakes, the other three having been acquired shortly before: one by Dr. Chuck Feltner, the well-known wreck hunter who pioneered the use of electronic position finding devices; the other two by the Coast Guard, who were evaluating the benefits of the devices on Lake Erie.

A whole new world opened for the diver/shipwreck hunter with the use of this new technology. The presence of GPS equipment has made the job of returning to identical locations even more accurate. For the first time, a shipwreck diver did not have to spend most of each spring relocating known sites, miles from shore, to dive. Divers could return to the site using a set of coordinates previously obtained. A whole new world had opened up to divers, charter boat operators, and anyone with two to three thousand dollars (nowadays, just a hundred dollars or so) to spend on one of these systems.

Over the years, and with the establishment of a research company, I have been involved in the discovery and documentation of well over 90 underwater sites. There was always an interest in our new findings, and groups all over the Great Lakes region, on both sides of the border, were interested in hearing about our discoveries and seeing the results of our work. I hope my role has served to enrich our understanding of the days when the Great Lakes played a more active role in our economy and in the lives of so many people who lived in the hundreds of lakeshore communities along these shores.

It is said that that some 16,000 ships have found a watery grave since La Salle first plied the Great Lakes waters with that other mystery ship, the *Griffon*. In the grand scheme of things, so little has been done; there is so much more to do. Many of us are fascinated by Great Lakes marine history, and one only needs to discover a virgin, intact wooden sailing vessel to stir the imagination.

I have been fortunate to be married to Mickey, who has willingly accepted and supported my love of the Great Lakes, its history, and the solving of mysteries beneath our "Inland Seas." It is the greatest of adventures to be able to share the experience with fellow divers who have made the transition to become wreck hunters and underwater explorers. People of modest means but with much dedication to the task at hand have been able to enjoy world-class discovery and underwater exploration, going where no one has gone before. Great Lakes history comes alive, and we have been able to share it with countless others.

Paul Carroll is to be commended for his efforts in documenting this tale of the elusive *Wexford*. He has answered many questions, clarified a number of uncertainties, pricked a little bit of conscience for how to handle future discoveries, and most certainly sparked an interest for others to pursue further studies and to conduct more research about our marine heritage. Enjoy his book. It will be an intriguing good read.

In closing, I offer you Dr. Clive Cussler's comments from his NUMA website: "To those of you who seek lost objects of history, I wish you the best of luck. They're out there, and they're whispering."[1]

David L. Trotter
Undersea Research Associates
Canton, Michigan

ACKNOWLEDGEMENTS

During the period of research for this book, the following persons and organizations have provided information, direction, support, or assistance.

I am indebted to my dear wife, Mary, of course, for her endless patience and her unwavering tolerance of my passion for marine heritage. It is an absolute mystery to her how I can always seem to remember the details of some remote historical trivia, yet so easily forget the more mundane, yet critical elements of daily living in matters that should be routine!

This work would not have been possible without the assistance and support of research made available through Peter Englebert, the Ontario marine archeologist with the Ministry of Citizenship, Culture and Recreation, at the time of the wreck discovery. Peter was able to provide funds to assist the Goderich Marine Heritage Committee and its members with the massive land-based research task that had been undertaken. While I accepted that responsibility as a personal goal on behalf of the committee, Mr. Englebert's support was invaluable. Peter hired a competent and enthusiastic historical researcher and genealogist, Ken McLeod of Ottawa, to gather documentation related to the loss of the *Wexford* and to forward copies of that information to us for our use. Ken worked meticulously to review records generally inaccessible to those of us located out here in the "boonies." He researched files in

Library and Archives Canada, the Transport Canada Library, and the Marine Museum of the Great Lakes in Kingston. Peter also conducted research on his own, in efforts to support our needs.

Even with the use of all the material provided, additional work could still be undertaken, but one reaches a limit, after which the task of pulling it all together must be done. Seldom has a week gone by in the final stages of editing where some additional person hasn't reported new information or offered another clue to help unravel the many remaining mysteries about this ship and the horrific storm.

In the words of Ron Beaupre, a distinguished Ontario marine historian, "When you shake the tree, the cherries begin to fall."[1] I have tried to shake the tree. There will be lots of new "fruit" to harvest, ready for follow-up research and more writing, no sooner than the current task can be completed. The debates will surely continue about what actually did or did not happen. Some of those arguments will be heated.

The role of key members of the Goderich Marine Heritage Committee must also be noted. I cannot underscore sufficiently the enthusiasm, 24-7, that was brought to the table by Jan Hawley. Her boundless energy and her exuberance for the search, discovery, and research follow-up were contagious. So were the excitement and the commitment of Bob Carey, a long-time hunter for the shipwreck *Wexford*. Jan even engaged her sister Debra Anderson to assist us with some on-site research at the University of Western Ontario. The contributions of Brent Bamford, who sought out the original builder's plan from Sunderland, and of Karen Sturdy, who provided me with a hard to find copy of the Goderich Inquest transcript, are also noted. In particular, Karen must be commended for the many hours she spent, pen in hand, in efforts to make the largely illegible transcript photocopies more readable.

Patricia Hamilton and Jeremy Allin at the Huron County Museum have provided support and assistance with access to records and images. Likewise, Melissa Shaw of the Collingwood Museum, Kim Forbes of the Sault Ste. Marie Museum, Marlo Broad of the Alpena Public Library system, and others in similar organizations have made it possible to acquire many new images that have been mostly unseen by the general public. Reg Thompson of the Goderich Public Library has been of great assistance in the struggle to find first names in several cases where only initials were used in newspaper reports.

The late Audrey and Bill Barlow, the late Captain A.R. (Uncle Roy) Munday, the late Robert Courtney, as well as Bob McGreevy, Ron Beaupre, Hank Winsor, Mike and Georgann Wachter, Mike Spears, Peter Sturdy, Glen Gardiner, Owen Delve, and Keith Homan are among those who made images available for use in this book. Glen Gardiner went out of his way to help solve some last-minute image problems, as did Elizabeth Profit at *Elizabeth's Art Gallery*, Goderich, who spent some after-hours, weekend photo shop time tweaking an important image for the colour plates section so that it could be included.

David L. Trotter of Undersea Research Associates, a well-known shipwreck aficionado who has found more shipwrecks on the Great Lakes than any other person, was an inspiration. His drive, determination, and quiet counsel have been most supportive over these last 10 years, in my sporadic efforts to get this job done. His knowledge and expertise have been valuable, not only to me in my current task, but also to the marine community in the Goderich–Lake Huron area as the search continues for the *James Carruthers* and the *Argus*,[2] both yet to surrender their location after their loss in the infamous storm. The support of the original side-scanning crews should also be acknowledged.

Well-known Great Lakes researchers and historians, including Brendon Baillod, Cris Kohl, Chris Pemberton, Patrick Folkes, William Deedler, Walter Lewis, David Swayze, Stan McLellan, John Weichel, and Dan Sullivan of the Wisconsin Marine Historical Society, always answered email and telephone requests and helped steer me toward the answers I was seeking, especially in the early days of my work, almost a decade ago.

Walter Lewis, David Swayze, and Brendon Baillod warrant special mention for the selfless work they do on behalf of the marine heritage community across the continent and beyond. These three marine historians maintain Internet websites that have amassed lifetimes of research documentation and provide links for lesser students of marine history, like myself, for access to an almost unlimited knowledge base. I cannot estimate how many times I have made a quick electronic trip to one of their websites to verify a fact or to seek direction for a next step. They deserve gold medals for their lifelong commitment on our collective behalf. Their contributions are invaluable. Canadians should be especially proud of the work undertaken by Walter Lewis, and those who have contributed to *www.maritimehistoryofthegreatlakes.ca*, including Bill McNeil and Rick Neilson.

Captain C "Bud" Robinson and his wife Jeanette have been acquaintances of mine for many years. Now residing in the Tobermory area, Bud has provided invaluable support and guidance as I have pulled this project together, especially with technical details, and with corrections of some of the misinformation, false presumptions, and errors that inevitably surface with the hype and the enthusiasm that follows such an exciting discovery as finding a shipwreck that has been missing for 87 years. His astute powers of observation have drawn out otherwise unnoticeable details — his knowledge is based on the experience of more than 40 years at sea. Bud has unselfishly shared his magnificent artwork; most notably his piece entitled *The Last Sighting*, which shows the *Wexford* in the excruciating throes of the storm offshore from the Goderich Lighthouse. His amazing talent for cleaning up old photos with modern digital tools on his computer salvaged some beautiful images for me, important in the history of this ship, that otherwise would have been unusable. Quite frankly, it would not have been possible to complete this book without Bud's generous assistance.

I must extend gratitude to Robert McGreevy, well-known American marine artist, named 2004 Historian of the Year by the Detroit Marine Historical Society, for access to two of his more than 300 paintings of Great Lakes ships. As well, I must also acknowledge William Nieuwland, an artist acquaintance and Friend of the *Wexford*, from nearby Grand Bend. These artists have created spectacular images of the *Wexford* in her final moments that convey that unholy wedlock of beauty and terror on the storm-swept seas with dramatic intensity. These renderings truly speak a thousand words.

From the Friends of the *Wexford* in Grand Bend, I must also acknowledge the interest and support of wreck-finder Don Chalmers and activist/writer David Bannister, who has allowed me to use his own summary of the events in those early days as an appendix in this book.

Acknowledgements

From the diving community, Doug Taleski, Steve Wilke, Jim and Pat Stayer, Dan Thomas, Paul Schaus, and Jim Clarey, along with those mentioned in the text of the manuscript, provided information or pointed me in the right direction on matters related to the wreck itself. Dr. Peter McLean Millar has offered encouragement and additional insights. Paul Padfield, a local diver, warrants commendation for his diligence in the creation of visual survey records for the *Wexford*. Paul and his son, with help from some divers from Deep 3 Scuba, London, completed the first underwater maps or plans of the wreck, and identified key areas that required further detailed study. Paul's work has been meticulous. And, of course, Bob Carey, longtime *Wexford* hunter, must be acknowledged for his diligent persistence and his unbridled enthusiasm for the whole project, as holder of the official survey licence for the wreck documentation.

Mike and Georgann Wachter, of *Erie Wrecks* fame, the best-known divers on Lake Erie, and guests of one of our Goderich Marine Heritage Festivals held a few years ago, offered insight into the state of the *Wexford* as she sits today, and provided access to a series of wonderful still photographs of the wreck, as well as some underwater video that I have consulted during my research.

Lawrence Brander, Les Begarnie, and Mike Hughes, all of whom consented to be interviewed about the widely proclaimed Bill Humphries *Wexford* discovery of the 1970s, must also be recognized.

Brian Prince, current president of Save Ontario Shipwrecks (SOS), has been unselfish in sharing thoughts about shipwreck preservation efforts, the involvement of the SOS (of which I am a member) in the evolution of legislation, and its partnership with government agencies in protecting our underwater heritage and educating the diving public about low-impact diving.

My good friend and sailing colleague, Don Bamford, with whom I have interrupted this *Wexford* quest to co-author two books, has also been a helpful inspiration as I complete this current project. Other friends, including Ron Lee, Jay Poulter, Robin Wilson, and Mike Scott, have responded to a number of oddball enquiries for help on short notice, back in the days when I was active with the local side-scanning group and still pulling my basic research files together. A sailing acquaintance,

Mike Earle, has taken time to complete a sophisticated mathematical analysis of the flotation capacities of ice-encrusted metal.

A neighbour, Captain Laird Fulford, offered a few wise comments that he has probably long forgotten; retired mariner Doug Graham offered insights into the numerous area Mac/McDonald clans; and acquaintance Phil Gemeinhardt, a collector of shipwreck memorabilia and member of the Bayfield Historical Society, shared important information about *Wexford* artifacts and his own search for materials washed up along the shoreline after the Great Storm.

The editing and publishing process requires diligent attention to detail. Once again it is necessary to acknowledge the guidance of publisher Barry Penhale from the wonderful publishing house, Natural Heritage Books,

The Wexford *under repair in Collingwood Harbour, recorded as being there in the "late season, 1903." Note the old-style fisherman-type anchors slung over the bow and four lifeboat stations, two of which were removed in this refitting. This photograph is from the Huron Institute Collection and is the second earliest photo of the newly arrived ship at the time of her refitting at the Collingwood Shipyards. The image shows important details about her early structure before changes made in 1904.* Courtesy of Collingwood Museum, X974-731-1.

a member of the Dundurn Group, and his partner, Jane Gibson, whose penchant for detail in the editing process is remarkable. They are both masters of their art. My copy editor, Allison Hirst, has also offered her amazing talent for ensuring coherence and consistency throughout the text. Her powers of observation and co-relation are astounding. Her work has certainly strengthened the text. Captain Robinson, marine historian Ron Beaupre, and Mel Wilson, a retired engineer and toolmaker from the British Mercantile Service, were also kind enough to read the manuscript at its final stages; Bud and Ron for technical aspects related to marine terminology and Mel for accuracy of the language of the sea and lexicon.

As the final editing process began, I decided that we should have one more look, in the United Kingdom, for any additional records that might shed new light on the *Wexford*'s appearance or shipping history. I had already exhausted the possibility of finding new photographic records in Sunderland, where she was built, but hired a researcher, Merilyn Hywel-Jones, through my good friend Jocelyn Wingfield, both of whom helped me with research for the book *Four Years on the Great Lakes: The Journal of Lieutenant David Wingfield, RN.* (Merilyn dug up Wingfield's actual naval service record for me and my co-author, Don Bamford.) While it was apparent that the collection at the National Maritime Museum did not hold any records related to our *Wexford*, it was still possible that the London Guildhall Library might hold a surprise or two. She found references noting that the *Wexford* was registered at Liverpool, rather than London, from 1890–1900, and that the period during which the *Wexford* was sold to a French company (in 1900), she was registered as the *Elise* in Dunquerque (Dunkirk). There were no photographs or pictorial records from this era. A further search by Jeremy Smith, assistant librarian at the London Metropolitan Archives, also revealed no new information. A last ditch effort has been undertaken at Liverpool. I am awaiting information from the Merseyside Maritime Museum at Liverpool to see if their archives contain any additional relevant information.

There are others whose names I have surely missed. There was such a flurry of helpful activity after the announcement of the wreck of the *Wexford* being found. One enthusiastic Canadian diver, for example, sent me exceptional underwater photos to be used in any way I saw fit, but his name, for whatever reason, does not appear in my records anywhere. In the mass of material I have collected, I have been able to document sources, including page numbers, where available, for most citations. In a few cases, news clippings have been given to me without the name of the source newspaper, or without a page number. In these cases, I have used the information, but indicated in a note that the data is unsourced. If I have inadvertently left out a necessary credit, please contact me or the publisher to have the omission rectified in the event that there are future reprints of this book.

Finally, I wish to acknowledge the support of the Corporation of the County of Huron Heritage Fund, the Corporation of the Town of Goderich, and the Huron County Historical Society for their generous financial support, which has made the inclusion of the colour plates section of this book possible.

For all of this support, I am truly grateful.

PROLOGUE

My late uncle, Captain Albert Roy Munday (1919–2008) was a dedicated seaman. He knew the waters of the Great Lakes well, having plied their full extent over many years. He also knew the temperament of the oceans, salty channels, and the adjacent seas — gleaned from the war years, when he served in the Royal Canadian Navy, from 1939 through the mid-1940s.

A British citizen, he had come to Canada with his parents, Bertram Roy Munday and Daisy May Whitehouse, when he was an infant. My grandparents had decided to emigrate in order to embark on a new life in this country after the ravages of the Great War. Throughout his childhood, he lived within sight of Lake Huron. A natural attraction to the Goderich waterfront, with its busy mix of sailing ships, tugs, and lakers, steered his life toward a full career on the water.

"Sol" or "Solomon," as he was called by his associates and close friends, worked the old fishing schooners and the later tugs with colourful mariners like Reddy MacDonald of the famous MacDonald lifesaving clan. He served on the *J.T. Wing*, the last lumber schooner to carry timber to Goderich Harbour in the 1930s. He was a leading seaman and anti-aircraft gunner in the Royal Canadian Navy during the Second World War, serving on five ships, with the most time spent on the *Ottawa*, which he helped to commission in 1943 and to decommission in 1945.

Captain Albert Roy Munday as a young man. Roy is relaxing on deck, leaning against the gaff-rigged boom on lumber schooner the J.T. Wing, *circa 1940.*
Courtesy of Mary Munday.

Sol joined the crew of a laker after the war, and worked his way through the ranks to become captain, acquiring his master's ticket in 1973, in time for that season's opening. He concluded his 49th year on the water at lay-up 1983, and worked relief assignments for the next few years. Throughout his nearly 20 years of retirement, he was an avid ship-model builder, crafting detailed and cherished replicas of lakers, naval vessels, tugs, and schooners. His work can be found in halls, private homes, and museums across Canada and the United States. One of his creations is even on display in England. His final model, his rendition of the *Wexford*, was completed in his 83rd year, in a time of failing eyesight and deteriorating health. It was a gift for me, as he knew my passion for the sea and my love for marine history.

I had the chance to gam with him, in his later years, about some of the perils he had encountered on the seas. The following are three of his personal memories. I have paraphrased the words he shared about situations relevant to introducing the story of the *Wexford*.

Roy's Worst Storm

The closest call I ever had was on Superior — late one season on the old steamer *Goderich*. The forecast called for northwest gales and snow. It would be a fearsome trip, so we anchored up behind Pie Island.[1] We weren't alone. We were lying with some 730s[2] — all the big ones had decided to wait out the storm, as well — even the Fitz [the *Edmund Fitzgerald*] was here. And I figured if they were here, I should be waiting in a lee along with them, to the best of my ability, too. It would be the sensible thing to do.

Ours was about 550 feet — the same length as the *James Carruthers*. We waited out the night, and the mate came to me and said, "Cap, some of the 730s look like they're getting on their way. Do you think we should weigh up and set out, too?"

I queried him about the weather — and although there might be some improvement, he thought, I was convinced it was not yet time to leave. *This just might be another sucker hole*, I thought.

I told him, "Call down to the engineer, get the engines warmed up, get the crew ready — and wake me in a couple of hours. I'll make my final decision then. Let's let these big fellows get out there. We'll see how they're doing. And if it sounds good, we'll follow along."

Well, in two hours the mate woke me. He said that some more of the big ones had set out — and on the radio, it didn't sound too bad. So I told him we'd haul anchor and go. And it wasn't too bad. There was a heavy roll, but it was slow, and there wasn't any danger. As we listened to the radio, it sounded as though the big boys were doing okay, and there wasn't much to be worried about.

After an hour or two, the mate touched my shoulder and said, "Cap, have a look behind us." I turned and looked toward our stern, and I could see a wall of white — looked like a blizzard coming toward us.

The mate uttered, "Squall line?"

I stared. I'll bet my mouth was hanging open. "*Squall line?*" I responded, with a sense of desperation in my tone. "*That's a wall of water coming at us — sound an alarm. Get everyone ready.*"

And within a minute, that wall of rampaging water thundered over us, hitting dead on the stern quarter. The entire stern section strained. We lifted and turned — and started to roll. Everything around me came crashing to starboard. Books, papers, charts, coffee mugs, glasses — they all flew wildly, crashing against the downside wheelhouse bulkhead. If ever I felt close to death on my ship, this was surely the moment. This was the instant where the tempest would rule — or our good ship, with the grace of God, would overcome and withstand the fierce pounding of this giant sea. A rogue? I'd never seen one like this before. The liquid mercury actually poured out of the gyro,[3] we were over so far. The compass card was dislodged from its pivot. My two radar scanners went down. Surely, we were finished. The watery tomb below was sucking us down to our final demise.

Yet, ever so slowly, our good ship overcame the insult and the injury of this sudden brash assault and righted herself — but only to roll past her even keel to submerge the gunnels of the port side well below the surface, but for just an instant less, a moment short of the deep initial roll. And we rolled for a good half hour or more — ever so gradually regaining our stability.

Frightened? Of course I was frightened. But, was it over? Fortunately, my radios stayed up and I was able to talk to a big guy beyond me — a 730 somewhere out there who wanted to know how we were doing. He warned of more to come. And it had to be taken on the stern quarter — to turn away would take us to shore and aground. In this fury, we'd be broken up for sure. The gale had swung unexpectedly to the southwest. We weren't ready, nor was anyone else. But we survived. And if we'd gone down, there be nothing we could have done. Just swallowed by an angry sea. And gone.

Rudder Damage

Another time we were caught in a storm on Lake Erie. It's a little lake, but it can sure whip up a fury. We were off the Erie shoal, trying to make Port Colborne in raging gales, blinding snow, and crushing ice. We had much anguish making way — feared going aground. The Canadian Coast Guard had been ordered in to help. Their job was to assist ships

Through the various marine ages, ice in the rigging and the resultant
instability, sometimes called "top-hamper," posed big problems and created
great risks for mariners.
Courtesy of Captain Roy Munday.

carrying cargoes of most value first, unless lives were in danger on other
ships, and then get the other vessels to safety. If things went wrong, we'd
all be frozen in on the lake for the duration of winter. We carried a cargo
of grain, so we were first on their list.

We were being heaved so badly that the rudder was lifted right out of
her shoe. She was twisted around beyond her turning radius, forced by
the raging swells, and her rudderstock above was ripped from its quadrant and twisted like a pretzel. It was an iron bar, reinforced and almost
a foot through in thickness, wrenched and twisted in a fleeting moment
— in the blink of an eye, no steerage. None. People who think there is
little that can go wrong don't understand the power and the fury of the
sea — even on a little lake like Erie.

We were finally thrown up on the shoal. We sent the crew with axes
to cut us loose from the Coast Guard vessels. If they kept trying to pull us
loose, they would rip us apart. We would wait. They could free the other

After a winter storm of December 1907, an unidentified vessel, perhaps the Meaford, *is shown arriving at the security of Goderich Harbour after a rough ride on the stormy waves. It was a fearful time for master and crew, as tons of ice could accumulate and sometimes cause the vessels to list dangerously.*
Courtesy of Goderich Elevator and Transit Company Ltd., Annual Report, 1948.

ships. We could hold on until the storm abated, and get hauled off in calmer weather. We'd suffered enough damage already. To be impatient would certainly bring more distress. We'd had enough already.

Language of the Sea

The language of the sea is confusing. There is a vocabulary for the salt-water sailors and for those on the lakes. It's very different. We can't talk eye to eye and understand the real meaning, unless we both speak the same version. This is especially critical in times of crisis.

In one inquiry, following some ships breaking loose in a storm, a lawyer who used the language from the salty sea grilled me. The terminology just wouldn't match my own words. I told the judge I would answer no more questions until we could talk the language of the Great Lakes. This was a problem from Lake Huron. We had to use the freshwater words that would suit that case.

The judge agreed.[4]

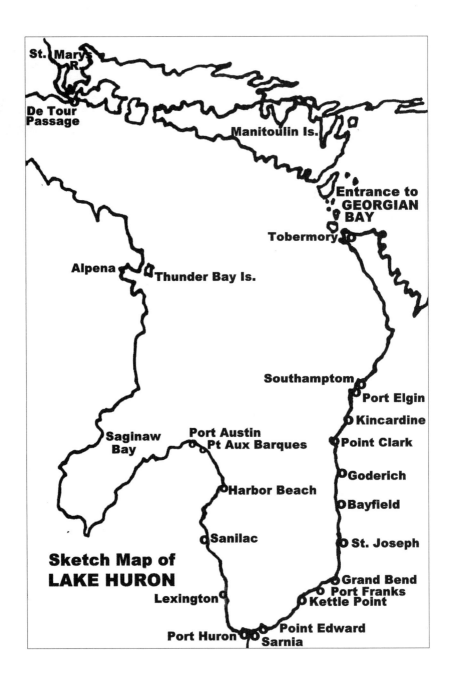

Sketch Map of
LAKE HURON

INTRODUCTION

"The only evidence that has been picked up on the beach at Port Frank [*sic*] so far which would indicate that the *Wexford* has gone down to the bottom is a card of the compass corrections[1] or chart which bears the name *Wexford*. It is also thought that some of the wreckage which is strewn along the shore from Goderich south is from the *Wexford* but this has not been definitely established."[2]

In the infamous Great Storm of 1913, more than 250 lives were lost. Most of those were on ships that "represented not only the best of [American and Canadian] lake practice, but of English and Scotch yards."[3] According to University of Western Ontario librarian and later university vice-president, the well-known journalist Fred Landon, who wrote about this maritime tragedy in his 1994 book, *Lake Huron*, "Sunday, November 9, 1913, is the blackest day in the history of navigation on the Great Lakes. The gales which swept the lakes region on that day sent ten stout ships to the bottom, drove more than a score of others ashore and took the lives of 235 sailors. No other storm of such destructive character has ever been recorded on these inland waters."[4]

Many books have been written about the Great Storm. Articles have appeared and reappeared in newspapers and magazines in every generation since that time. Even as we approach the centenary of this tragic event, these stories of almost 100 years ago are oft repeated. Each time, there is a new twist or another revelation to help unravel the mysteries of these tragic events that unfolded, without witnesses, and in the absence of any survivors to recount the stories. The tales are probably exaggerated to some degree, and certain facts get distorted or unintentionally misrepresented through the passion of the raconteur. Today, the stories of the storm have found their way onto the Internet and are beginning to show up in the newer electronic media. Video and computer-based productions are presenting gripping accounts with vivid imagery and frightening reality.

Over the years, most of the missing vessels have been located. The most recent, on Lake Huron, was the mystery ship *Wexford*, the only "salty" in the list of ships lost on Lake Huron. She was found quite by accident in August 2000 by Don Chalmers, who was fishing with a downrigger behind his sailboat, northwest of Grand Bend. Ironically, at the same time, Great Lakes shipwreck aficionado David Trotter of Undersea Research Associates was scanning the depths of Lake Huron, south of Goderich, off Black's Point, for the same wreck. The American sonar expert had been retained by the town of Goderich's Marine Heritage Committee to conduct side-scan searches for the *Wexford* in one of its several reputed hiding places.

There are two wrecks on Lake Huron that remain to be found: the carrier *Argus* (as footnoted earlier, perhaps it is the *Hydrus*) and the 550-foot (about 168-metre) Canadian-built freighter the *James Carruthers*. At least one of these is expected to "give up" soon. According to Dave Trotter, "They'll be found when they are ready to be found, just as their sister, the *Wexford*, was found in August of the year 2000."[5]

The purpose of this work, the culmination of my own personal research and writing, with support from those mentioned in the Acknowledgements, along with many of the more significant anecdotal reports of others, is to tell the story of the *Wexford*. It will be a combination of historical fact — mostly correct, I hope — and some speculation about what may have happened on her last fateful journey. Perhaps another researcher will alter these stories at a future date, when new information is found — locating her rudder, for example, or parts of

Dave Trotter and Klein side-scan equipment, searching for the Wexford *in August 2000. In his 40-year history of wreck hunting, Trotter has discovered over 90 wreck sites, most of which were marine in origin. He also has been involved in several successful finds after aviation tragedies.*
Photos by the author.

The Wexford *is shown approaching an unknown harbour. The profile presented here was from her later years, a view seen by many as the vessel made her way from port to port.*
Courtesy of Ron Beaupre, National Archives Canada, # 144150.

her pilothouse, or any of its contents, would be quite revealing. Some of the alternative scenarios of what caused her final demise are hotly debated. I will try to offer a perspective from opposing sides, but we are all entitled to an opinion. If, in my passion for telling a complete story, I have neglected to acknowledge a source correctly, or made any other error, I accept full responsibility, and ask that I or my publisher be notified so that such acknowledgement or correction can be included in future editions.

In any event, I will share what I believe could be true. Only the *Wexford*, or the spectres of her crew, could reveal the genuine realities.[6] With some degree of apology, I will also express a few opinions — mostly related to events in the current century. I trust that I can do so with the necessary diplomacy, so that no person involved in any aspect of the events following her discovery will carry ill feelings or malice about my effort. The truth is that not everything was done correctly, and, at times, spontaneity ruled the day.

There are instances where I have taken some liberties with the manner of presenting certain information. I *do* want to respect the traditions of sound historical research and writing, but it is sometimes impossible to present certain "missing pieces" without a degree of speculation. For example, we have much "circumstantial evidence" of how the *Wexford* spent her final hours, but we have no first-person account, nor did anyone witness the terrible struggle that she and her crew encountered before she foundered. We must, therefore, based on a careful examination of the evidence, construct a scenario that we believe *most likely to have happened*. I have done that with utmost care, yet my own conclusions are that of one observer. Others, just as they have done with the speculations about how the *Edmund Fitzgerald* was lost (and that debate continues to this day), will offer alternate opinions and no doubt challenge my findings.

As well, the keeping of a personal diary by the captains and many crew members of these ships was a common practice. At least two such booklets were recovered after the Great Storm as the flotsam washed in along the shorelines. In discussions with my late uncle Roy Munday, a laker captain of some 35 years, in dialogue with other mariners, and in respect of my own practice as a sailor — keeping a personal ship's log for over 40 years — it is almost a certainty that young Bruce Cameron kept such a diary. Yet none was ever found. After due consideration, and my own experience with the challenges of difficult storms, I have constructed a few diary entries that reflect, I am certain, the kind of fear and uncertainty the fledgling master would have experienced.

In respect to the storm itself, I was not there to see it. But I have had my own direct experience with raging tempests that kept me at the wheel of my *SolSean* for up to 27 uninterrupted hours. In this case, the accounts of this "white hurricane" are best told in the words of those who survived to tell their tales. Out of respect for their observations, and for their astounding anecdotes, I have taken the liberty of including several accounts in their entirety. They may be longer than might be the normally accepted tradition for historical writing, but they are accurate and complete accounts. I beg your indulgence for including these references.

A Note about Numeration, Compass Directions, Spelling, and Visuals

Whether to use Imperial measurement or the metric system (System International or SI) for numeration always presents a challenge in historical writing. Particularly in writing Canadian history, the maritime tradition has always been expressed in Imperial terminology, yet today's standard is to use the metric equivalents wherever possible. The matter remains confusing. Take the formats used on Canadian Hydrographic Services nautical charts, for example, where water depths are listed in feet, metres, and fathoms, while distances are measured in a complex combination of statute and nautical miles along with standard feet and yards. Wherever possible, for ease of reading, the use of historical maritime terminology has been retained. In all cases where I have quoted from other sources, I have left the measurement units alone. With respect to the historic use of a capital letter to begin the names for compass directions, I have tried to use the contemporary fashion of presenting these words and their variations with lower case letters, but have preserved the manner of spelling, usually with a capital letter, in quotations as they were originally, but not always consistently, made. With respect to the convention of writing out the smaller numbers as full words, I have retained the maritime tradition of using figures in most cases.

With respect to the mix of spelling conventions, between the Canadian and American versions, I have tried to use the variation consistent with the country of origin. When a quotation is made from an American source, I have retained the American spelling. The best example is in the repeated use of the word *harbor/harbour*. Even in the transcript for the Goderich Inquest, 1913, it is spelled both ways. Both Canadian mariners and American officials testified. In early Canadian newspaper stories, both spellings are used at random, it seems.

Also, by today's standards, a number of images included in this text would be deemed to be inferior. Given the technology of the time, the amateur origins of the material, and the frail condition of some of the historically important visuals that have survived, I have requested that they be included in this book to create a more complete record of what ought to be preserved and to be shared.

Research Updates

For those wishing to keep up with new information as it becomes available, I maintain a website at *www.shipwreckwexford.ca*. The site is updated periodically with additional research findings as they are confirmed.

"*Wexford* Found Off Grand Bend" by Tim Cumming

The Goderich Signal-Star, September 6, 2000

Two cellular phone calls were made to the *Goderich Signal-Star* newsroom on Friday afternoon and it was hard to understand the words through the poor reception. The excited voice breaking up over the lines belonged to Bob Carey. The usually reserved chair of the Goderich Marine Heritage Committee was speaking with the excitement of a child on Christmas morning.

The words on the voice-mail message might not have been clear but there was no question about the meaning. After 87 years hidden at the bottom of Lake Huron, the *Wexford* had been found. It was as if Elvis Presley himself had walked onto the Goderich Square.

What is the *Wexford*? It was one of only three lost ships left to be found from the Great Storm of November 1913. Until last week!

The ocean-going steamer had become a tomb for the 26-year-old[1] captain and his fellow sailors who served on the vessel's ill-fated journey, which started when the vessel left Fort William with a load of steel rails.[2] Built in 1883, the roughly 260-foot steamer was the pride of the William Doxford & Sons Company of Sunderland, England. It was built in 1883. It was launched as the *Wexford* and the name was changed to *Elise* in

1890 before being renamed *Wexford* in 1894. That name *Wexford* will be new to some people, but not for long. The vessel may soon become a major draw to scuba diving and marine heritage enthusiasts.

"It will open up another page of Great Lakes history," said Carey. "It's opened up this whole Ontario west coast as a dive centre; it's just unbelievable."

Serendipity, the ability to make wonderful discoveries by accident, was the word applied by Brent Bamford, acting president of the Goderich chapter of Save Ontario Shipwrecks (SOS). "It sort of makes you believe there's a destiny or a fate," he said. Long before Hollywood would popularize the concept of a "perfect storm," the Great Storm of 1913 was the storm of unrivaled proportions.

The storm around November 7–12 has been referred to as the White Hurricane and the Big Blow. The *Wexford* went down after the cruel twist of fate, which left Lake Huron resembling a boiling cauldron.

There were a couple of odd twists of fate last week when the *Wexford* was discovered. The ship, which had remained hidden for 87 years, picked a strange time to reappear. Her discovery was almost to the day that Great Lakes searcher David Trotter arrived in Goderich with advanced side-scan sonar, ready to map out the bottom of the lake in a search for shipwrecks.

Trotter is the owner of Undersea Research Associates. He is the equivalent of a marine detective, having found more than 60 Great Lakes shipwrecks.[3] He spent about ten years tracking down the *Minnedosa*, which he says is the biggest schooner ever built in Canada. Trotter, who is beginning his fourth decade of searching for shipwrecks, came to Goderich from his home in the Detroit suburb of Canton, Michigan. He brought advanced, commercial-grade side-scan sonar equipment to track down the *Wexford*.

It was a humble fisherman with an inexpensive fish finder who made the big catch, however. Donald Chalmers, who is staying at Green Haven Trailer Park in Grand Bend, wasn't specifically looking for the *Wexford*. The London resident and avid fisherman was actually out downrigging for salmon but he knew by looking at his fish finder that he had caught something bigger than a salmon.

Dave Trotter and the side-scan crew on the Danel Mac *in August 2000. From left to right: Dave Trotter, Brent Bamford, Jay Poulter, and Bob Carey. Effective side-scanning requires a great commitment and long hours of repetitive but systematic survey work.*
Photo by the author.

"Part of fishing is looking for structures down on the bottom," he said. "You watch for anomalies on the bottom … when this showed up (I realized) this was not natural." He was northwest of Grand Bend about eight miles when the fish finder indicated there was something there. The ordinary fish finder gave enough detail to see the contour of the hull.

It was another interesting twist to the *Wexford* saga that the man who found the steamer just happened to be a close acquaintance and former co-worker of Carey. "Look at the number of fishermen who go out here every day … of all the people who could have been there to snag that, it was someone who knew Bob," marvelled Bamford. "What are the chances of the two of them knowing each other?"

"The wreck wanted to be found," said Carey.

The ship's discoverer, Chalmers, also has other links to the *Wexford* story. His father-in-law, 93-year-old John Manore, was a commercial fisherman for many years. John's father was Christopher Columbus "Cub" Manore. The great storms of 1913 ripped Cub Manore's fish shanties right off the shore.

"John remembers his father telling him stories about the damage from the storm," said Chalmers. The soft-spoken Carey has an ever-present smile and a polite, quiet manner. When it comes to the *Wexford*, however, there is no reserve in him. His wife, Barb, says he even has *Wexford* parties in the wintertime. He has a map there marked with the final destination of lost Lake Huron ships and coordinates for the prospective location of the *Wexford*.

"Every waking minute, when you're not working, you're after it," he said of his near obsession. It came as no surprise then, that the normally low-key Carey was the most excited of anyone when news of the *Wexford*'s discovery came his way. He spoke Friday sporting a sunburned face and a smile from ear-to-ear, having recently dived on the ship he is convinced is the *Wexford*.

Carey and his fellow divers were ecstatic to find the well-preserved relic sitting upright on the bottom of the lake, as if it had been gently placed there by an unseen hand.

"This one's just perfect," said Chalmers. "It's like it was just set there on a pedestal."

Carey agrees with the assessment. "It's one of the best ships that I've ever seen," he said after his dive. Carey's hair may be greying but his boyish enthusiasm shone through last week after swimming through a boat he has sought for almost a decade. He dove on the ship with Chalmers and Bamford. "We were the first ones on that ship since 1913," Carey said.

Trotter wasn't part of the original discovery but his presence in Goderich during the momentous event provided the opportunity to take some sonar pictures of the vessel and the surrounding topography.

"It was like a dream for all this to come together," said Carey. "We've been looking for this for years." There have been reports of the *Wexford*'s discovery in the past but they either weren't substantiated or proved false. There is the chance this wreck could prove to be a ship other than the *Wexford* but the men who have dived on it are adamant that this is the real McCoy.

"There's no question what it is, absolutely none," said Chalmers.

The bed of the lake is provincial Crown land, so the vessel is the property of the province. The marine heritage committee had a licence[4] to search for the ship, but they will now have to obtain a licence through the Ministry of Recreation and Culture to do an official survey and to document the artifacts inside.

"Divers won't be able to touch the artifacts while the vessel is being surveyed," said Carey. "We've really got to educate people not to take artifacts," he said, repeating the diver's adage "take only pictures, leave only bubbles."

Is shipwreck searching over for Carey? It doesn't appear so. He feels knowledge gained from the location of the *Wexford* could help locate other ships. The chance discovery of the *Wexford* just has Carey wanting to find the *James Carruthers*, near Point Clark,[5] now one of only two undiscovered 1913 wrecks.

"The discovery of the *Wexford* was destined to be," insists Bamford. "It was the perfect day for the perfect find for the perfect dive with the perfect team."

The apparent discovery of the steamer *Wexford*, south of Bayfield and north of Grand Bend, may have disappointed some people who had hoped to find the ship closer to Goderich. Her discovery last week, however, could provide momentum for plans of the town of Goderich, and

The Wexford *being dipped in her forward hatches at the first concrete storage towers for the Goderich Elevator Company, 1903. This is the first known photograph of the* Wexford *after her arrival on the Great Lakes. It has been preserved in the Huron Institute Collection at the Collingwood Museum. According to archivists at the Sunderland Library, located in the city where the* Wexford *was built, there are no earlier photographic records available of her at that location.* Courtesy of Collingwood Museum. Access # 974-724-1.

its Marine Heritage Committee, to make this part of Lake Huron a scuba diving tourism destination.

"There could be an influx of divers as early as spring of next year," said Bob Carey, Chair of the Goderich Marine Heritage Committee. "It's not just the U.S. and Canada, it's international status, you'll have people from England diving on it … they'll want to know what their grandfathers built."

"The Town of Goderich is obviously interested in both marine heritage and bringing tourism to town," said Paul Carroll of the Huron County Historical Society.

The *Wexford* may have been the "Holy Grail" sought by the Marine Heritage Committee but members say there are many other potential shipwrecks waiting to be discovered.

"The activities of the committee since its inception less than two years ago has created a whole new awareness of marine heritage in the population of Goderich," said Brent Bamford, acting president of the Goderich chapter of Save Ontario Shipwrecks (SOS). "Many local residents are only just now becoming aware of Goderich's history as a major shipbuilder," he said.

The discovery of the *Wexford* prompted an impromptu champagne toast by divers and members of the shipwreck community. "It's like it was meant to be," said Jan Hawley, Secretary of the Marine Heritage Committee.

The man who discovered the vessel, Donald Chalmers, couldn't say enough about the state of the ship. "It's far and away the best wreck I've

Don Chalmers, the sailor who found the long-lost wreck while fishing with a downrigger.
Courtesy of David Bannister.

Celebrating the discovery of the Wexford, *Goderich, August 2000. From left to right: Paul Carroll; Brent Bamford; Stan Connelly; Bob Carey; Ellen Connelly, deputy mayor of the town of Goderich; Dave and Mickey Trotter; Jan Hawley; Paul Schaus; and Robin Wilson. Absent from the photo was Keith Homan, who assisted in the search and made an early dive on the newly found wreck.*
Photo from the Paul Carroll Collection.

ever seen for diving," he said. "I would think it would create some tourism for the area — it's an absolutely gorgeous wreck." He speaks not only as the man who discovered the find but as a diving enthusiast since 1955. "I've been on a lot of wrecks and this is absolutely the best I've ever seen."

What do Ford employees do when they're not hard at work? They head to the lakes to look for shipwrecks, it seems. The remarkable discovery of the English-built steamer *Wexford* is largely a Ford motor-company story. The man who discovered the vessel, Donald Chalmers, worked as a maintenance supervisor at the Ford assembly plant in St. Thomas for 30 years. Meanwhile, while Chalmers was discovering the boat, legendary Great Lakes shipwreck-finder David Trotter was on his way to Goderich.[6] Trotter, in an interesting twist to this story, is also a Ford man. He is a retired administrator with Ford Credit in Dearborn.

51

CHAPTER 1

Historical Perspectives:
Great Britain to the Great Lakes

They that go down to the sea in ships,
that do business in great waters;
These see the works of the LORD,
and his wonders in the deep.
For he commandeth, and raiseth the stormy wind,
which lifteth up the waves thereof.
                                    — Psalm 107:23–25

The *Wexford*: A History

The shipbuilding firm of William Doxford & Sons built the *Wexford* at Sunderland near the Scottish border on the northeast coast of England. Shipbuilders since 1840, they had accumulated almost a half-century of experience in their craft. The shipping environment on the River Wear was a good choice for the prospective owners of this new packet freighter. Not only were builders well experienced, but the presence of chandlers and equipment suppliers was bountiful. The *Wexford* keel was laid at the very heart of a shipbuilding region, in place for over 500 years, as but one of some 128 ships built on the River Wear that year.

From the evidence provided on her order papers,[1] signed on September 4, 1882, by Messrs. R.M. Hudson & Company,[2] of the same location, she was to be a fine and well-equipped vessel. Hull number 145, the well-decked steamer was to carry a single deck of steel, with four large hatchways covered with stout boards and canvas. An enclosed bridge was designed over the whole length of the two-cylinder, 207-horsepower engine — built at the same yards — and boiler space to provide a secure power plant. She was planned with an "open top gallant fcle" [*sic*] and "a hood over steering gear aft."[3]

She was to be a two-masted schooner. The deck would be strengthened with two longitudinal stringers, attached to web frames that ranged from 12 to 16 feet apart. Provision was made for 406 tons of water ballast below the holds. She may have been able to carry additional water ballast elsewhere, in her cargo holds and in the fore and after peak tanks. There were to be five bulkheads cemented in place. Crew space was provided in the bow, with entry through a hood from the open deck. Cabin space for the "old man"[4] was located forward and below the pilothouse, amidships, while officers were housed in space near the stern.

This photo of the Wexford *in the Welland Canal is a favourite image with many marine history buffs. It was made into a postcard that became popular for decades after the Great Storm.*
Courtesy of the late Audrey Barlow. Enhancements by Captain "Bud" Robinson.

The steamer Corunna, *built in 1891 by Ramage and Ferguson in Leith, Scotland, ran for the Leith, Hull and Hamburg Steam Packet Company Line of Scotland before coming to the Great Lakes under the ownership of C.H.F. Plummer and the Canadian Lake Transportation Company in 1907. She had a colourful history, not unlike the* Wexford, *and bears an uncanny resemblance to that vessel. She, like the* Wexford, *was rebuilt, with a new Scotch boiler installed by the Great Lakes Engineering Works, Ecorse, Michigan, in 1918. In 1930 she was purchased by the Corunna Steamship Company, Fort William, Ontario. In this era, many ships of similar design were built at the shipyards at the River Tyne, just to the north of Sunderland and the River Wear.*
Courtesy of the C. Patrick Labadie Collection/Thunder Bay National Marine Sanctuary, Alpena MI, 39243-39256.

The *Wexford* was built in the era that bridged the period between the great age of wooden sailing ships and the new era of large steam-powered, freight-carrying vessels made of iron and steel. Her internal design, crafted of steel girders and ribs, was the best combination of engineering design that married the old traditions with new practices — state-of-the-art for this time. When her new spar deck was added in 1884, the builders used web frames instead of beams to support the new

The Cherub. *A steam-powered, sailing gunboat, stationed at Goderich in 1866, during the Irish-American Fenian Raids, carried a sailing rig quite different from the schooner-rigged* Wexford. *This image shows her bearing square-rigged sails on the forward main mast. The main power for both vessels was a coal-fired, steam-powered engine.*
Photo from the Paul Carroll Collection.

construction. The engineering combined new approaches to structure with old. The altered drawings from 1883 refer to tween decks space created after this addition.

The fact that she was built with two large masts, long booms, and a full suit of sails, and that part of her upper deck was crafted of pine, bore witness to the reluctance of her builders to leave entirely the traditions of a maritime age that was fast coming to a close. Ship insurers often preferred the additional safety factors afforded by carrying a suit of sails.

The 250-foot keel was laid, beginning October 9, 1882, and she was ready for launch on March 24, 1883. After her decks were fitted out and interiors finished, her sea trials were completed by May 29, 1883. With only minor alterations, including some "machinery repairs," she sailed away in the hands of her owners on that same date.

Table 1: *Wexford* Specifications

Author's Note: Readers will observe no less than three different lengths given for the *Wexford*. They are all essentially correct. The "B. P." (between perpendiculars) is the length measured at the summer load line from fore side of the stem to the aft side of the rudder post. The "O.A." (overall length) is the distance measured between the forward-most and aft-most extensions on a vessel. The minor variation in the O.A. length is most likely a function of using slightly different extremes as starting points.

Information from Lloyd's Register, 1904–05:

Steel, screw steamer, 250' x 40. 1' x 16.7'

Built 1883, W. Doxford and Sons, Sunderland, A&CP official # C87342, ex *Elise*, ex *Wexford*

Registered at Port of London, classified in Great Lakes register special survey No. 3–11, 1895

Liverpool special survey No. 1, 1900, Dunkirk

Steel deck, spar deck, web frames (yellow pine decking noted on Collingwood drawings)

2,104 gross tons; 2,043 under deck tons; 1,340 net tons

Flat keel, cellular construction, double bottom, 5 bulkheads cemented water ballast after peak

Tank new donkey boiler, 1901

Engine 2 cylinder compound, 33" & 62" x 42", 200 nominal horsepower

Lloyd's Register 1913:

Engine 3 cylinder compound, 18", 30" & 51" x 42", 210 nominal horsepower new Scotch boilers 6/04 – 12d x 121

Engine altered to triple expansion, 1904 at Collingwood, SB&E Co. Ltd., Ontario

John O. Greenwood in Namesakes 1910–1913:

Hull No. 145, 257" x 40'1" x 16'7", Draft 23.7

3 compartments – capacity 675, 825, 1175. 2800 gross tons

Hatches 4 24 x 14

The Collingwood Bulletin April 16, 1903 page 8 (Marine News):

Particulars of the steamer *Wexford* which Capt. W.J. Bassett has purchased in the Old Country for the Western Steamship Company have come to hand. The steamer is a steel ship 258 ft. 6 in. in length beam 40 feet and a depth of hole (sic) to upper deck 24 feet. The steamer is classed 100 A 1 by Lloyds. She is what is known as a flushed deck ship and has main and spar decks and is so arranged as to carry a large amount of water ballast when necessary. The steamer is also fitted with steam winches, steam steering gear and hand and steam windlasses. She has a carrying capacity of 3,000 tons of freight of 100,000 bushels of wheat which is greater than any canal size steamer at present on the lakes. Capt. Bassett will commence to load the steamer tomorrow on the Thames at London with a cargo for Hamilton, Montreal and Fort William and he expects to sail for Montreal on Wednesday next.

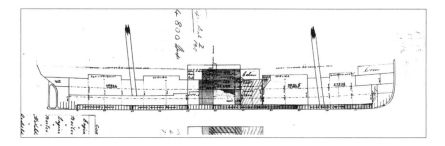

Order Plan for the Wexford, *showing the deck profile with spar deck, as added in 1884 by William Doxford & Sons Boatyards, River Wear, Sunderland. The ship plan for the* Wexford *was typical of many used at this time along the western seaboard of the British Isles.* Photo scanned from Ships Particulars Book, *held by the Tyne and Wear Archives of Sunderland, with permission of the Sunderland Public Library, England.*
Courtesy of Brent Bamford.

There is evidence,[5] in the form of handwritten, pencilled notes on the order sheet, that she returned to the Doxford yards 16 months later, in September 1884, for work on a seven foot high spar deck.[6] Part of this new construction to convert her to a flush-deck steamer seems to have allowed for an increase in coal capacity in the reserve bunker and would have altered her forward deck arrangement in particular. The fuel capacity appears to have been increased by some 50 tons of coal after the deck modifications.

There have been questions as to whether her galley was located midships or aft, with arguments posed to conjecture either position. It is generally assumed that the galley was located aft. According to diver Paul Schaus, "There were many broken and intact dishes on port side near the stern."[7] This observation would support the stern location of the galley and dining area for crew. There are secondary smokestacks or funnels in both locations. Early photographs show a large stack, sometimes casually but erroneously described as a "galley stack." In one later picture, with the new name of the shipping company, Western Steamship Co. Ltd., added at the bow, under the name *Wexford*, a minor change appears to have been made in the midship coal-bunker ventilator configuration. She carried a directional ventilator as a cap instead of a rope-suspended canvas hood, as shown in one very early picture. It is also possible that

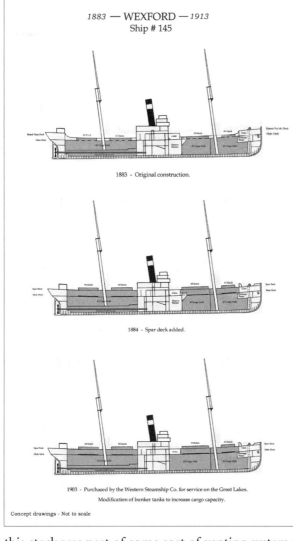

1883 — WEXFORD — 1913
Ship # 145

1883 - Original construction.

1884 - Spar deck added.

1903 - Purchased by the Western Steamship Co. for service on the Great Lakes.
Modification of bunker tanks to increase cargo capacity.

Concept drawings - Not to scale

These successive profiles show the configuration of the Wexford *as she evolved. The first is as-built in 1883. In the second, the 1884 spar deck as added was normally constructed of lighter material than the main deck below, and consequently had to be given a lighter draft when loaded. Only passengers and lighter cargo would normally be carried here. In the third drawing, the probable alteration made in the 1904 re-fit at Collingwood is shown.*
Courtesy of Captain "Bud" Robinson.

this stack was part of some sort of venting system to draw methane off the coal stored in the bunkers below, to reduce or eliminate the possibility of explosion. Another possibility is that it simply provided a way to draw off heat, smoke, and fumes from the coal-fired boilers in the engine room that supported the secondary donkey boiler.

The *Wexford* was a steel-hulled, 2,100-ton package freighter. Prior to the addition of her spar deck, she was rated at 1,626.91 tons. Her length between perpendiculars — bow stem and rudder post — was 250 feet, with a 40-foot beam. She carried a depth of just under 24 feet, after the addition of the spar deck. The builders' specifications show her as slightly less than 259 feet[8] in length and some 19 feet in depth, before the spar deck. Her revised light draft, in 1884, was 7 feet 10 inches aft, and 7 feet 8 inches forward. Loaded, she carried up to 15 feet 3 inches before the spar deck was added; afterwards, 20 feet 8 inches was shown in the plans. Photographic records show her loaded on the Great Lakes at between 16 and 18 feet. The original plans show that she could carry 2,500 — and some reports say up to 3,000 — tons of freight, as well as over 400 tons of coal. The pilothouse deck was constructed of three-inch yellow pine. She carried a "hurricane deck" or open platform, extending through and above the wooden enclosure we are calling a pilothouse, protected only by stanchions, with a rail, often covered by weather-cloths for protection from the elements.

Her name, *Wexford*, was the same as the name taken by a town and a county in southern Ireland. The name *Wexford* had been carried proudly on many a seafaring transom since the early 1600s, when the British Navy ruled the seas.

Viking refugees from Denmark founded Wexford Town in Ireland around the year 850 AD. They were attracted by its handy location near the mouth of the River Slaney. The Viking name *Waesfjord* means "sandy harbour." The Vikings fortified the harbour town with a defensive mound and a wall, and also allowed a Gaelic–Irish village to be established outside their own walled settlement. Wexford was a handy port for Vikings to break their journey when sailing along the east coast of Ireland between the several other Viking settlements, such as Limerick, Cork, Waterford, Arklow, Wicklow, and Dublin. The shallow Wexford harbour also facilitated salt farming, salt being a very important trading item to the Vikings.

The Normans captured the town just after their first landings in the year 1169 AD, and later improved on the Viking wall, extending it to include the Gaelic–Irish settlement, as well. Tragically, Oliver Cromwell also included Wexford in his "1649–1650 Irish Tour"[9] and three-quarters of the two thousand inhabitants were put to the sword, including all the town's Franciscan friars — the standard treatment for towns that refused to surrender to Cromwell. During the 1798 Rebellion, rebels made a determined stand in Wexford Town before they were defeated by the British Army. It is not clear why the name *Wexford* was used to name several British seafaring vessels over the centuries. It may have been to honour and to personify the courageous, daring, and defiant stand taken by the village inhabitants in the 1798 Irish Rebellion.

For five years the steamer *Wexford* plied the South American trade routes to and from Argentina, uneventfully, under her first master, William Richardson. A skipper with 10 solid years of experience as a ship's master, Richardson hailed from Sunderland, and had most likely watched his vessel materialize in the Doxford ways before he applied to become her first captain. It is likely that he recommended the spar deck modifications made to her late in the season of 1884, as noted earlier. He remained as her skipper until 1888, at which time a 35-year-old Scot, Thomas Walker, a master since '83, took over the helm.

It was clear that this "cabins amidships" steamer, a centre pilothouse packet freighter, sometimes also called a "centre-island" steamer, was well-suited to traverse the ocean routes from north to south Atlantic. She could conduct herself well in the constantly blowing trades, the gentle and erratic doldrums, and the occasional ocean gale. Her steam-driven engine, the single screw, and the benefit gained from carrying a schooner rig with gaff-rigged sails, worked well in tandem to carry her loads to southern climes and return. The twin-masted sailing rig gave added stability in the long, rolling ocean swells — and sometimes a good push with offshore trades on the quarter. The strong wooden booms, carried on each mast, doubled as deck cranes to help load and unload bales of cargo, packed below the four planked and canvas-covered hatchways.

As a package freighter, she probably carried manufactured goods, including textiles, porcelain, cutlery, and tableware from mills and foundries across the heavily industrialized districts of England. On her return voyages, she would be loaded with cane sugar, bananas, raw rubber, wool, mutton, citrus, tallow, tannin, tung oil, tea, and other exotic cargo to meet an enthusiastic demand back at home. The tween deck area would have contained packaged freight and lighter payloads, while her main holds would carry bulk cargo. No bills of lading have yet surfaced to confirm the exact details of her cargo at this time.

William Deal, crew member of the Wexford *during her South American passages, shown at age 60.*
Courtesy of descendant Keith Deal.

During her first 15 years as an ocean freighter, she also made passage to the Mediterranean Sea. No details have been discovered to confirm her destinations or her cargo under the direction of Master Knox Mogelstine, her skipper from 1891 to 1895.[10] In spite of the fact that Mogelstine had been the master of several wrecked vessels prior to his role on the *Wexford*, this period of time was also uneventful for the British freighter.

Under Master James Sloggett, she made many trips to and from South America in 1896 and 1897. Sloggett was born in Plymouth in 1844, and became a ship's master at age 30. The *Wexford* continued to ply the southerly routes until 1897, after which, in probable need of repair and in a time of falling freight rates, she was sold in 1898. She was renamed *Elise* by her new owner, a Monsieur Dubuisson of Dunkirk, France. Within a few years the new owner found her to be a business liability for the French firm. In 1901 she required the refit of her auxiliary don-key boiler.[11] She returned to London, England, and, by 1903, was sold yet again to the Western Steamship Company from Toronto. She was relocated to the Great Lakes, continuing to be registered out of London under her original name, *Wexford*. It is an interesting side note that the Western Steamship purchased a second vessel,[12] the *J.A. McKee*, a similar size vessel, built in England, at Newcastle-On-Tyne by Swan, Hunter and Richardson in 1908. The voyage of the *McKee* in the 1913 Great Storm is addressed, in part, later in this account.

The new owner of the *Wexford*, William J. Bassett, managing director for the company, travelled to England to take personal charge and provide supervision for Captain George Thomas on the long voyage home to Canada. The following account, from *The Collingwood Bulletin* of April 16, 1903, tells the story:

> Particulars of the steamer *Wexford* which Capt. W.J. Bassett has purchased in the Old Country for the Western Steamship Company have come to hand. The steamer is a steel ship, 258 [feet] 6 [inches] in length, beam 40 feet and a depth of hole [sic] to upper deck 24 feet. The steamer is classed as "100 A1" by Lloyds. She is what is known as a flushed deck ship and has main and spar decks and is so arranged as to carry a large amount of water ballast when necessary. The steamer is also fitted with steam winches, steam steering gear and hand and steam windlasses. She has a carrying capacity of 3,000 tons of freight of 100,000 bushels of wheat which is greater than any canal size steamer at present on the lakes. Capt. Bassett will commence to load the steamer tomorrow on the Thames at London with a cargo for Hamilton, Montreal and Fort William and he expects to sail for Montreal on Wednesday next.
>
> Bassett signed on as "Purser" — to be paid the nominal wage of £1 for the voyage — probably to meet the requirements of the British Board of Trade — to account for all crew on a foreign-going ship. He joined a crew of 22 plus the Captain, George Thomas, and her Mate, S.

Colborne. The crew was a mixed collection of nationalities. Nine hailed from England, four from Sweden, three from Norway, two from Finland, two from France, two from Germany, one from Holland, one from Denmark, along with Bassett from Ontario, Canada.

During a stop at Dunkirk, France, a crewmember, H.G. Bentley, was discharged "… and left in hospital on account of sickness (scarletina) and that the balance of his wages £3 17.4 has been paid and his effects delivered to the hospital." — signed John (undecipherable), British Vice Consul. The Vice Consul "sanctioned the engagement" of her new crew for overseas passage, and certified the Agreement and Account of Crew, April 6, 1903, which contained these details.[13]

Certificate of Endorsement for 1903 Transatlantic Voyage of Wexford. *The process of "clearing out" was a formal review of a ship's particulars, crew, and conditions aboard, always authenticated by government officials at the departure point.* Courtesy of Library and Archives Canada, R184-202-5-E, 1903.

Several interesting terms of service were noted:

> At the Master's option, no grog allowed on the voyage. Provisions included a sufficient supply of water, bread, beef, pork, flour, peas, rice, condensed milk, tea and cocoa, for the trip. No cash shall be advanced aboard or liberty granted other than at the pleasure of the Master. The seamen and firemen are to keep their respective forecastles in a clean and sanitary condition and leave them so at the end of the voyage under a penalty of 5/ [shillings][14] — per man for each case of neglect.
>
> Should any crew fail to join at the time specified in the agreement, the Master may engage substitutes at once. The crew shall be decreed complete with 21 hands all told. The fireman shall supply the galley with coals.
>
> Anyone using offensive or abusive language to Master or Officers will be fined 10/ — anyone found asleep or absent when on the lookout will be fined 5/ per offence.[15]

Such were the Articles of Agreement for the crew when the *Wexford* departed Dunkirk, France, on April 8, 1903, headed for Montreal, via London.

An interesting requirement, in handwritten notes on page one of the Agreement and Account of Crew for the trip was an employment guarantee for all crew members upon their arrival in Canada: "[O]n arrival at port of destination the crew agree to be discharged and reshipped on Canadian articles in the same capacities and at the current Canadian wages for any period not exceeding nine months terminating in Canada."[16]

It was rumoured that she was in trouble and had to stop in at the Azores to take on fuel to ensure that she would arrive home securely. The two-masted schooner rig was still intact at this time, and she may have used her canvas as a power assist and to add stability on the huge ocean swells. In any event, a telegraph from Mr. Bassett to his wife, at

Collingwood, Ontario, on Georgian Bay, Lake Huron, confirmed that all was well, and she need not worry.

Again, according to *The Collingwood Bulletin*, May 14, 1903:

> On Saturday, Mrs. Bassett received the following cable-gram from her husband, Capt. W.J. Bassett, who is bringing out the steamer *Wexford* for the Western Lakes Steamship Company. — "Port Delgada, Azores — Have put in here today. Short of coal. Will leave after coaling. Strong gale with heavy sea." The steamer was not in trouble as reported around town.

The rest of her transatlantic journey was uneventful, and she arrived in Montreal on May 4, 1903, spending two days there. She was discharged at this port by mutual consent, under seal of the Shipping Master's Office, Montreal, signed by the vice consul.[17]

As noted by *The Collingwood Bulletin* of May 28, 1903:

> Capt. W.J. Bassett arrived with the steamer *Wexford* at Father Point[18] on Wednesday last and at Montreal on Friday. The steamer had a full load of freight for Canadian ports. The *Wexford* was bought by the Western Steamship Company and was brought out by Capt. George Thomas. The steamer is schooner rigged and was built in 1883 in Sunderland. Subsequently, she was engaged in the British and French trade. She is of 1,340 tons register, 250 feet in length, 40 feet in breadth and 23 feet deep. She is fitted with a (3 cylinder, triple expansion) compound engine of 200 horsepower. The steamer will immediately engage in the freight business of the upper lakes.

Once on the lakes, her first cargo of inter-lake origin was unloaded at Goderich. On June 25, 1903, the *Bulletin* reported that: "The Western

The Wexford *is shown dockside at an unknown location. If a boat is unable to get dockage at the inner harbour piers near loading and unloading facilities, she was often forced to wait in the less protected outer harbour areas.*
Courtesy of Ron Beaupre/ Library and Archives Canada, PA-213341.

Steamship Company's new steamer *Wexford*, Capt. W.J. Bassett, arrived at Goderich on Saturday with her first cargo from one lake port to another. The cargo consisted of grain taken aboard at Fort William."

When it became apparent that she required a major refitting, Bassett contracted for major works to be undertaken following her first season on the lakes. She was to be taken to the Collingwood Shipyards — ironically, the concept of which was conceived in 1882, at the same time as R.M. Hudson was engaged in planning discussions with the Doxford shipyards in Sunderland, to build the centre pilothouse freighter.

According to the *Detroit Post and Tribune* of May 2, 1882: "Collingwood has in contemplation the building of a dry dock and shipyard, and the council is prepared to submit a by-law granting a very liberal bonus to any person or persons who will undertake to build, equip and properly run said dry dock and shipyard." Collingwood had become the key shipbuilding yard on the Canadian Upper Lakes, and remained the industry leader until its demise in the 1980s. The winter berthing yard for the *Wexford* was normally Collingwood Harbour.

The Wexford *is shown at the Collingwood Shipbuilding Company Yards at the opening of navigation season in 1909. This overhead shot provides a clear image of the deck plan of the centre island ship design in the middle period of her tenure as a bulk freighter, carrying mostly cargoes of grain on the Great Lakes.*
Courtesy of the Library and Archives Canada, C006-767.

The *Wexford* was placed in dry dock in 1904 for major restorative works and an extensive refitting at the Collingwood Shipyards. Her boilers and engine were replaced by the Collingwood Shipbuilding and Engine Company Limited, which won the contract for her boilers first, and then her engine. According to newspapers, a "gang of men are [*sic*] engaged in taking down the old engines and preparing for the removal of the boilers."[19] She had two new "Scotch" boilers installed and a triple expansion engine, made in Collingwood. While the engine was similar to other marine engines, it differed from the usual design in that the piston rod and crosshead were separate. The connecting rod had a wedge-type upper end — and the thrust block carried adjustable collars.

Following those upgrades, she routinely made passage from Thunder Bay, apparently unloading steel and reloading wheat at Fort William for the trip downbound to the elevators at the Port of Goderich. There remains the question as to whether she actually carried deck cargo, such as steel rails for the railroad industry. There are no available Canadian records for this cargo, but most American history sources cite that the *Wexford* carried steel rails as part of her circuit from Lake Superior through ports on Lake Huron, Georgian Bay, and the lower lakes. No documentation is provided for these claims. Her log for 1903 was thought to be available

This three-cylinder Doty engine is similar to a much larger triple-expansion engine fitted to the Wexford *in 1904. The engine shown was built in Goderich. These engines, remarkable for their simplicity and versatility, were manufactured in many sizes.*
Courtesy of the late Graham MacDonald.

at the National Archives,[20] but the document there makes no reference to cargo at all. The deck configuration does not seem to give credence to this claim. It is possible, according to Captain Bud, that she could have carried rails on her tween deck, in this case on the old main deck then below the newer spar deck, or indeed in the bottom of the main cargo holds if necessary to keep her centre of gravity low. If she did carry rails on her tween deck, this would have raised her centre of gravity, compounding any problem after storm ice accumulation. Perhaps we can rely on the word of her owner to settle the matter? During the Goderich Inquest, owner and manager of the Western Steamship Company, Captain J.W. Bassett, stated, "She has only carried two cargoes of ore, never any package freight and never carried deck loads."[21]

The *Wexford* was a well-known Goderich, Georgian Bay, and Lake Huron vessel. Her centre pilothouse, cabin-amidships design, large twin masts (finally stripped of her full suit of sail), and the flared bow "salty" lines made her easy to recognize and to remember. Unlike her counterparts

Two traditional lakers, with fore- and aft-cabin structures, are shown wintering at Goderich, circa 1920, next to a smaller "cabins amidships" vessel. Lakeports such as Goderich, Sarnia, and Collingwood were the site of large numbers of lake boats laid up for shipkeeping each winter. Goderich Harbour would often host more than 20 vessels for the winter season.
Courtesy of Huron County Museum and Historic Gaol.

— boxy-looking lake freighters, long and plain, with their cabins found fore and aft, leaving a long, plain and open deck space — she was much more visually appealing.

Her master and senior officers, sometimes accompanied by the unofficial passengers onboard, would stand atop the pilothouse on the open lee, cloth-clad hurricane deck, waving to spectators and dockworkers as she proudly entered port. Members of her young crew hailed from the lakeshore town of Goderich and other communities along the Huron shoreline, but most hailed from Collingwood, on Georgian Bay, where she rested during most winters as part of the storage fleet in that harbour. On occasion she also wintered in the Goderich harbour.

Her business success for the Western Steamship Company was sometimes called into question. The Goderich Coroner's Inquest, following the storm in 1913, raised questions about her repair history and her time supposedly out of service — running aground, hitting the docks, and losing propeller blades on repeated occasions. In one wreck report from 1910 she was reported as held up in the "Soo" in December 1909 with "trifling damage" and a partial loss of her cargo of grain. Her owner, defending her safety record, said, "The *Wexford* has only been in drydock about six times in 10 years."[22]

The *Collingwood Enterprise* of August 21, 1913, reported that:

> On Aug. 17, the SS *Wexford* went aground abreast of Lime Island[23] in the fog. On Friday night she was released from her grounding at 9 p.m. after lightering 50,000 bushels of wheat. Water had leaked into #1 and 2 cargo holds [wetting approximately 20,000 bushels of grain]. Pumps were used in the forward hold. A diver went to examine the vessel's injuries and make temporary repairs so the vessel could continue to Goderich. The 50,000 bushels of wheat [lightered] would wait for transport and delivery by the first available ship from the company owning the *Wexford* [Western Steamship Co.]. Mr. F.D. Root, the manager of the Great Lakes Towing Co., was representing the insurance company.

Capt. J.B. Foote [of Toronto] was looking after the Western Steamship Company's interests. The vessel was expected to get away on the 18th of August.[24]

In the *Saturday Evening News*, another Collingwood newspaper (August 30, 1913), it was reported that the "*Wexford* came in from Goderich Wednesday morning and immediately went into dry dock. A large number of plates would have to be replaced." This event, the last known mishap before her November voyage, may have contributed to the hasty retirement of her skipper, Captain George Playter. According to a newspaper report, Playter became ill and went home for the balance of the season.

The Wexford, *right, is shown in dry dock in Collingwood beside the passenger steamer* Germanic, *owned by the Northern Navigation Company. The* Wexford *had run aground, damaging a number of plates. The* Germanic *had survived a serious collision with a fishing tug, the* Victoria K., *which she cut in two and sent to the bottom. Both vessels were undergoing repairs. Date unknown.*
Courtesy of the C. Patrick Labadie Collection/Thunder Bay National Marine Sanctuary, Alpena, MI, # 156067-156090.

The *Wexford*, laden with 96,000 bushels of grain from Fort William, and her crew, said to be 22 in number,[25] left the dock at Sault Ste. Marie, Ontario, early Saturday morning, November 8, 1913, bound for Goderich. The *Collingwood Enterprise* of that day reported that "The steamer *Wexford* was last seen on Saturday last when the steamer *City of Midland* passed her in Hay Lake [now named Lake Nicolet] while the former was lying at anchor, apparently she had later passed on down the river and gone out from Detour heading for Goderich." The same account stated that she "took on coal at Detour and started down the lake well South of Duck Island on a line for Georgian Bay."

We know that she was seen once again, somewhere north of Point Clark, by the steamer *Kaministiquia*, and one questionable report has her much farther west in view of the northbound *H.B. Hawgood*.

Her captain was Frank Bruce Cameron, born September 4, 1889. A sailor, he was the second son of lake port captain and Master Mariner Alex Campbell Cameron. Bruce was certified as a mate in Collingwood in 1910, and acquired his master's papers, Certificate No. 6713, in 1912, qualifying him to act as a master of steam-freight vessels on the Great Lakes. A young man, he was only 24 years and two months old when he

The Goderich Lighthouse, circa 1900, showing the storm-signal tower as it would have appeared in 1913. The lighthouse grounds were used as a grazing yard for farm animals at that time. From its first construction in the mid-1800s, the lighthouse had been improved and refined until around 1890, at which time it seemed to enter a period of decline. Major improvements were planned for after 1910, but were not completed until political necessity dictated betterment of the lighthouse following the 1913 storm.
Courtesy of Duncan and Linda Jewell.

assumed the master's role. The year before, on February 29, 1912, he had married his young bride, Blanche Moore.

Cameron was a talented young hockey player of some renown and had the scars to prove it. During a playoff game against Cobourg in late February 1910, while playing defence for the Collingwood Shipbuilders, he bloodied the ice with a slashed artery on his left foot.[24] According to the newspapers of the day, the team went on to win the first of nine Ontario Championships (Ontario Hockey Association, Intermediate "A").[26]

Being assigned the captain's role on the *Wexford* was his first — and final — marine role as a ship's master. He assumed command of the *Wexford* in 1913, following the sudden retirement of her skipper in the last weeks of October. The glowing pride that surely could be seen in the face and eyes of his young bride, Blanche, would soon flicker and die. By mid-November, tears of sorrow and despair would replace her broad smiles and the sparkling eyes that had marked her aura of marital bliss.

CHAPTER 2

The Skipper's Log

Let only the young come,
Says the sea.
Let them kiss my face
And hear me.
I am the last word
And I tell
Where storms and stars come from.

> — Carl Sandburg, from *Young Sea*

Captain Bruce Cameron's View:
The Skipper's Personal Log[1]

Although there was always a ship's log to keep records of trips, maintenance, and other particulars up to date, and there was a bill of lading for each trip, such as the one found in Bruce Cameron's pocket when his body was recovered, ship captains and other crew sometimes kept their own personal diary as a log of their trips and their feelings about events that transpired. A good example is the diary of young Captain Edward McConkey of the packet (or package freighter) *Regina*, now held by the

Huron County Museum in Goderich.[2] It was found in a pocket on his body when it finally washed ashore in August 1914. The diary was returned to his wife, who dried each page carefully by placing a tissue between each leaf. It remained in the family for years until it was donated to the Huron County Museum by McConkey's daughter Amy, in June of 1984. Amy, who was seven years old at the time of the storm, said she "remembers how her sorrowing mother would sit on the side of the bed, misty-eyed, reading the words which Ed had written during the months of 1913."[3]

The diary is a small, pocket-sized, leather-bound volume, with hand-written entries recounting daily events, feelings about the weather, and thoughts about family. It is written in a MILES COMBINATION DIARY, MEMORANDUM & COMPENDIUM OF USEFUL INFORMATION — a commercial, blank journal used for such purposes. McConkey filled in the personal information section at the beginning of the diary, stating his employment by the Interlake Line of Toronto,[4] his weight at 186 pounds, his height at 5 feet 8½ inches, shoe size 7½, and hat size of 7 1/8. He lists detailed expenses, both of a personal nature and for the ship. He writes observations about ships seen travelling "up and down," and includes comments to confirm the behaviour and disposition of the crew. For example, May 31, 1913: "Boyer and Reid drunk again." He also records the dates of letters received and sent to his wife, Amanda, as well as the occasions on which he was able to telegraph messages to her. The weather sometimes bothered him. On November 3, a few days before the storm, he enters, "hard pull. anxious. Not to [sic] much fuel." His final entry was written Friday, November 7, at Sombra, where he noted, "loading hay. Cloudy S." The entry for November 8 was blank.

In one incident, he describes the progress of a nephew, Bert, taken onboard the last time Captain Ed left home, to mentor him through a "drinking habit." According to daughter Amy, "Pappa had to sack the cook and his helper for having whiskey onboard — Bert took over the work and did very well. Bert's progress toward 'becoming a man' ended in the wintry gales of 1913 — somewhere on Lake Huron, along with his advocate and mentor Captain McConkey."[5]

It was clear that McConkey pined for the presence of his wife. In his diary entries for September 1913, he "wired Amanda at Kingston" just before leaving the dock, arranging for her to join him onboard the next day at Toronto. "Amanda aboard," he writes. "Wish she were going for a round trip, but weather disagreeable. I am going to have her go as far as Hamilton anyway." He leaves Hamilton with Amanda still onboard, leaving her at Port Dalhousie. In spite of his extra time with her, he writes, "Amanda going to leave me here.... Oh how blue I feel."[6] In the words of his daughter, as she wrote in June 1978, "After seventy years the pages are frail and the writing becomes more faint each year. The gilded 1913, boldly inscribed, is no longer bright and shiny. But these memories can now live forever."[7]

After the storm, a diary written by "youthful fair-haired" Walter McInnes, a wheelsman on the *Regina*, was also found. As reported in the news:

> McInnes was a good boy. That is indicated by the diary which he kept. It is evident that the mother was the boy's idol, for carefully written in the pages of the little book are his complete accounts, the money expended for tobacco and underwear, the little incidentals, and other items denoting thrift on the part of the dead youth.
>
> But, better still is the record kept by this youthful sailor of the money sent home to his mother. The reporter, together with the Coroner Clark, separated a pile of money order receipts which were found in the dead youth's pocket. His memorandum book showed that he sent his mother during the season over $400.... His record was one that any mother could be proud of. Last night he lay silent and still between the forms of two of his shipmates, and there was a smile of contentment on his face.[8]

Although there is no such record for Bruce Cameron, the youthful, newly married, and freshly appointed master must surely have reflected on the important things in his life, as well as the issues of the moment, as he undertook this first, and fateful, voyage. An enthusiastic newcomer would most likely carry a diary to record these exciting events in his new position of leadership onboard. Let us conjecture what he might have written, based on considerable sailing experience and knowledge of Lake Huron:

On this uncompleted voyage, only 11 entries:

Entry 1: November 7, afternoon.
The passage from Thunder Bay has been quiet. The pleasant autumn weather persists, in spite of the lateness in time. This trip may not be our last run, after all. Although Blanche will not be happy about that — and I'm sure the gang on the shipyards' team will want me pulling my weight on the ice in the scrimmages to come. That ankle that got badly cut up three years back is still bothering me when the glass goes down. It's the cold in the air, I guess. Maybe Bassett will want another run up the lake and back — to make up for the damage costs.

Entry 2: November 7, evening.
We're fairly tight to the line [plimsoll] with 96,000 bushels in the hold. But the bilges are dry. The new plates after Playter's big mishap on Lime Island must have been fastened tightly and well — no sign of anything in our bilges. The guys at the yards know how to flatten those rivets. Have to wonder how he'd let her wander that far off course, especially in the fog. Steering chains seem tight, so it can't be that kind of problem. But then, it wasn't the first time he'd put her up — and then, hitting the docks earlier on was a strange move, too. This old girl doesn't deserve that kind of treatment. She's sure had her moments — but comes through every time.

78

Entry 3: November 8, morning.
The barometer dropped a real heller, in a very short time. Amazing. And the southwest wind with almost single-digit temperatures is really unusual. Must be an Arctic front twisting in around the lakes. It doesn't seem to matter which direction, the winds on Superior pile up the swells in no time. Our heading to the Soo can be maintained, although the roll coming in on the starboard bow may shift a bit of our cargo. Shouldn't hurt. The breakers are sparkling white against the sky — kind of a treat to watch.

Entry 4: November 8, afternoon.
Plan on pulling into Hay Lake. Let's wait to find out what's really going on. Weather doesn't seem quite right. Getting quiet again. Maybe should send a letter to Blanche when we stop at De Tour for coal.

Entry 5: November 8, evening.
If it gets any colder, I'll have to warn the crew to watch for ice on the deck — too easy to get hurt. Although that's not likely. It's too early for it to build up. And it's been too warm. A great Fall ... early November — and the first real cold snap. Wonder what it's like at home?

Entry 6: November 9, 3:00 a.m.
Wind's still freshening; up and down. Gusting heavily, but only at times. The big guys are on their way. Guess we'll go.

Entry 7: November 9, dawn.
I'll bet Wilmott and his mate are happy they bought passage home to England before they started this trip. Even if we do one more run, they'll make their departure date

— December 6 — with no trouble at all. Wonder when Jimmy Glen has his booked? Wants to pick up his wife and bring her back to Goderich before the new season begins.

These cold blasts will be old hat to Solliere, our Swede who just joined in September — a good deck hand; works hard.

Entry 8: November 9, 10:00 a.m.
Settled again; almost calm. Strange.

Entry 9: November 9, 11:00 a.m.
Acknowledged the *Kaministiquia* a few miles north of Point Clark. The *McKee* should be around here somewhere too.

Decks Awash — these two photographs were taken from the W.H. Truesdale *in 1936 by the late Captain James McCannel. "Catching fish in the smokestack" was the saying used to describe massive waves rolling over the decks and superstructures of lake boats. Note the lifeline cable strung from bridge to engine house. Moving along this cable was the only means of fore-and-aft communication. One can only imagine the horror that must be experienced by crew members during intense storms.*
Courtesy of the Captain "Bud" Robinson Collection.

Entry 10: November 9, noon.
Wow, a real change. Wind's swung right around to NNW and blasting even harder. Gale force. Got new ice and snow building up on deck. Amazing — have to watch what's coming from behind us.

Entry 11: November 9, 2:00 p.m.
Piling up. Ice on the cables is amazing. Should be off Goderich; it's really bad! Blanche, I love you dearly.

No more entries.

CHAPTER 3

The Final Voyage

With that, he gathered the cloud, and seizing his trident in
his hands, stirred up the sea, and roused the tempest blast of
every wind, and hid the land and sea with vapour: and dark-
ness swooped from the sky. The East Wind and South Wind
clashed together, and the stormy West Wind, and the heaven-
born North Wind, drove a vast wave before him.

— Lord Poseidon, upon meeting Odysseus, raising a storm.

Homer, from *The Odyssey*, Book Five.

Just One More Voyage — For This Season!

While the drums and cones of the signal towers at the Sault and all
other stations down the lake warned of heavy storms, there was no
indication as to the extent of the feral "white hurricane" that would
follow. Even if the signals were up before the storm, they were not seen
to be sufficient to keep the captains in. "These signals were simply used
as guides to navigation," later claimed a witness at the inquest. He went
on to affirm that captains would have gone out at their own risk and

they alone were responsible: "I would have gone out myself," concluded Captain Whitney of the Lake Carriers' Association.[1]

There was even a deceiving break in the early November gale that morning — a window that might allow safe passage to their Goderich destination. The barometer was rising. And, in the one humorous statement, also made at the inquest following the storm, a witness affirmed that "sailors hung their hats over the barometers so they could not see it going down."[2] Several captains must have agreed, for they all departed from the safety of the Sault Locks. At the other end of the lake, other vessels headed north, away from the security of the St. Clair River, at about the same time.

In its annual report for 1913, the Lake Carriers' Association refers to the misleading conflict of the elements that prompted these

The Turret Chief *is shown entering Goderich Harbour on a quiet afternoon. She was lost on Lake Superior during the Great Storm, but was recovered the next year. She was one of the famous "turret-hulled" vessels built at the Doxford Shipyards in Sunderland in 1896. The word* turret *is thought to be a mispronunciation of the word* terrace, *first assigned by Doxford to name the shape of the bulging side of the hull. The fattened hull would permit more cargo to be carried, thus enabling higher profit margins for the owners.*
Courtesy of Huron County Museum and Historic Gaol, # 987-0012-008.

departures. Their report for November 8 states, in reference to Lake Superior, where the storm had its origins, that "Vessels generally remained in port on that lake during the day or sought shelter along the north shore. During a lull of a few hours, in which it appeared that the sea was going down, and that the worst of the blow was over [vessels] put out."[3] For Lake Huron: "The northwest gale had practically died down to a breeze of about fifteen miles from the northwest, the sea being quiet.... Obviously, in such a condition, there was nothing to disturb an experienced navigator on the course that vessels usually follow in crossing this lake."[4]

It is imperative to remember the complex navigation skills required of these early mariners. Today, with the assistance of computerized GPS devices to pin down locations to within a few yards, full-colour electronic chart plotters that show one's exact position and course on an LCD computer screen, triple-scan depth-sounders that actually show the bottom contours as 3D images, electronic fluxgate compasses, and sophisticated autopilot steering devices, one would have to be a bit of a dolt not to find one's way on the water. But in those earlier days, navigation depended on the insight of an experienced mariner, who required a refined set of skills to determine the vessel's position using paper charts, a magnetic compass, a "lead line"[5] to measure depths, and complex manual calculations. It took a combination of intuition, mathematics, and observation skills, often in periods of foul weather conditions and little or no visibility, to find your way. It is little wonder there could be problems.

So Captain Cameron steamed through the Sault Locks, too. According to the *Detroit News*, November 13, 1913, the *Wexford* "passed down at the Soo in company with the *Willis King* and others which have since arrived in Port Huron, but nothing has been heard of her." But for some reason he chose to drop a hook at Hay Lake[6] before heading farther south to De Tour, where he took on coal before the passage south across the stormy waters of Lake Huron to his destination at Goderich. The *Wexford* was seen lying at anchor at Hay Lake by the steamer *City of Midland* as the latter ship passed her by.

Cameron must have been wary that Lake Huron was not yet fit for the safe passage to Goderich. He may also have had concern about safely

This image of the Wexford, *thought to be taken in Fort William, was a popular postcard image in the lake-faring community. The lighter colour of the lower half of her hull was actually a rusty red, the colour of a much-used anti-fouling paint used at the time to keep boat hulls free of algae and scum.*
Courtesy of the C. Patrick Labadie Collection/Thunder Bay National Marine Sanctuary, Alpena, MI, # 156067-156088.

entering the Goderich harbour. There was a widely held concern that this port was not a safe haven. The narrow entrance made it extremely difficult to enter in heavy weather. As company owner Bassett stated deridingly during the inquest, "Your harbour here is like many others. It is a political $2.50 harbour, just good enough to hold the vote."[7]

Captain Whitney, who was the dock superintendent at Ashtabula, a major shipping and commercial Ohio port on Lake Erie, said, while appearing at the Goderich Inquest as Chairman of the Lake Carriers' Association, that he had examined the foghorn, and as he considered it insufficient and inadequate, he would not care to attempt to enter this port in a storm. He suggested that one should be placed at the end of the pier and operated with the use of compressed air, similar to the ones in use at the American harbours.

As other ships passed him by that fateful night, Cameron must have mustered the courage to proceed, hauled anchor, and begun the journey down. As a novice master of only three weeks, he would not wish to be seen as unworthy of his new charge. It may be that his hesitancy set the stage for the tragedy that followed. Had he continued in company of those other ships that passed through at the Soo, he may well have reached his destination just ahead of the terrible storm.[8]

Captain Stephen of the steamer *Kaministiquia*, dubbed the "storm king"[9] by hundreds of Goderich folk lining the docks to meet his freighter when it arrived safely at Goderich, saw the *Wexford* in fair weather, some 15 miles north of Point Clark about 10:30 Sunday morning, November 9. This sighting, some 30 to 35 miles north of her destination, the Port of Goderich, is the last time the vessel was definitively seen. She must have left her protected anchorage early the previous evening.

In another report, given in a television interview in 2002 by the then-elderly wheelsman Ed Kanaby of the *H.B. Hawgood*, Kanaby suggested that they sighted the *Wexford* as the *Hawgood* struggled northward, but much farther south and west than the *Wexford* ever should have been. "On the way up, looking to the east, there was another little boat there. I didn't know what it was, but later somebody said that it was the *Wexford*."[10] This location, presumed to be south of Harbor Beach (also called Sand Beach), Michigan — immediately across the lake, opposite Goderich — does not seem like a plausible location for the *Wexford* to be seen.

At that time, late Sunday morning on November 9, residents of the Point Clark area reported, according to old-timer Gordon Jamieson, that on their way to church that morning, "The lake was as calm as glass … by the time church was over, it was obvious that no boat could be safe in the water."[11]

William Ruffle, foreman at the Goderich Elevator, claims that he saw the *Wexford* off Goderich, where she "lay fighting the gale."[12] William Niven made a startling statement that he saw "rockets shoot up three times on Sunday."[13] She was thought to be heard several times later that day. There were reports of her whistles and foghorns in the late afternoon. Ruffle again reported hearing what might have been distress signals close

The ice-shrouded Wexford *as photographed in Collingwood, December 1906. The peril of ice-covered decks is often understated. In this condition, vessels are top-heavy and sometimes difficult to manoeuvre in heavy seas. This photograph, with its combination of ice in the rigging and steam from its boilers, has a mystical quality that is almost ghost-like.*
Courtesy of Hank Winsor.

to 4:00 a.m. At the inquest there was considerable controversy about what may have been seen and heard.

A newspaper article in *The London Free Press*, dated November 15, 1913, disputed earlier reports that the *Wexford* had fought the horrible gale off Goderich Harbour. It said "not a great deal of credence is placed in the report that the lost steamer *Wexford* lay fighting the gale off Goderich." In spite of claims of her sighting by William Ruffle, other persons hearing whistles and distress calls, and the insistence of William Niven seeing rockets on three separate occasions on Sunday, the article cites, "There was no effort to launch the lifeboat normally used to conduct rescues at such times. The volunteer crew of the lifeboat is summoned by means of the foghorn. It was admitted that the foghorn did not sound all day Sunday. The fact that it did not call the lifeboat crew probably saved their lives. Captain Malcolm McDonald is in charge of the lifeboat. His son, Donald, was on the *Wexford*. Captain McDonald would have gone out, storm or no storm, if he had known the *Wexford* and his boy were out there."[14]

That the foghorn did not sound became a contentious issue from the time the storm abated. The lighthouse keeper, Captain William Robinson, adamantly declared that he had been instructed by civil servant superiors that it was not his place to have the foghorn sound. Robinson further remarked that "the foghorn is no good anyway, and the town should have a better one."[15] Other sailors expressed the opinion that it would not have made any difference, as the vessel could not make the port in such a storm.

In the aftermath of the storm, reports of masts protruding from the water were circulated through the community — one sighting supposedly by the crew of the tug *Horton* searching for survivors near Black's Point, and a second observation by a farmer, Charles James Slocombe Naftel, and his son Knyvet Naftel, about six miles south of Goderich. *The London Free Press* reported a rudder ashore, four miles south of Goderich.[16]

This image of bodies on the beach was taken shortly after the storm. While the exact location is unknown, this tragic sight is what greeted searchers as they combed the lakeshore looking for survivors. The original photograph is from the Historical Collection of the Great Lakes, Bowling Green State University, Bowling Green, Ohio. Courtesy of Huron County Museum and Historic Gaol.

Captain William J. Bassett, president of the shipping company, told his daughter, Mrs. Alex Qua, that a number of bodies had washed ashore and there was no doubt in his mind that the *Wexford* was lost.[17] Bassett contacted the authorities, suggesting that the identification task would be made easier if the bodies from the same ship were taken to one centre. The bodies from the *Carruthers* were mostly taken to Goderich; those for the *Argus* to Kincardine.[18] From the *Wexford*, it seemed, bodies were processed through several centres, including Thedford, Zurich, and Goderich.[19] The body of Captain Bruce Cameron, found at Kettle Point,[20] was taken to Thedford.

Five bodies wearing *Wexford* life jackets washed ashore at the Robert Turnbull[21] farm south of St. Joseph. Turnbull, a farmer along that part of the shore, occasioned to visit the beach to inspect for erosion damage and to seek out flotsam from the tempest. He is said to have spied a log, which came in with each successive wave, and which was sucked back by the undertow. A white mark on the log drew his attention. He looked closer and finally came right down to the beach. The "log" was a dead man.[22]

This was the first of five bodies to be discovered that day. Two more followed in the next 48 hours. All were taken to Zurich and were positively identified by "a party of Collingwood men who journeyed by train … to make the identifications."[23] It is said that the bodies were laid out along the street at the front of the Westlake Mortuary to make it easier for inspection and identification by the many company representatives, relatives, and friends who travelled through the small communities along the lakeshore. Family members arrived to inspect the corpses, hoping against all hope not to find a loved one who had perhaps somehow survived the tempest.

A lifeboat, also washed ashore near St. Joseph and examined by William J. Bassett, the owner, carried contents still intact and unused. The state of emergency packages confirmed that this boat had not been used or occupied. Other wreckage was examined but no reports are noted to confirm its origin. The second lifeboat was never found — at least until reports provided in 2002 by Reverend Edward C. Haslip of Leamington, Ontario, who reported, quite coincidentally, "Some wreckage including a *Wexford* lifeboat, came ashore at Point Edward, and my

An unidentified crew member holds an oar from a Wexford *lifeboat collected after the storm by the search vessel, the tug* Horton. *The whereabouts of this oar is not known. A second oar, collected by Paul Creve, is owned by Phil Gemeinhardt of Bayfield.*
Courtesy of Ron Beaupre.

Scavengers would encounter piles of wreckage such as this along the Huron shore and remove anything valuable, if it could be done without attracting attention. Photo taken after the storm.
Courtesy of Huron County Museum and Historic Gaol.

grandfather being a farmer, towed the lifeboat home and used it for a pig pen. *Regina* lifeboats also made good pig pens," he recounted in a letter written in March 2002.[24]

Haslip lived for 53 years at the Point Edward location where his father was a commercial fisherman. He spoke about the many passages of the steamer *Wexford* by the waterfront location, in and out of the River St. Clair. "Parts of hatch covers, spars, doors, life jackets and freight came ashore. The *Wexford*'s wreckage included all this," he claimed.[25] Haslip also claimed that the body of Bruce Cameron was found at Kettle Point. It is not known whether he is citing newspaper reports of the day, corroborating already reported information, or simply passing along hearsay.

Initially, the gruesome task of recovering bodies from the Wexford *was undertaken by formal search parties. But as time wore on, farmers, upon finding corpses of sailors washed up long after the storm, would remove the remains for a quiet and respectful private burial along the lake-bank bluffs. This image, taken near Black's Point, south of Goderich, is originally from the Historical Collection of the Great Lakes, Bowling Green State University, Bowling Green, Ohio.*
Courtesy of Huron County Museum and Historic Gaol.

In late March 2002, Anne Talbot, great-granddaughter of Harry Talbot, and granddaughter of Edward Leonard Talbot, described their farm, purchased in 1916, two and a half miles south of Bayfield, Lot 6, Lake Road West, where for years a *Wexford* lifebelt hung in the driving shed: "The preserver was a white canvas covering a cork-like material. The title SS *Wexford* was stencilled on it with black letters approximately three inches high. My brother did tell me he took it back to the lake to play with it, but it sank, so he retrieved it. It was disposed of in 1987 when the farm was sold outside the family."[26] The life jacket was supposedly found hanging in the branches of a tree along the lake bank at the back of the farm, prior to, or around 1916. Anne has promised to report any additional information from her 99-year-old aunt, to round out this intriguing tale.

The *Wexford* was never seen again. But the mounting evidence seemed to indicate she suffered extreme trauma well north of her current resting place[27] at the bottom of Lake Huron, offshore from St. Joseph.

Her Last Hours: An Outline of the Sinking Sequence, the Loss of Crew, and Immediate Subsequent Events

The following sequence is but one reconstruction, part of which reflects on my conclusions based on all of the available evidence following the review of newspaper articles, the transcript of the Goderich Inquest, and local information to identify how the *Wexford* might have foundered. There are several theories offered by different historians, all of which vary in some manner. Some points have been debated by mariners for years, not unlike the speculations about what actually happened to the *Edmund Fitzgerald*, which is still being discussed. We will never really know, we can only speculate; there were no survivors. Some explanations that seem relevant and some contrary opinions have been added:

- Enters the storm front just past noon, November 9, off Point Clark, 20 nautical miles north of Goderich, after a period of relative calm.

- Approaches Goderich Harbour sometime after 2:00 p.m., November 9. Cameron tries to assess whether breakwall opening is accessible; sounds whistles.
- Hangs offshore, waiting for a break in weather and visibility; spray has begun to freeze on deck; snowstorm has intensified, reducing visibility.
- Sounds whistles — 4:00 p.m. No mention was made at the inquest or in the news reports, whether these were the standard fog signals — three distinct blasts at one minute intervals — or otherwise.
- Sets off rockets to attract attention — at dark — hopes for foghorn to guide her through.
- Cook Wilmott, not without a great concern about the night ahead, prepares a meal for the crew. A large quantity of eggs is boiled hard. They'll be easy to grab in unstable conditions — and good for high energy for the hard work that lies ahead. The crew had better eat. They will no longer be able to make their way to the stern galley location to pick up a meal or a snack.[28]
- Sounds whistles repeatedly. According to a report in *The Collingwood Bulletin*, November 20, 1913, W.J. Bassett commented that the *Wexford* had been "blowing her signals from two o'clock in the afternoon of Sunday until eight o'clock at night. During all of that time the foghorn at Goderich had never sounded once…. If the fog horn had blown during that time, my steamer, in all probability would have been lost, but the poor boys might have been saved."
- May have fired more rockets.
- Continues to seek refuge — gradually falls south, pushed by the northerly winds.
- Cameron found great difficulty to control his vessel in massive, rolling waves and hurricane winds. Large amounts of ice had accumulated on lifelines, deck, and pilothouse; forward deck shows signs of collapse. (This was part of the spar deck, added in 1884.) The lighter web frames were just not strong enough

to hold the burden of tons of ice. Some historians dispute this observation, suggesting that the deck collapsed when she hit the bottom hard, bow first. The matter of her spar deck failing was also raised at the inquest.

- Anchor windlass becomes inoperable. Some historians suggest that crew simply could not get forward to operate them. Cameron may have wished to drop anchor to hold the stricken vessel in deep water offshore. With severe ice buildup, anchors and chains could be frozen in their hawse pipes.
- Thrown hard against bottom in a trough between massive rollers — off treacherous Black's Point — damages hull — begins to take on water through ruptured bilges. Wet cargo of grain swells, adding more weight and strain on her bulkheads.
- Breaks rudder — lost; ripped from its post by slamming into massive submerged rock.
- Damages screw and throws at least one propeller blade.
- Rolls hard broadside; no steerage, strains all topside rigging, now heavily burdened with ice. Bow facing shore: railings are bent over deck on port side; bent away from ship on starboard side from seas sweeping over her. Rolls, rolls, and rolls, but somehow retains her upright position.
- Loses smokestack; ice-laden steel cable shrouds and stays snap in roll.[29] There are credible reports that her funnel rolled up onto the shore by Naftel's Creek, below the bluff where Knyvet Naftel claimed to have sighted the twin masts offshore, through the icy fog, during the day, sometime after the storm. A descendant of the Naftel clan recalls seeing what could have been the rusted remains of that same stack as he walked the beach, in his youth, in the 1950s and 1960s.[30] How would a heavy piece of metal, which would normally go straight to the bottom if it were unshipped from the *Wexford*, float? Could it be a function of how much white ice and snow had encrusted the stack before it toppled? Did the weight of ice and snow contribute to its loss? A detailed analysis of the physics of the flotation capacities of ice is warranted.[31]

Consider this comment from Captain Bud, October 6, 2009:

If the stack parted from the deck, I doubt if all wire shrouds would let go immediately. Considerable damage would result with a runaway heavy steel stack, superstructure, vents, engine room skylights, bunker hatches, perhaps cargo hatches, etc. Then with it down, it could come in contact with the cold water as she rolled from port to starboard. The frigid temperature would be cause for icing, completely sealing an open top or bottom. Then after a considerable build up the remaining shrouds parted, stack entered the water and floated as a spar buoy would after parting the chains. It could make landfall in this way also. Perhaps both ends became sealed, or the coating theory. Whatever. It's possible.[32]

Author Paul Carroll is shown with section of metal pipe sleeve, one of several found along the shoreline near Naftel's Creek. The suggestion that a heavy steel cylinder such as a ship's funnel could actually float ashore caused an amazing response of incredulity from experienced marine historians.
Photo by Kalen Carroll.

- Loses steam — draft-fed burner boiler could not hold fire without its stack. It is also possible that the boiler fires had gone out some time before.
- Heavy smoke below; some ports were opened.
- Rolled hard broadside; green water adds new layers to icy shroud on decks.
- Ice buildup becomes treacherous; boilers continue to cool; interior becomes inhospitably cold.
- Pilothouse and hurricane deck began to distort from weight of ice; Cameron and mates seek security below; work their way through engine room and tween deck space to officers' quarters, near stern deck. Deck lifeline cable no longer accessible.
- *Wexford* loses full upper pilothouse and hurricane deck.
- One lifeboat breaks free from davits; floats to Point Edward, where it is retrieved by a farmer, taken home, and turned upside down to use as a pigsty, along with another from the *McGean*.
- Takes on water through ruptured openings in deck.
- Deck hatches remain covered; air trapped below; cargo still provides flotation.
- Crew in protected areas: amidships, bow, stern; some crew has been swept away.
- Awash at deck line by morning.
- Water conditions abate during the afternoon of November 10 — surviving crew attempts to abandon ship.
- Somehow loses only remaining lifeboat, which washes up at Taylor's Grove, three miles south of St. Joseph. A later inspection of the lifeboat by shipping company owner Bassett suggests that the lifeboat was never occupied.
- Masts sighted, apparently on November 11 or 12, by Knyvet Naftel from shore and from the search-tug *Horton* from Goderich. "The crew of a tug sent out to search for possible survivors afloat on life rafts returned without having sighted any bodies. They reported, however, that three miles off Black's Point, six miles south of Goderich, they had found spars and rigging, believed to be of the *Wexford*, protruding from the water."[33]

The question of whether these reports are true bears greatly on theories that the foredeck did not collapse until she hit the bottom, bow down, as some historians insist was the case. That she floated awash, decks below surface, and drifted to her present location, settling rather gently on the bottom, particularly with the apparent absence of any significant debris field, is an option that also has to be considered. Some authorities are very skeptical as to whether it would even be possible for the *Wexford* to float upright, awash, in such a manner, with her masts showing above the water's surface.

• Pilothouse rubble washes ashore at Hicks' Farm, Cut Line Road; contents and equipment pilfered; ship's clock stolen. Folklore about the amount of the pilothouse that washed varies from just one board, on which these items were mounted together, to large, broken pieces of the structure being found.

Farmer Hicks, and others who lived adjacent to the farm at the extreme west end of the Cut Line — the road that runs from Holmesville to Highway 21 — quietly recounted the plunder of the pilothouse remains as washed ashore after the storm, below the Hick's farm. Small sections of the pilothouse remained sufficiently intact to allow the salvage — or theft, depending on one's point of view — of furnishings and equipment washed overboard when the pilothouse was wrent from the hull. A ship's clock is asserted to be among the booty. It is claimed still to be held locally — the current owner, who was reluctant to make its presence broadly known, recently passed away. "It is a Crosby Steam Gage and Valve Company device, marked with a No. 7 — perhaps a model number — on its back," according to collector Phil Gemeinhardt of Bayfield.[34] The brass timepiece is consistent with those sold in London in the 1880s, when the rapidly expanding Crosby Company from Boston operated a major ship-supply business at 75 Queen Victoria Street, in the British location. There is no doubt that other instrumentation — gauges, valves, and whistles — originated from the same chandlery. Gemeinhardt insists that the items found were all attached to one board.

According to the late Captain Roy Munday of the town of Goderich, in an interview with the author, March 20, 2002, he once had the "engine room clock" in his hands — brought over by his neighbour, the late Leonard Hicks, who sought assistance to get it running again. Roy claims all he did was to insert and turn an appropriate key from his own collection, and it began to tick again. The clock, according to Munday, was found by Leonard's grandfather, stuck in the ice close to shore near the Hicks' farm, originally attached to a board, with a steam gauge as part of the appurtenances. The clock he describes was larger in diameter than eight inches, and contained an open centre through which one could see the clockworks. According to Captain Munday, Maurice, Leonard's father, used the clock as a toy, rolling it with a hoop around the farm and barnyards for entertainment. It was allegedly sold to the late Clark Chisholm, formerly of Goderich, for the sum of $50, when Leonard needed money to quench an apparent thirst. Phil Gemeinhardt continues to query its present whereabouts.

- Remaining crew follows lifeboat and leave *Wexford*; seek shore in freezing cold water.
- Five bodies wash up at Turnbull farm, five miles south of St. Joseph; two more in same area later. Five identified apparently, according to *London Free Press* reports. Collingwood papers suggest 11 bodies found in total.
- Remaining bodies wash offshore with wind shift to southeast.
- Captain Bruce Cameron remains onboard.
- Hull begins final descent; bow first, possibly carrying some crew trapped under forecastle hood.
- Cameron perishes from exposure; body leaves ship with flotsam.
- Body of Bruce Cameron floats to Kettle Point.
- Bodies from Turnbull farm taken to Zurich; said to be identified by a party of men from Collingwood. Inquest at Blake, near Zurich, conducted by a Dr. A.B. Campbell of Hensall.[35] Sailors died from exposure, not drowning.

- Bodies from Kettle Point taken to Thedford. Inquest conducted by Dr. H.S. Clerke of Thedford. Records of inquest have not been found.
- Brother of 2nd Engineer Lougheed searches along the shore between Bayfield and Grand Bend. He has inspected the lifeboat and many piles of rubble — oil barrels, oilcans, and pieces of cabin work.
- Owner William J. Bassett arrives to inspect lifeboat and view bodies.
- Party of residents from Collingwood identifies all Zurich bodies.
- Body of Bruce Cameron is returned home for large funeral.
- Vessel owner submits insurance claim for $107,300; presumed to be paid as a total loss.[36]

William Deal, shown second from the right, with his companion crew of Chelmsford, *circa 1880s. Later he was a deckhand on the* Wexford. *Members of this crew would have moved on to work on packet freighters such as the* Wexford *as the days of sail turned into the age of steam.*
Courtesy of Keith Deal.

Thus unfolded the untimely demise of the *Wexford*. She had been taken by what is considered to be the ultimate storm recorded for Lake Huron. Her loss, among the many other ships that went to the bottom that fateful night, created a mournful memory for family, friends, and the marine communities around the lakes, many of whom lost fathers, brothers, and sons in this terrible storm. A hundred years later, her name is still well-known in the lexicon of the Great Lakes marine community.

CHAPTER 4

The Crew List: November 1913

How will they tell the shipwreck
When winter shakes the door,
Till the children ask, "But the forty?
Did they come back no more?"

Emily Dickinson, from "Life"

Master and Crew List for the *Wexford* — On Her Last Voyage

Estimates of *Wexford* crew numbers vary from 17 to 24. The numbers are not consistent. The number 17, as reported by the Lake Carriers' Association in its 1913 *Annual Report*, was certainly too low. Crew lists were not necessarily kept in a meticulous manner at this time, nor were records of passengers kept consistently.

The Globe and Mail of November 11, 1913, under the headline "No Names Yet Given," reported:

> Mr. Albert E.J. Blackman, Secretary Treasurer of the company, informed the *Globe* last night that he had a list

of the deckhands, but he would not divulge the names until he had been authorized to do so by Captain Bassett, who had left for Goderich to make a full investigation.

"The ordinary crew on lake freighters are a roving lot," said Mr. Blackman, "and for that reason I do not think it would be wise to make known the names. Many changes are made monthly, and it was quite possible that might have been the case with some of the deckhands lost in the wreck."

While this photo shows the harbour full of ice, it is not known whether the Wexford's *final run of the season had been made. Likely she was preparing to* "lay-up" *for the season. Photo not dated.*
Courtesy of the C. Patrick Labadie Collection/Thunder Bay National Marine Sanctuary, Alpena, MI, # 156067-156086.

It is ironic that one of the earliest estimates, appearing in a news report in *The London Free Press*, at the time of the storm was 23, very close to the number 21 (or 22, depending on which MacDonalds were actually onboard) identified, to this date, in my own research findings. It is also the number that is most consistent with the documents that review the size of crew that accompanied her on the crossing from

Britain. When she made her Atlantic crossing from London in 1903 — starting in at Dunkirk and stopping at the Azores — the Agreement and Account of Crew records lists a crew of 19 persons, plus captain, mate, and the new owner. Crossing the English Channel, however, there may have been more crew members onboard. Apparently, according to the folklore, they were a hardy and cosmopolitan group, hailing from seaports across England to Denmark, Finland, Norway, Sweden, Germany, Holland, and France.

The final official document ever found to attest to the crew of the *Wexford* was a payroll report dated September 13, 1913, issued by the Western Steamship Company immediately following the storm. It was sadly out of date and listed those paid off. It did not provide any accurate account of those who might have been onboard. Captain Cameron did not submit any further report to the company. Any such record kept onboard would have been lost when the ship foundered.

Marine historian Skip Gillham[1] wrote in *The Goderich Signal-Star* on November 6, 1996, that one sailor was spared when he missed boarding at Fort William. Gillham also indicates, "All hands, including 2 passengers, were lost." I have been unable to identify, for certain, the name of a second passenger. Perhaps that person is the 23rd crew member, the number onboard as reported by the *Free Press*.

There is a tombstone at Maitland Cemetery in Goderich that shows the burial spot of five unidentified sailors. The only identification, now marked with stones at the foot of each grave, gives the name of the ship from which each sailor was thought to have come, and one showing only the location where the body was found. It is not likely that any of these men hailed from the *Wexford*. All but one had life jackets carrying the name of the ship on which each mariner had served, save one, whose footstone simply reads "Kintail," a location too far north for the *Wexford* or her flotsam to be found.

According to *The Signal* of November 20, 1913:

> The bodies of five unidentified victims of the Great Lakes disaster were interred in Maitland Cemetery this afternoon in a plot donated by the town council at its

last meeting on Monday evening. Rev. Geo. E. Ross conducted the funeral and was assisted by Rev. J[ames] E.
Ford and Rev. W[illiam] K. Hager. Rev. J[ames] B[oath]
Fotheringham [later archdeacon of Huron] was unable
to attend owing to an accident last week. The town
council attended in a body. At the same time two bodies
were also buried at Kincardine.

It is still a mystery that the bodies of Capt. Cameron[2]
of the steamer *Wexford* and Mr. Donald McDonald have
not been recovered. It is the belief of some that they are
incarcerated in the hull of their ship at the bottom of
the lake.

Elgin Hendrick, a relative of Robert Turnbull, a farmer near St.
Joseph, to the north of Grand Bend, said that there were bodies from
the *Charles S. Price*, another Great Lakes freighter, as well as those from

*The Sailors' Tombstone in the Maitland Cemetery, Goderich. This frequently
visited gravesite is easily found. Upon entering the main portion of the cemetery,
in the first section, look to the right side just round the first curve.*
Photo by Neil Hamilton for the Huron County Museum and Historic Gaol.

the *Wexford*, washed ashore in the St. Joseph to Grand Bend area. The bodies were stored in neighbouring barns until they could be identified. Some were never identified and were buried in unmarked graves in the Grand Bend cemetery. The local folklore in Bayfield suggests that a number of bodies were collected from along the shoreline below that community, as well. They were taken to the local undertakers, Harry and Alfie Erwin, who operated their business on the main street, in a building now located across the road. A designated structure, it is preserved by the Bayfield Historical Society and used as the Bayfield Archives. According to an article published by the historical society, and recently updated by Ralph Gillians (society president), the furniture store and undertaking business provided "the initial resting place for the bodies that were picked up off the beach after the great storm of 1913 until the numbers were so great that they were moved to the Town Hall."[3] According to society archivist Ralph Laviolette, some of these bodies were relocated to mortuaries at Goderich and Thedford, but no documentation has been found to verify this claim.

As identified earlier, Coroner A.B. Campbell of Hensall conducted the inquests on the bodies found on the shores south from St. Joseph, in the hamlet of Blake, near Zurich. His report (no copy found) apparently declared that the deaths were an act of providence and no blame could be assigned.[4] All bodies recovered had apparently died of exposure — not by drowning. There are photographic records of the bodies laid out for identification on the main street in Zurich, in front of the local mortuary.[5] The victims, 23 in total, but with one possible exception, were as follows:

Frank Bruce Cameron: Master, of Collingwood. One of seven bodies said to be found at Kettle Point[6] and taken to Thedford. He is said to have started sailing at age 14. Cameron crewed on several vessels in various positions out of Collingwood. He was the second son of the late Captain Alex C. Cameron, who testified at the Goderich Inquest. The details about the discovery of Cameron's body have not been documented in any detail. It was suggested that he could be identified by the scar on his ankle left by the hockey injury he had received a year or two earlier.

According to the president of the Western Steamship Company, Albert E.J. Blackman, "Captain Cameron was one of the most capable Masters on the lakes."[7]

James McCutcheon: First Mate, first thought to be onboard. According to an article in *The Owen Sound Sun Times*, November 9, 1963, McCutcheon, the first mate, stepped ashore when the ship was upbound through Detroit to send a money order home, and "when he rushed down to the pier the *Wexford* had sailed. His tardiness saved his life, and Mr. McCutcheon lived for many years to come."[8] A contrary view is offered in the *Detroit Free Press*, November 15, 1913, under the headline "Kindness of Friends Gives Mate Death Trip." The article tells about the mate being "accidentally left ashore when the *Wexford* cleared for Fort William. He was without funds but his many friends about the grain elevators made up a purse enabling him to catch the boat at Sault Ste. Marie. He is believed to have been aboard for the fatal trip." Was this actually someone else, yet unnamed? *The Saturday News*, Collingwood, November 15, 1913, in a front-page story suggests, "Mayor Gilpin today sent James McCutcheon, who was formerly mate on the *Wexford*, and Samuel J. Bailey to the scene of the disaster with instructions to take whatever steps were necessary toward securing the bodies of victims from Collingwood and assisting in the search for those not yet found." It is apparent that Mate McCutcheon must have found a safer way home.

Archibald "Archie" Brooks: Second Mate/Acting First Mate[9] of Collingwood, "in the absence of Mate McCutcheon who left the vessel three weeks ago and is now in Collingwood."[10] Found at St Joseph: "a young man and had sailed for several seasons. Last year he occupied the same position on this boat."

Ferguson: Second Mate, of Collingwood.[11]

Rogers: Second Officer.[12]

James "Jimmie" George Scott: Chief Engineer, of Collingwood. Married, three children; brother of Captain Frank Scott, master of the steamer *Collingwood* of the Farrar Line; had sailed for several years — found at St. Joseph. This was to be his last year of sailing. "At the urgent request of his wife, he had determined to turn his attention to farming and only recently had arranged for the sale of his home to Capt. Charles Baker of the steamer *Leafield*, who in turn was giving a farm in part payment."[13]

Richard "Victor" Lougheed: Assistant Second Engineer, of Collingwood. Thirty-nine years old with 22 years of experience — native of Owen Sound; married to a Miss Dickinson. A brother, Mr. A.H. Lougheed, "has walked and re-walked along the shore of Lake Huron through snow and over the rough country lying between Bayfield and Grand Bend, always with the picture of his brother in mind."[14]

He inspected the lifeboat of the *Wexford* that had washed ashore, and saw plenty of evidence in oil barrels, oil cans, pieces of cabin work to convince him that the *Wexford* had been wrecked. The wreckage was being placed in piles along the shore where it was found. The roads in the vicinity are very bad. Until Friday [14th] they had been pretty well frozen, and in some places they had to be dug up.[15]

The ice bridge that spanned the mouth of the Grand Bend River gave way on Friday, making it impossible to cross now without a boat.[16]

Orrin "Orin"[17] Gordon: Wheelsman, of Collingwood, age 16, unmarried son of Mr. and Mrs. Charles Gordon. Body found; he had held the same position on the *Wexford* in 1912.

Alan (or Allan) Dodson: Watchman, of Collingwood. Body found; he was an Englishman.[18] His funeral was fairly elaborate as he was a former member of the 35th Regiment Bugle Band. The full membership of the band turned out, as did two full companies of the regiment, whose members also paraded in the procession that led to the cemetery after services at the Collingwood All Saints Church. "The casket was covered with a Union Jack and Alan's Bugle and cap rested on it, as did one cross of yellow rosses [*sic*] from Miss Deer, the girl he was to have married."[19]

John Deplonty: Watchman, listed in the September 13 payroll report issued by the company.

Donald McDonald, a crew member on the Wexford. *Donald's body was never recovered and was first thought to have been "incarcerated" within the hull along with the body of Captain Cameron. Cameron's remains were later found at Kettle Point.* Courtesy of Doug Graham.

Donald McDonald:[20] Crew, cousin to Murdoch McDonald of Goderich. Son of Captain Malcolm who supervised the lifeboat crew at Goderich Harbour. There was not a Roderick McDonald onboard, according to Doug Graham of Goderich,[21] who claims that even the tombstone engravers got mixed up, especially confusing the names of Roderick and Ronald, with the headstone showing the name of the former, while the footstone on the same grave shows the name of the latter. To add further to the confusion, information relayed by a Mr. MacDonald, descendant of Bob Carey, as noted below, also suggested the name of a Ronald "Roddy" MacDonald. It is not likely there was a third MacDonald onboard (these said to be spelled *Mac* — see section below). A John McDonald, Sault Ste. Marie, Michigan, was part of the crew of the *Argus*, also lost in the storm. The confusion abounds!

Murdoch McDonald: Twenty-five years old, a passenger from Goderich. On return from a pleasure trip to Fort William on the *Turret Chief*, Murdoch McDonald lived on Quebec Street, son of the late Norman McDonald and his wife, Annie.[22] He left six brothers, all of Goderich: Angus, Daniel, Norman, Lorne, Roy, and Malcolm. His body was found at St. Joseph.[22]

> Although the days of large funerals have passed, yet the funeral of Murdoch McDonald, one of the wreck victims, which took place on Saturday [November 15] was largely attended and the cortege as it moved slowly from the family residence on Quebec Street to Maitland Cemetery cast a gloom over the whole town. Some 22 carriages were in the procession. Rev. George E. Ross, pastor of Knox Church, which the deceased attended, conducted the funeral service.
>
> A short time before the storm, he went from here to Fort William with a friend on a pleasure trip on the *Turret Chief* and was returning from this trip on the *Wexford* when the storm came up and wrecked the steamer.
>
> The floral tributes were very beautiful and testified to the high esteem which the deceased commanded here.[23]

According to wreck hunter Bob Carey, a former schooldays chum reported to him that a Judy MacDonald was married to Malcolm ("Mac" as reported) and they live in London. "Malcolm's family apparently came from Goderich and he had three uncles who perished during the great storm: Malcolm MacDonald, Ronald "Roddy" MacDonald, and Donald

Here, some members of the MacDonald marine family of Quebec Street, Goderich, pose for a portrait with their father, Norman, standing (centre). Murdoch, who was lost on the Wexford, *is seated. He is flanked by brothers Roy "Plug" Malcolm (left) and Lorne "Husky" (right), who also died young in an accident onboard a ship at Goderich Harbour. Missing are sister "Pearly" and brothers Angus, Norman, and Daniel.*
Photo from the family collection of Doug Graham.

MacDonald. His aunt still remembers bodies washed up on shore after the storm. Malcolm apparently also had another uncle, unnamed, who perished during that same storm on Lake Erie."[24] I have not been able to identify the second passenger alleged to have been onboard.

George Wilmott (or "Wilmot"): Cook, of Collingwood. He had purchased tickets in Collingwood for a December 16 return to Bristol, England, on the *Royal Edward*.[25]

One explanation for all the apothecary-type bottles found on the wreck may be in *True Tales of the Great Lakes*, by Dwight Boyer: "A friend of Glenn's was George Wilmott, the vessel's cook, an older and somewhat dyspeptic gentleman who prided himself on his collection of patent medicine literature while assuring others that it was no reflection on his culinary skills."[26]

Mrs. George Wilmot(t): Stewardess, of Collingwood.[27]

James Glen (or Glenn): Crew, of Goderich. Only in Canada a few months, he had worked on the *Wexford* for most of his time here. This trip was to be his last before going back to Scotland to bring his wife to this country; identified by his brother-in-law; found at St. Joseph.[28]

Jim Maxwell: Crew, was born on a farm near Brentwood, Ontario, son of Harold and Mary Jane Scott Maxwell. He was an engineer, in charge of the heating and electrical plants for a Detroit theatre before sailing on lake freighters. His younger brother sailed as an engineer on oil tankers for Mobil for 35 years, where according to his niece, "He never learned how to swim, despite being torpedoed three times during World War II."[29]

Solliere Caesar (Or Cesare): Deckhand. A Swede, he had just signed on in September. Body found.[30]

George Peere: Crew. Body found. Although he is listed as part of the crew of the *Leafield*, lost on Lake Superior,[31] other accounts group him with the bodies of the *Wexford*.[32] Peere was believed to be a recent immigrant from Old Windsor in England. He had letters from a Miss Elliott in his pockets.

Walter Berwin.[33]

James Flynn.[34]

Gordon Allan: Crew. Found at St. Joseph and identified by Coroner Campbell.[35]

Charles Peters: Crew. Found at St. Joseph and identified by an invoice found in his pocket from a New York publishing house, and a tattoo of the Union Jack on the back of his right hand.[36]

Thomas Spiers (also Speers): Buried in All Saints Cemetery, "Not a Collingwood boy," but, at the request of the Mayor Gilpin to Captain

Bassett, owner of the *Wexford*, his unclaimed body was to be sent to Collingwood for burial.[37]

According to the author's neighbour, Walter McIlwain, also a resident along Black's Point Road where wreckage and bodies floated ashore after the storm, our former barber, the late Percy Johnston of Goderich, insisted that he actually viewed footprints in the snow leading up to a body wearing a *Wexford* life jacket. This is the only comment[38] that I have ever encountered to suggest that there may have been at least one survivor to reach the shore alive before he succumbed to exposure.

A former crew member, Alf Carver, sailed with the *Wexford* in 1912 but was not onboard for the 1913 season. According to Patrick Folkes, a Bruce County historian, "I do recall speaking with the late Alf Carver, of Tobermory, who told me he sailed on the *Wexford* in 1912 and was damn glad he wasn't on her the next season. He went through the Great Storm on Lake Superior on another ship."[39]

A Reward for Recovery

An incentive for bodies to be turned in was deemed necessary. Local folklore suggests that several sailors whose bodies washed ashore were dragged up the lake bank and interred in the most appropriate nearby spot. A reward system was devised. An arrangement between Edward Norman (E.N.) Lewis, MP, former mayor of Goderich, and the Lake Carriers' Association provided a reward of $25[40] for each body recovered. The members of the Relief Committee, in partnership with the Lake Carriers, called for all persons living along the lakeshore in a distance of about 150 miles, extending from Sarnia to Southampton, to report the finding of bodies or wreckage, to the headquarters (at Goderich) at the expense of the association.

CHAPTER 5

A Memorial: November 16, 1913

In a solitude of the sea
Deep from human vanity,
And the Pride of Life that planned her, stilly couches she.
Steel chambers, late the pyres
Of her salamandrine fires,
Cold currents thrid, and turn to rhythmic tidal lyres.
— Thomas Hardy, from *The Convergence of the Twain* (1912)
— lines on the loss of the *Titanic*.

On Sunday November 16, a large gathering of friends and relatives joined with families in mourning of those lost in the savage storm. About 1,400 persons attended at the Knox Presbyterian Church. Earlier, the mayor had issued a proclamation for citizens to attend the memorial service on this Sunday afternoon.

All in attendance bowed their heads, and stood in silent sorrow as the "great organ pealed forth the dirges from the *Dead March in Saul*." According to *The Signal* of November 20, 1913: "It might not be an exaggeration to say that many a noble and manly heart with considerable

Table 2: Ships and Lives Lost (Great Lakes), 1892–1912
Table and text from *The Collingwood Bulletin*, December 25, 1913 (page 3).

Year	Ships Wrecked	Ships A Total Loss	Lives Lost	Value in Millions
1892	367	68	138	1.7
1893	325	51	102	1.8
1894	334	79	110	2.0
1895	265	41	76	1.8
1896	358	66	31	1.6
1897	236	34	18	1.0
1898	209	33	27	1.0
1899	305	65	57	2.0
1900	261	40	15	0.9
1901	284	45	79	1.5
1902	311	58	62	2.0
1903	247	48	62	1.3
1904	233	49	19	1.6
1905	267	46	10	1.8
1906	364	78	116	3.0
1907	415	55	32	32.3
1908	327	32	42	2.1
1909	365	48	76	2.5
1910	424	34	95	3.5
1911	291	30	56	3.3
1912	280	26	9	1.6

Number of Ships and Lives Lost on the Great Lakes in Twenty Years Preceding the 1913 Great Storm

Although the toll appears to be yearly on the decrease, the toll of this year, 1913, will be far greater than for many years past. The number of lives lost in recent years has not been as great compared with the number of sailors involved accounted for by the increased efficiency of the life-saving service. The lives given as lost do not include accidents to seamen, except through shipwrecks.

It is hard to realize the terrible toll of the lakes. We have heard of the thousands that have lost their lives battling against the mighty waters of the ocean, but only occasionally is the exacting demand of the Great Lakes brought to our notice.

Fourteen thousand man-made vessels launched in all the glory, have proudly sailed from port and have headed into many a gale, but in the end acknowledged a master of the lashing, raging waters of the greatest friend this continent has.

"It is a good servant, but a harsh master," weeped [*sic*] one old man, last week, as he saw the beaten, bruised and frozen remains of his son laid to rest, and remembered the calamity of the *Asia* of thirty years before when his brother, returning from an evening of pleasure, went down into the open jaws of the lake with a hundred others.

---

difficulty suppressed the ready tear. The scene was most affecting and a whisper could be heard all over the church."

The newspaper account continued:

> The edifice was filled to capacity and the eager worshippers desirous to pay tribute to the dead crowded in and sat on the steps of the aisles. The council and officials for both the town and the county attended in a body. All the fraternal Societies in the town were present. The service was conducted by the church pastor, Rev. George E. Ross, assisted by rectors from all of the other local churches.
>
> To the strains of "Father I know that all my life is portioned out for me" the united choir, numbering about 100 strong, marched onto their places. Sadly, but lustily, the choir and congregation then sang "God Moves in Mysterious Ways."
>
> The local account for the Lakes Disaster Fund of Canada was enriched by a collection of $141.22.
>
> The sermon, by Reverend J.B. Fotheringham, St. George's Anglican Church, offered a moving commentary based on Job, chapter 14, verse 19: "The waters wear the

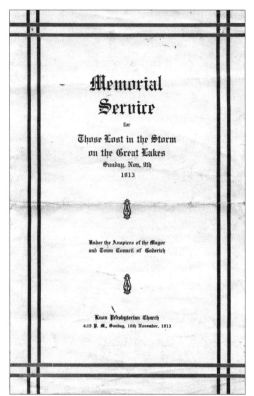

Memorial Service

for

Those Lost in the Storm
on the Great Lakes

Sunday, Nov. 9th
1913

Under the Auspices of the Mayor
and Town Council of Goderich

Knox Presbyterian Church
4:15 P. M., Sunday, 16th November, 1913

Cover from the Order of Service, November 16, 1913, memorial at Knox Presbyterian Church, Goderich. Very few copies of the original memorabilia from the days following the Great Storm seem to have survived. The Order of Service was printed in dark purple or mauve-coloured ink on an off-white paper and was quite a decorative document. The author also owns a small card printed with the words of an original commemorative poem that was read by the poet and distributed at a public gathering held to raise money for the Lakes Disaster Fund. Photo from the Paul Carroll Collection.

stones: thou washest away the things which grow out of the dust of the earth; and thou destroyest the hope of man."

"We stand at the open grave and we gather at the foot of the cross," commenced Mr. Fotheringham, "to look into the grave and to speak sympathy to the ones that are mourning the loss of their loved ones.... This has been a dark week for Goderich, for this country, for this province, and for the whole Dominion. It has been our fate to walk along the shores of Lake Huron and see the results of the winds. There was seen wreckage, timbers, and furnishings of ships, which were thought to be sufficient for the waves. And there we have picked up the bodies of those who have perished in this awful storm. In consequence many a bewildered mother with her child will walk through this world alone.

This day as we gather within the house of Our God, we mourn for them, and our tears are tributes to the lost. We believe in a world of order, but when we see the forces of nature, which to the observing eye, seem to be uncontrollable, we are for a time, apt to cry: "Where is the God who rules?"[1]

To the Unknown Dead: Goderich Gives Unidentified Sailors a Public Funeral

There were five hearses supplied by the Brophey Bros. Funeral Home on West Street, drawn by teams of fine thoroughbred horses and followed by the members of town council and other prominent dignitaries. They "slowly wended their way through the streets of the town. The 33rd Regiment band, led by Mr. J.B. Hunter, with funeral tread, played the Dead March in Saul."[2] The streets were lined with people as everybody

Preparing to honour the unknown dead. The horse-drawn hearses were lined up on West Street outside Brophey Brothers Funeral Home just beyond the top of Harbour Hill, in preparation for a grand but sombre parade to Maitland Cemetery, some miles distant from the mortuary location.
Courtesy of Huron County Museum and Historic Gaol.

Procession on the Square, Goderich. With the band in the lead, teams of fine thoroughbred horses draw hearses carrying the coffins of unknown sailors who perished in the Great Storm.
Courtesy of Huron County Museum and Historic Gaol.

seemed to turn out to pay their respects along with the merchants who all "had their blinds drawn through the ceremony."[3]

In the words of Reverend George Ross, one of the three officiating ministers:

> Our hearts have been deeply touched by the sad course of events that has brought us hither today. The recent disaster on the Great Lakes has wrought havoc to many a strong ship; scores of brave and hardy seamen have found a watery grave, and the shadow of death has settled like a pall upon our whole community.
>
> Throughout our province, as well as at lake ports of our neighbouring republic, and far away across the sea where loved ones dwell, there is heartache and sorrow in many a home. Not a single survivor lives to tell the tale

of that awful night from any of the ships that went down to death. Stark and stiff the stalwart forms of but a few have been borne ashore on the crest of the restless wave. But no other message, save that of floating wreckage gives any token of their fate. And as we listen to the surf that breaks day and night upon our shore it seems to chant a requiem for our departed brethren of the lake ...

Our gathering today is extremely pathetic. It is our sad duty to commend to this resting place the bodies of these unidentified and unclaimed dead. Their names are not known to us. Death has sealed their lips and they cannot tell us whence they come or whose they are. Their hardy hands are helplessly by their side and they are unable to point us to their distant home [*sic*] or beckon dear ones to their side ...

In committing "dust to dust" we are not unmindful that somewhere there are doubtless loved ones who know not. Possibly a mother who wonders why some message from her boy is so long delayed; perchance a sweetheart who may be counting the days till the navigation season ends and anticipated joys destined never to be realized on earth shall be; or some faithful wife it may be far across the sea, expecting with her little band of dependent children some message by each disappointing mail.[4]

With the assistance of no less than 18 honorary pallbearers from the marine community, the five comrades were placed side by side in the five open graves. A wooden cross carrying the name of the vessel to which each belonged, or, in one case, the location and number assigned to the body, was erected over each chamber. In more recent years, a single, large memorial stone has been erected, bearing only the word SAILORS.

Memorial services were held throughout the province, especially in the lakeshore communities where marine activity played an important role in the lives of area families and in the local economy. At one such service in Toronto, a James B. Potter, superintendent of the Upper

Canada Tract Society's Mission to Sailors, who was a passenger on the *Huronic*, which had run aground off Whitefish Point on Lake Superior, told of the terrible force of the storm in graphic language:

> Snow and sleet blinded us. The decks and engine room were solid ice. The ship was an iceberg. The wind blew 80 miles an hour and the snow striking the pitching vessel froze as it struck. The ship tossed and lurched and creaked and trembled. It was a terrible sea, a wicked sea, such as I never saw before. Inside the ship, men were thrown like toys and furniture was broken to bits. It was tremendously terrible.[5]

As decades of successive Novembers have unfolded, memorial services have been held to commemorate the losses in this horrific, yet natural event. Even today, as we approach the centenary of the Great Storm, tributes such as the annual Mariners' Service at Knox Presbyterian Church in Goderich continue to attract a large attendance each year.

CHAPTER 6

Weather Forecasting in 1913: Descriptions of the Storm

Down came the storm, and smote amain
The vessel in its strength;
She shuddered and paused, like a frighted steed,
Then leaped her cable's length.

The breakers were right beneath her bows,
She drifted a dreary wreck,
And a whooping billow swept the crew
Like icicles from her deck.
— Henry Wadsworth Longfellow, from *Wreck of the Hesperus*

Signal Towers

In the days before telegraph and telephone service, lightkeepers and others responsible for weather notices to mariners used a system of signal towers. The Propeller Club, a marine heritage preservation society, has built a replica at Southampton. The system of signal towers persisted until after the Great Storm of 1913, when loud controversy raged over the reporting system, its accuracy and timeliness. A photograph of the lighthouse at Goderich, around 1900, shows the original signal pole, in use since at least the 1880s. In this case, the light was ignited from the location at the top of the bluff, while the signal horn was activated from the water station below, at the harbour. There was no means of communicating between the two until after 1913.

The following extract is from *Schools and Colleges of Ontario: 1792–1910*, Volume 3, by J.G. Hodgins, 1910, from the Magnetic and Meteorological Observatory, Toronto, a "Dominion Government" facility:

If a storm is brewing on the Lakes, or on the Atlantic, or Pacific, Storm Signals are sent out. At the various Harbour Ports, Mariners may know by looking at the Signal Mast

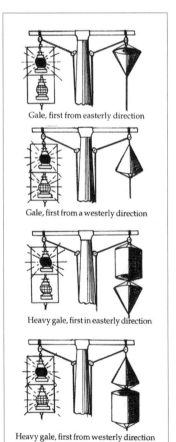

Gale, first from easterly direction

Gale, first from a westerly direction

Heavy gale, first in easterly direction

Heavy gale, first from westerly direction

Storm signals used along Lake Huron. Signals as illustrated by the Southampton Propeller Club. From top to bottom, the lights and lanterns are arranged in combinations to show: 1. A gale, first from an easterly direction; 2. A gale, first from a westerly direction; 3. A heavy gale, first from an easterly direction; and 4. A heavy gale, first from a westerly direction. Experienced mariners would understand how the cycle of wind directions would normally unfold in such storms.

Courtesy of the Southampton Marine Heritage Society.

whether there is peril on the deep that day or not. Drums and Cones are the Signals used.

The Cone displayed alone means a moderate gale; the Drum and Cone mean a heavy gale; the peak of the Cone downward means a southerly, or easterly Wind; the peak of the Cone upwards means northerly or west-erly Winds.

In certain locations, such as at the Soo Locks or where vessels transit locations, and pass by both American and Canadian signal locations, the information might be confusing. Not only was there a different system of display, but there was also the probability that forecasts may have dif-fered. Skippers, as was the case in the hours preceding the Great Storm, would often rely more heavily on their own steering station barometers as the most accurate forecast of what lay ahead. The American Storm Signals, at the time, were as follows:

At noon on Friday, November 7 [1913], Coast Guard Stations and weather bureau offices in ports along Lake Superior hoisted white pennants above square red flags with black centers.[1]

Late in the afternoon lighted lanterns replaced the flags at Coast Guard stations and weather posts. But instead of white lanterns above red ones, carrying word that the storm was still a nor'wester, there were red lanterns, one at the top and one at the bottom, with a white lantern in between. This warning, not often hoisted, told that a hurricane, with winds of seventy-four miles an hour and over, was on the way.[2]

On the Canadian side, it is clear that the signal system was woefully inadequate to warn sailors of the impending disaster that might face them on the open waters of the lakes. The signal system, even at its extreme posting, could show only the signs for a heavy gale — with winds from

41–47 knots — while the hurricane predicted on the American side saw winds in excess of 74 knots. It was quite a significant difference.

It was a big storm, affecting much of the eastern North American continent: "The line of freezing temperature will extend almost to the Georgia–Florida line, and frosts are likely in Florida down to the twenty-sixth parallel."[3]

Radio Equipment?

An interesting side note relates to the equipping of ships with radios or radiotelephone equipment. There was considerable debate at this time as to the veracity of such installations. The shipowners seemed to prefer that such equipment be installed onboard — better to track the time and distance travelled by the masters. But, on the other hand, it was suggested by the masters that the ulterior motive of the shipowners was simply to spy on the captain and his crew, and that there was little to be gained by maintaining this means of constant communication.

It is clear, at least for those ships already at sea, that the forecast revisions and updates that foretold the impending doom, could have been easily transferred to vessels in transit, providing at least the opportunity to seek shelter in some appropriate location before the cataclysm was to be unleashed. In fact, some vessels may have carried radiotelephone equipment. Although the general sense, on the Canadian side, suggested that vessels "should have been" equipped, some American reports tell us that radio equipment had been onboard ore carriers and some other vessels since 1905.

In his summary to the jury at the Goderich Inquest, Coroner Archibald Cross Hunter suggested that some system of wireless telegraphy, had it been available there, would have been very useful. The arguments "for" or "against" may be moot points. The storm arose with such vicious ferocity that there was no hope for anyone, save those few ships who survived, surely, with some sort of divine intervention or amazing good luck.

The White Hurricane

So many times, as authors write about a fierce storm, these lines from *The Iliad of Homer* are cited:

White are the decks with foam; the winds aloud
Howl o'er the masts, and sing thro' ev'ry shroud:
Pale, trembling, tired, the sailors freeze with fears;
And instant death on every wave appears.[4]

The story of the Great Storm of November 1913 has been told and retold many times, in newspaper accounts, local histories from communities

Wexford is docked at Collingwood Harbour, next to the steamer Arthur Orr, at the end of the shipping season, December 10, year illegible. It had obviously been an uncomfortable trip for captains and crew. Once again, ice in the rigging played havoc with the stability and manoeuvrability of the vessel.
Courtesy of Collingwood Museum, X974-675-1.

along the lakeshores, in documentary texts, and in marine histories. In this new age of information technology, one can find web pages on the Internet dedicated to the meteorological events of that fateful week, and you can purchase video documentaries telling the tales about this storm described by some writers as a "white hurricane" on the Great Lakes.

Captain George Playter, master of the *Wexford* until mid-October 1913, quoted in *The Owen Sound Times* in a commemorative article published on November 9, 1963, declared:

> It was the craziest storm ever. You couldn't figure it out and the weather experts were all wrong until the full force of the storm broke clean across Lake Superior, Lake Huron and Georgian Bay. Skippers got the "go ahead" 12 hours before the big blow, but when the barometer dropped like a stone in 40 minutes there was hardly time to hoist storm signals. The hoisting of storm signals meant nothing then because the ships had cleared from three dozen ports from Superior to Goderich and it was too late.
>
> I sat at home in Collingwood and watched the barometer. The arrow dropped until it bent. I never saw it so low in 55 years of sailing and I knew in my heart that the toll would be bad.

By the time the barometer returned to some semblance of being normal, between 175 and 200 lives were lost on Lake Huron, up to 250 in total on all the lakes. The Lake Carriers' Association[5] reported, "As nearly as can be traced, 235 sailors lost their lives in this storm, 44 of them on Lake Superior, seven on Lake Michigan, six on Lake Erie, and 178 of them on Lake Huron."[6] Ten ships lost all hands, and 20 were driven ashore in the 16-hour blow. Records are inconsistent with respect to the true numbers of sailors lost.

In a most colourful account of the storm, with respect to events in and near Goderich Harbour, Jim Hunter, the organist at the Knox

Presbyterian Church, wrote the following comments in a letter written many years after the storm:

> There was a little island in Goderich harbour then, since dredged out, and I remember the way the great seas piled over the breakwater, poured into the harbour, and picked up the harbour tug and chucked her on the mud-flat of this little island. The next one would sweep her off and surge her into deep water. And the next would suck her back again.
>
> The MacDonald boys had a little fish tug in the harbour at the time of the Great Gale, and the seas that were running picked their tug up and landed it high if not dry on the pier and there it stayed. 'S a fact.
>
> After the gale, when sailor after sailor was being washed up all glazed in his lifebelt and oilskins, the story got around that there was a reward of fifteen dollars for every body found. We schoolboys used to search the beach north and south like boy scouts on an Indian trail. What we would do if we found a body was less on our mind than what we could do with fifteen dollars.
>
> One day when the whisper went round "There's another found," I hung around the door of the Morgue.
>
> "Here," said the caretaker, "see if you know this poor fellow."
>
> He took me into where half a dozen overcoated, oilskinned, mittened men lay dead on the slabs, with wet towels covering their poor wave-battered faces. He switched the towel from the latest, who was still dripping Lake Huron water, and propped him up. I let a yell out of me and ran faster than I ever dreamed I could. I was cured of all desire to make fifteen dollars by finding a dead man.
>
> I knew the crew of the lost *Wexford* well, and also men in the lost *Carruthers*. Both those steamers went

past Goderich in the height of the storm. They couldn't come in on account of the sea that was running. They couldn't make the harbour entrance. Perhaps they were lost trying to turn around, and falling [sic] into a trough.

The most remarkable experience I know of in that gale was that of the *Kaministiquia* and the *McKee* of the Western Transport line. The *Kaministiquia* was bound up the lake, light, and the *McKee* was coming down loaded with grain. Neither was able to get into shelter, and both had to ride out the gale in the lake. They manoeuvred so as to come alongside one another and make fast, with all their heavy fenders supplemented by big cedar posts and dock-logs, hung between them. The *Kaministiquia*, sitting high in the water, was brought down to the *McKee*'s level by flooding her ballast tanks. One was headed one way, the other the other, and the one kept her propeller turning over ahead and the other astern. So they rolled the gale out, nosing or backing into it, and they came through safely. But all those oak and cedar fenders between them were chewed down into match splinters, and wooden wale-strakes along their sides were scrubbed down flush with the steel plating.[7]

The Lake Carriers' Association probably carries the most accurate documentation of ships and crew lost — but only for its own members. Of their total membership of 19,553 recorded in 1913, the association lost 153 sailors in the Great Storm, paying out some $18,245.60 in welfare plan benefits to the survivors of the 132 members enrolled in the plan. The names, capacities, ships, amounts paid, and other details are documented in the annual report for 1913. What a pity that such records were not kept for all sailors on all ships. In the case of our own *Wexford*, as noted previously, estimates vary from about 17 to 24 persons having been onboard at the time of her sinking. I have not found any records showing compensation amounts paid to the survivors of those who perished on the *Wexford,* but I do note that funerary tributes were placed by the shipowners.

A vivid description of the storm was published in the *Village Squire* magazine in 1981, and republished by the Huron County Historical Society in 1988.[8] Excerpts are provided here to share regional historian Dean Robinson's perception of this catastrophic event:

> It was one of those mornings when you could just feel it in your bones. At least Milton Smith of Port Huron did, as he looked at the weatherboard in Cleveland's harbour.
>
> It was Saturday, November 8, 1913, and Smith, an assistant engineer, signed off the 524-foot coal carrier *Charles S. Price.* He didn't like leaving his mates, especially his good friend Arz McIntosh, a wheelsman from St. Clair, but sometimes you must do what you feel is right. McIntosh, who had been having trouble with his eyes, was ready to call it a season, too, but then elected to make at least one more run. He needed the money for a possible operation.
>
> The weather information that helped Smith to decide to leave was no secret. On the previous day, a dirty blow had come up on Lake Superior. It was a nor'wester and by noon coast guard stations were flying flags that spelled storm warnings. In the afternoon winds reached fifty miles an hour and carried with them a blizzard. And at night the coast guard station lanterns warned of an approaching hurricane, something unusual on the Great Lakes.
>
> The fall of the year traditionally brings bad weather to those who ply the Lakes, some years worse than others. But an extra run or two before ice clogs the shipping lanes can make for a financially merrier Christmas for all concerned: the company, the captain, and the crew. The gales of November were and are simply a part of the job. There was no doubt a sigh of relief among many

captains later that Saturday when the storm on Superior subsided. Carriers in port or sheltered in the St. Marys River began moving down into Lake Huron and those similarly at ease in Lake Erie and in the Detroit and St. Clair Rivers continued north up into Huron.

Early Sunday morning second mate Howard Mackley mailed a letter to his wife as the *Charles S. Price* passed Detroit. A short time later, as the steamer fought her way up the St. Clair River, Mackley pulled the ship's whistle to salute his wife, who was waving from the dock at their St. Clair home. Such was customary. Warding off the hard weather, dozens of friends and relatives went to the docks that morning in the many ports along Huron.

All Saturday night and well into Sunday ships came into Huron from the St. Clair River, the Straits of Mackinac, and the St. Marys River. But the lull on Superior that had coaxed them onward was false.

Later that Sabbath and in the early hours of Monday, November 10, the Great Lakes, particularly Huron and Erie, and their shorelines, were savagely beaten by winds and snow. An eight-year park project in Chicago was destroyed in as many hours. At Port Huron there was an estimated $100,000 [1913 dollars] damage to shoreline properties, where roofs were torn off, trees uprooted, and concrete walks swept away. The mouth of the Port Huron canal was blocked by 640,000 cubic feet of sand that washed over a protective breakwall.

Blizzards paralyzed traffic. Streetcars were stranded, scheduled trains cancelled. By Sunday, telegraph and telephone lines had been knocked out in Ontario and Michigan. Around Huron snow was piled four feet deep. Cleveland was rendered immobile by twenty-two inches of the white stuff, and in that same city, at 4:40 p.m. Sunday, the wind was clocked for a full minute at seventy-nine miles an hour. For the next nine hours it was a steady sixty to sixty-two miles an hour. Down at the docks two-inch mooring cables were snapped and barges broke loose.

The people who had been at the docks in the morning slept uneasily that night. Near Goderich, a family who had been away from their Colborne Township farm arrived home Sunday night and discovered their chickens had been blown into the wire netting of their enclosure and frozen to death. Early in the week that followed, snow was piled so high across Huron County roads that rail fences had to be parted so children could be drawn to school across open fields.

With communications knocked out it was some time before those on land learned that at least eighteen vessels were bearing the brunt of nature's worst out on Huron. Another two dozen struggled on Superior, Michigan, Erie and their adjoining rivers, bays and canals.

Two steamers, one northbound, the other south, made full passage on Huron during that wild night. Under Capt. James B. Watts, the *J.F. Durston* took almost forty hours to go from the Lake Huron lightship up to Mackinaw, a run that usually needs about twenty-two hours. When he tied up at 1:00 p.m. Monday, the *Durston* was coated in about one thousand tons of ice. In this report, Capt. Watts said, "I have been sailing for thirty-three years and for the last twenty-three years have been Master on steam vessels. November 9 was the worst storm I was ever in during my sailing career.... They can talk about life lines, sounding machines and patent logs; they are no good to a man in weather like November 9." Salvation for the *Durston* stemmed from Capt. Watts' ability to keep her headed into the storm and retain control.

Not so fortunate were at least sixteen other vessels on Huron. Some of them may have survived the

Sunday–Monday terror and even "hung on into Tuesday, but all of them yielded sooner or later." The lucky ones crashed ashore where many of their crews were saved. But from the eight ships that went to the bottom there were no survivors.

A welfare committee was established and set up headquarters at the Hotel Bedford in Goderich. Within days the Dominion Marine Association collected about $110,000 to provide relief for dependents of the men lost. The Lake Carriers' Association obtained detailed descriptions of most of the missing from relatives, to help with identifications. It also issued a twenty-five-dollar reward for each body found.

While the shoreline from Kettle Point to Kincardine was combed by searchers on foot, the tug *Horton* patrolled the water close to shore as far north as Cape Hurd. At the same time, the Canadian revenue cutter *Lambton* cruised the open lake, about twenty-five miles offshore…. The loss of life and property was undoubtedly due to the unprecedented character of the storm. Too, there was no radio or radar in those days, and communications … were poor.

The financial damage that occurred could not begin to compare, however, to the losses in human life. It is estimated that approximately 240 lives were lost. Sixty bodies washed up on shore between Sarnia and Goderich. At Thedford, when the Woodhall Funeral Home was filled, the excess casualties were placed on the concrete floor of a barn across the street. Special orders were sent to London for more caskets.

It would have been difficult to avoid this tragedy. The fierce November gales were viewed as being "part of the job." And, with technology being as primitive as it was, radar and communications systems would not have been sufficient to prevent the disastrous effects of the

If work on deck were possible in these cold and wintry conditions, full storm gear, as cumbersome as it might be, would be an absolute necessity.
Photo courtesy of the late Captain Roy Munday.

storm. Hopefully, technology has improved enough to prevent this type of tragedy from ever happening again.

In *Hay Township Highlights*, a local history compiled for the same geographic area as the Robert Turnbull farm mentioned previously, the storm is described as follows:

> The worst storm ever recorded on the Great Lakes took place on November 9, 1913. That storm claimed over two hundred lives and destroyed 12 lake freighters, eight of which sank in the waters of Lake Huron.
> Warning flags had been posted on the upper lakes on November 7, when the storm blew up in the state of Minnesota. Storm flags were hung out at ports all along the Great Lakes but then there seemed to be a lull in the storm. Because lake captains and their crews wanted to complete the last runs of the season, they set out from

ports around the lakes, little imagining that the coming storm would reach hurricane proportions.

In Huron County, the 60 to 70 [miles per hour] winds brought up to four feet of snow in 16 hours. The storm was eventually called a hurricane and remains unmatched in historical records. On the lake, the winds caused up to 40-foot waves. These same winds kept changing direction, so that the wind frequently blew one way while the seas ran in the opposite direction. These opposing forces subjected the ships to incredible punishment, making it impossible to keep the bow of the ship into the wind. Lake Huron would claim the heaviest loss of human life.[9]

In the November 10, 1913 edition of *The London Free Press*, it was reported that "the storm varied from point to point of the compass, keeping for the most part between NW and NE." It was clear that it was a massive and complicated weather system that moved in.

In her volume *Off Watch*, the story of her travels as the purser's daughter, published in 1957, Anna G. Young wrote extensively about the Great Storm:

Old mariners had thought a vessel could not live in such a storm (as the one encountered in November 1913). Captain Foote said he hoped never to see another but in the storm of 1913, as Master of the *Hamonic*, he was to meet his most severe test.

There was a measure of false security in the nearness of the ports and the comparatively short trips. Wireless was in its infancy and freight boats were not equipped with it.

Captain W[illiam] A[lfred] Geddes recalls how the water in the Niagara River rose thirty-two feet above normal. He was Master of the *City of Ottawa* heading for

Cleveland. The wind was blowing hard from the north as he passed Long Point. He put the ship on the centre light of the Cleveland Viaduct, the light was forty feet high but he couldn't see the piers. Letting go both anchors, she pulled up not a foot off the dock.

Chief Engineer Harry Moore of Owen Sound described his experience on the *Paipoonge* with Captain N. Foote of Collingwood her Master:

We cleared from Goderich the evening of November 8, 1913. Lake Huron was comparatively calm but the Captain said to me the barometer was the lowest he ever saw it and we could expect something to come out of that. We crossed the lake but found few boats had taken shelter in Harbor Beach so we headed north at full speed and joined an American squadron. We got to the Sault River in the morning and fuelled at Lime Island.

The wind by now had reached hurricane proportions. We all vowed the river was far enough to navigate until the wind abated. The clouds were as low as the masthead and we had difficulty locking through at the Soo; the water was low on account of high winds. At least fifty ships had been lying between the Soo and Whitefish for thirty-six hours, from the ninth of November. When we arrived they were covered with ice. About the time we got there, seven of them pulled out and headed north toward Michipicoten. We joined that mad flotilla but when we got as far as Coppermine our Captain decided he was going back regardless of what the other ships did.

We seemed to be jumping up and down in the same hole and not making any visible progress. When we turned, five other ships turned too. They followed us right back into the Sault River.

The other two blew across the Lake and, luckily, found some degree of shelter behind some ore docks at Marquette, Michigan, on the south shore. These ships were the *Winona and Midland King.*

From Chief Moore's perspective:

All right, we're talking about the same place: It was jammed when we got there, all the ships were looking for a holding ground. We had a collision with the steamer *Fairmount* but it fortunately wasn't serious; no real damage done. We rested that night in comparative comfort. Next morning the wind had died down but mountainous seas were still running and these took many hours to subside. On Point Iroquois, a large 600-foot boat was piled up on shore. We saw another on Parisienne Island and the *Huronic* was sitting on the sand of Whitefish Point, high and safe.

When we got to Port Arthur we learned about all manner of mysteries.... Lack of communication hindered reports for days. We had been reported lost but were one of the lucky ones instead. We were told the new 10,000 ton freighter *H.B. Smith* was lost with all hands.

By the time we reached the shelter of the Sault River ... the wind was blowing one way while the sea was running the other. The waves were thirty-five feet high, shorter than usual with gale winds, but they sometimes hit three and four at a time. When the gale ripped the lightship *Huron* from her anchorage and sent her aground two miles above the mouth of the St. Clair River some of the ships set their course by her, not knowing she was grounded and three of them went ashore as a consequence. Maybe saved them, can't tell.

There were features of the ships themselves that made them more vulnerable. The investigation recommended more length and a wider beam with added power. They wouldn't be so much at the mercy of the waves. They were heavily loaded for it was the end of the season and there were one hundred million bushels to be shipped one thousand miles, only twenty-foot channels, sometimes. Our canals are shallow, our season is short, freight rates are low. The largeness of their hold is more and more indispensable. The ships lost were certain types, satisfying government requirements, at that time, and they just couldn't out-manoeuver those heavy seas.

My own experience was typical of many November storms for, coming down Lake Superior from Duluth on November 27, 1924, the *Hamonic* seemed to be the only ship on that stormy sea. Father [Anna Young's father Hugh] had been engaged in establishing the freight system there that season and I begged to return to Sarnia by boat while he cleared up last business and followed by rail. The weather report was good; it had been a wonderfully open, late fall so I had my wish. It was a fair run to the Lakehead where we loaded at Fort William and sailed in late afternoon with 2,200 tons of flour in addition to the 500 tons of bran and flour we had already taken from Duluth. The sirens of tugs and other ships blew the farewell salute to the *Hamonic* and finally the watchman's foghorn, on the end of the pier, gave us her blessing. We kept away from Thunder Cape and Thunder Bay Harbour, slipped by the Passage Island to the open Lake.

With the tossing of the ship the hairpins began falling out of my hair, I wasn't taking any chances on picking them up. We were in for a dirty night but I was anxious to qualify as another "last Tripper" and I could let a few more hairpins fall at the challenge. There was a lot of motion and the lights on our smokestack, as I looked aft, were swinging a wide arc. "Catching fish in the smokestack" had been a colourful phrase in my listening career but tonight it was a reality. I was the only woman on the ship.

We reached the Soo late the following day and lay in shelter until dawn. As we picked up Iroquois Point in Whitefish Bay I echoed the words of Captain Patenaude, "Good-bye Ol' Superior, you no get me now this year."[10]

The best meteorological description of the storm is found in an Internet posting by William R. Deedler, a United States weather historian,

This snapshot was found in the personal collection of my late uncle, a lifetime mariner who experienced every kind of weather on the sea. The image conveys an absolutely frightening situation on the stormy waters.
Courtesy of the late Captain Roy Munday.

in the Pontiac, Detroit, Michigan, area. He writes in extensive detail under the title "Hell Hath No Fury Like a Great Lakes Fall Storm" — Great Lakes White Hurricane November 1913. For those wishing to pursue a scientific description of this monster storm, they can review the website.[11]

What Was the Actual Height of the Waves?

I recently polled a few of the more senior members of the Southampton Propeller Club, at one of their warm, friendly and most hospitable, Wednesday afternoon, *weekly* meetings at the Walker House pub and hotel in their community, about the actual height of the waves during this tempest. Recognizing that calculations should be based on the distance from trough to crest, I asked whether it would be possible to have waves of the 35- to 40-foot heights described by lake masters and sailors of the time.

The answers suggested that the lake would have been furious, and savagely confused, but perhaps the suggestions of wave heights are easily exaggerated. They thought shore damage, in particular, although extensive in some areas, would have been much more profound along the lower-lake shorelines had the wave heights been as extreme as described. Other sources suggest that the Lake Huron bottom, being a gradual slope to the shoreline, would knock down large seas long before they reach the shoreline properties. Contrary opinions have also been expressed, suggesting that waves will become steeper and closer together as they approach the beaches. My own experience, sailing on the ocean, is that wave heights lessen as you approach the shore.

There is no doubt the waves were horrendous, and in company with the hurricane winds and the driving snow, would have created situations to wrest control from the ships' masters and turn vessel, cargo, and crew over to the mercy of the elements. The greatest villain was ice and snow. Hundreds of tons of the stuff would grip decks and superstructure in an icy death hold. Vessels would become top-heavy and impossible to control. They would certainly capsize and founder. The wrath of waves of 20 or even 25 feet would be sufficient to turn and topple vessels as short as the 250-foot *Wexford*, or to turn turtle the brand new and invincible 550-foot *James C. Carruthers.*

Captain A. Roy Munday, my late uncle, had almost a half-century of his life and work on the water. He spent five years on salt water during his service as an able seaman in the Second World War, Royal Canadian Navy, and the balance of his time on the Great Lakes. Fully 11 seasons were spent as master on various lakers of all size, travelling from the head of the lakes, in Superior, to the Gulf of St. Lawrence. Much of his time was spent on Lakes Huron and Superior — where he was caught in many vicious storms. He insisted that it is not possible to create 30-foot waves on these inland lakes. The fury of waves can be short and steep, but the tales of 30-, 35-, and 40-foot waves on Lake Huron are most surely exaggerated, according to him. He has been caught on the receiving end of rogue waves on Lake Superior in sustained 80-mile-per-hour winds — and wave heights may have reached 20 or just a few more feet in height, but the wave period and the critical spacing, which allowed for the occasional devastating and higher "rogue," was a more perilous factor in causing havoc for shipping, according to Roy.

Other contemporary masters, such as the aforementioned Captain Bud of Tobermory, would verify that waves of 30 feet or more could have been be experienced, mostly certainly on Lakes Huron, Michigan, and Superior, with an occasional rogue as part of the infamous "three sisters" grouping, that might reach 40 feet or even more. His worst experiences would have seen waves "more than once on Lake Superior, waves of 40 feet plus"[12] when he encountered the "three sisters" phenomenon.[13]

The one factor during the Great Storm that could well have produced the gigantic waves at the height of the storm was the wind direction — mostly from the north. They would have had the full fetch of Lake Huron to intensify and it is not out of the question that a so-called "once in a hundred year" wave event could have occurred. According to Captain Robinson, the waves would be "steep, ugly, and in quick succession. Such heights as reported by masters and crew of those vessels did take place, as it [the storm] had the full extent of the large body of water to create massive wave action. Anyway, I do believe the stories and letters of the events as told by those old-timers to be very near the truth."[14]

Any of these suggestions are not to belittle the comments of mariners of the day, or to challenge the observations of the Lake Carriers' Association as they wrote their reports in the aftermath of the storm. However, it would seem that more attention might have been paid to the peril created by accumulations of ice and frozen slush and the effect of the profoundly increased topside weight, or top-hamper,[15] on steerage and stability. Once covered with ice, these hulks were viewed as floating tombs or "floating hearses" as they were sometimes called.

The Captain C.D. Secord *at Sault Ste. Marie, Michigan, in an undated*
photograph. Once again, an ice-covered hull tells a tale of the terrible conditions
as the Secord *sought refuge at port.*
Courtesy of Huron County Museum and Historic Gaol, 982.0030.023.

Not enough has been researched or written about the role of ice and snow in these calamities. The buildup of the wintry shroud of slush and ice is rapid, according to today's skippers, and brings with it a significant addition of weight. As it solidifies, grabbing at lifelines and encasing them, entombing bollards, winches, deck companionways, and encapsulating other such equipment, these very structures, designed to

143

support the needs of crew and to protect them, become unrepentant barriers to immense crashing waves. Some of these fixtures would surely have snapped like matchsticks and been torn away from their footings. Others, such as cargo hatches, may actually be strengthened and held more securely. In addition, there is no doubt that the additional strain would lead to damage and destruction from stem to stern as the hours unfolded under such storm duress. I am convinced that the buildup of ice and snow played the key role in the loss of the *Wexford*, and have included such reference in my outline of the last moments of the ship in another chapter in this text.

The Wisconsin Marine Historical Society has published many accounts about the Great Storm of November 1913 in its publications over the years. Excerpts from the first-person accounts that follow first appeared in the March 1914 issue of *The Marine Review* and were republished in the *Marine Historian* in 1988.

Captain Stephen A. Lyons of the *J.H. Sheadle*[16] wrote a long and detailed account of his own recollections. He described the sequence of unusual changes in the wind as the storm unfolded, and offered speculations about events that must have transpired onboard the 10 ships that totally disappeared, the six that were driven onto beaches and were total losses, the 15 driven ashore and requiring extensive repair, and the untold number that had to return to shipyards to have rivets tightened that were sprung loose by the severe pounding of the waves against their hulls.

It is worth sharing his observations about one ship that survived:

> The experience of the steamer *H.M. Hanna Jr.*, which was thrown upon a reef near Port Austin light, must have been typical of the experience of all. The *Hanna* passed Port Huron about 5 o'clock Sunday morning, the weather being fair and clear, with a 15-mile breeze off the land, and a low barometer. She passed Harbor Beach about 11:30 a.m., the wind increasing meanwhile. The vessel passed Pointe Aux Barques about 2:00 p.m., and as the wind increased, she was hauled more to the northward to hold her head to the wind. As the day advanced,

Plate 1. *The Last Sighting*, oil, 2000, artist Captain C. "Bud" Robinson.

Plate 2. *The Wexford*, watercolour, 2001, artist Robert McGreevy.

Plate 3. *The Wexford*, acrylic, 2000, artist William Nieuwland.

Plate 4. *The Goderich Lighthouse, circa 1900*, watercolour, 2000, artist Paul Carroll.

Plate 5. *Grain Vessels at Goderich Harbour, colourized postcard, circa 1910.*

The Docks, Collingwood, Ont., Canada

Plate 6. The *Wexford* at Collingwood Harbour, colourized postcard, nd.

Unloading Wheat — Winter Scene, Goderich.

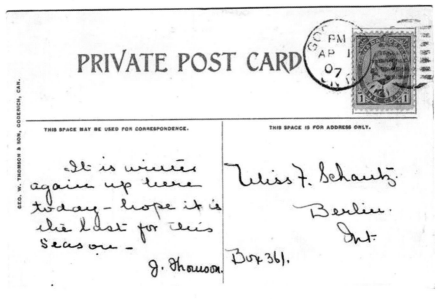

PRIVATE POST CARD

GEO. W. THOMSON & SON, GODERICH, CAN.

THIS SPACE MAY BE USED FOR CORRESPONDENCE.

THIS SPACE IS FOR ADDRESS ONLY.

It is winter
again up here
today – hope it is
the last for this
season –

J. Thomson.

Miss F. Schantz.
Berlin.
Ont.

Box 361.

Plate 7. The *Turret Chief* Shrouded in Ice, colourized postcard,
George W. Thomson and Son, Goderich, Canada, 1907.

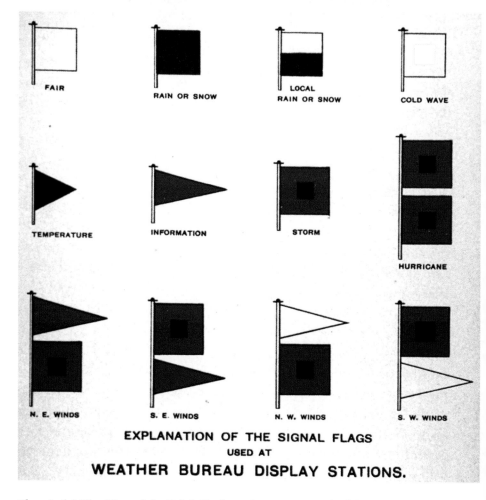

EXPLANATION OF THE SIGNAL FLAGS
USED AT
WEATHER BUREAU DISPLAY STATIONS.

Plate 8. (a) The Flag of the R.M. Hudson Company, 1912; (b) U.S. Weather Flags, 1899.

the snow got thicker and thicker, and the wind and sea so increased that the vessel began dropping off her course. Tremendous seas began to break over her, demolishing her after cabin, carrying away the starboard lifeboat, and tearing off the top of the pilothouse. About 8 o'clock at night the steward's wife was swept into the engine room by a particularly heavy sea, which struck the after quarters. Though the steamer was in good trim and her engine kept wide open, it was impossible to keep her headed into the sea, and she gradually went off into the trough. From that time on she wallowed heavily, with the seas breaking continuously over her, demolishing the crew's quarters aft and pouring tons of water into the engine room. Pumps and siphons were kept going to free her, and when the captain saw the Port Austin light close aboard, he threw out the port anchor to bring her head to the wind, but she continued to drift until she slammed upon the reef, where she pounded so badly that she broke in two. All her hatches were torn from her and her rivets sheared off the topsides as if they had been cut with chisel and hammer. The crew remained aboard the ship all day Monday, but as the seas were moderating on Tuesday morning, they were able to lower the port lifeboat and reach the shore. The balance of the crew was taken off by the lifesavers. Everybody aboard spoke in the highest praise of Mrs. Black, the cook, who foundered about in the galley in water waist-deep, trying to prepare meals for members of the crew. The *Hanna* was abandoned as a total constructive loss.

Captain Lyons offered his own speculations about the disappearance of the brand new 550-footer, the *James S. Carruthers*, which in itself was the largest and most valuable loss in the storm. He suggested that she must have been caught in a trough, rolled, and her cargo shifted, causing her to capsize and sink. Her location is still unknown to this day.

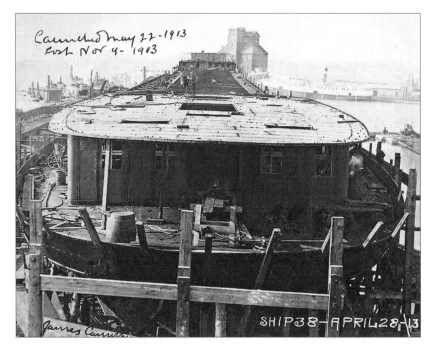

The mighty 550-foot James Carruthers, *launched in 1913, was invincible, according to her builders, her owners, and informed mariners. Shown here in the final stages of her construction, just before her "side launch" at the Collingwood Shipyards, she, too, was lost in the Great Storm. Her name joins the list of other so-called "invincible" ships — including the* Titanic *and the* Edmund Fitzgerald. Courtesy of Collingwood Museum, Accession No. x968.809.1

Lyons departed Fort William on the *Sheadle* on the February 6. While monitoring the unstable weather, he made the same observations — that the barometer had steadied enough that he was confident that safe passage could be made following his arrival at the Sault on the eighth, when he, in the company of several other vessels, departed to head down Lake Huron. The fledgling Captain Cameron of the *Wexford* was one of these drawn along by the crowd.

Things seemed fine for Lyons as he passed Presque Isle, and winds did not whip up until he reached Thunder Bay Island, off Alpena on the American shore. By now in a blinding blizzard, with raging seas, the ship course was adjusted so that she could run full before it, so as not to be knocked or rolled. With no visibility, and nothing but dead reckoning to determine his location, Lyons called for regular soundings to determine his position by calculating the depth. When he figured he was off Harbor Beach, he switched his course to due south to compensate for a slight wind shift, and kept running. The wind and the waves intensified.

At the regular time the cook had set up for supper, about 5:45 p.m., and the tables were ready. As the crew was called,

> a gigantic sea mounted our stern, flooding the fantail, sending torrents of water through the passageways on each side of the cabin, concaving the cabin, breaking the windows in the after cabin, washing our provisions out of the refrigerator and practically destroying them all, leaving us with one ham and a few potatoes. We had no tea or coffee. Our flour was turned into dough. The supper was swept off the tables and all the dishes smashed.
>
> Volumes of water came down on the engine through the upper skylights, and at all times there were from 4 to 6 feet of water in the cabin. Considerable damage was done to the interior of the cabin and fixtures. The after steel bulkhead of the cabin was buckled. All the skylights and windows were broken in. A small working boat on the top of the after cabin and mate's chadburn were washed away.

In another dramatic moment, the captain sent men to the aft cabins to secure the windows with shutters, for protection from the onslaught of huge waves washing aboard over the stern:

> They forced their way aft, braving the wind, sleet and seas, one hand grasping the life rail and the other the shutters. Reaching the after cabin in safety, they began securing the shutters, when another tremendous sea swept over the vessel, carrying away the shutters. The

men were forced to cling to whatever was nearest them to keep from being washed overboard; immediately a third sea, equally as severe, boarded the vessel, flooding the fantail and hurricane deck. The men attempted to reach the crews [*sic*] dining room, but could not make it, and only saved themselves by gripping the nearest object they could reach, indeed one of the wheelsmen was only saved from going over by accidentally falling as he endeavoured to grope his way to the rail, his foot catching in one of the bulwark braces, preventing him from being swept off. Another monster sea boarded the boat, tearing the man loose from the brace and landing him in the tow line, which had been washed from its after rack and was fouled on the deck.

In one dramatic moment, when struck by a rogue wave, "The heavy rolling tore adrift the binnacle on top of the pilothouse. After that it was extremely dangerous to be in the house, as this heavy object was hurled back and forth across the deck as the ship labored and rolled in the heavy sea."

Conditions must have been terrifying for the captain and his crew:

The rolling was very bad — I was lifted right off my feet. Only by the greatest effort were the second mate and myself able to hold onto the stanchions on the top house, our legs being parallel with the deck most of the time. Again and again she plunged forward, only to be baffled in her attempts to run before it, sometime fetching up standing and trembling from stem to stern. She was buffeted about by the tremendous seas, almost helpless, dipping her hatches in the water on either side, barrels of oil and paint getting adrift and smashing out the sides of the paint locker. The men were tossed around the wheelhouse at will. I feared her steering gear had given way, but fortunately on examination they proved to be all right.

The closest thing to an "official" description of the storm is found in the pages of the Annual Report 1913 by the Lake Carriers' Association. It cites a four-day period for this meteorological atrocity, from November 8 to 11. It started, according to that report, on the morning of November 8, first striking Lake Superior from the northwest. The blow was sufficient that vessels either stayed in port or sought shelter along the north shore. There was a lull of a few hours, thus tempting a few skippers to set out; but the gale broke out again, still from the northwest, with heavy seas, such as to cause the *H.B. Smith* and the *Leafield* to founder, both with all hands onboard:

By Sunday, the 9th, the tempest had calmed down to the degree that ships set out on Lake Huron, in a breeze being about fifteen miles per hour from the northwest, the sea being quiet, the barometer, however, remaining quite low.

By noon … a fresh wind began blowing from the North, shifting to Northeast, and increasing to become a raging gale. Five ships had entered the lake that morning, upbound. Four ships had sought a southerly route, entering (Lake Huron) at Detour Passage from the Soo. The *Hydrus* and the *Carruthers* appeared to be the early morning leaders. The *Regina*[17] and the *Wexford* followed them. All were lost, with all hands. The ships destroyed represented not only the best of great lakes practice but also of the high seas. The *Leafield* and the *Wexford* were typical "British tramps" and had both weathered gales in all parts of the world.

No lake Master can recall in all his experience a storm of such unprecedented violence with such rapid changes in the direction of wind and its gusts of such fearful speed.

Storms ordinarily of that velocity do not last over four or five hours, but this storm raged for sixteen hours continuously at an average velocity of sixty miles per hour with frequent spurts to seventy and over. Obviously with a wind of such long duration, the seas that were made were such not ordinarily familiar to the lakes. The testimony of Masters is that the waves were at least 35 feet high and followed each other in quick succession; three waves ordinarily coming one right after the other. They were considerably shorter than the waves that are usually formed by the ordinary gale. Being of such height and hurled with such force and such rapid succession, the ships must have been subject to incredible punishment. Masters also relate that the wind and sea were frequently in conflict, the wind blowing one way and the seas running in the opposite direction. This would indicate a storm of cyclonic character. It was unusual and unprecedented and it may be centuries before such combination of forces may be experienced again.[18]

In a very subtle and unobtrusive fashion, perhaps not to offend the "foreign" Canadian politicians, whose weather signal and reporting systems were somewhat incomplete, the report also suggested that the Weather Bureau reporting system might be modified to indicate more clearly what might be expected than did the current system. Let us remember that the signal system of the day reported only a "gale" as the maximum type or characteristic of a storm. The American system provided for "hurricane" reports. There is little doubt that the Canadian system in place in 1913 was inadequate to report the so-called "white hurricane" that was unleashed.

Finally, nothing appears in the literature about the presence of so-called "rogue" waves during this tempest. There are many reports of giant waves appearing out of place and unexpectedly in ocean settings. These events are sometimes mistakenly identified as "tidal" waves, but they are not. Waves are an almost constant feature on any sizeable body of water.

On Lake Superior there is a phenomenon called the "three sisters," as discussed earlier, where three large waves in succession, close together, each worse in impact than the last, culminating in a final assault more harmful than normal because a ship would likely not have time to recover from the effects of the first two passing by.

Wind blowing across the surface is the causal factor for most waves. Friction and the driving force of the wind combine to form a series of hillocks and trenches across the surface. Although it appears that these waves are moving, the water itself is not. It generally just moves up and down. Ralph Doolin, author of an article published by *SailNet*,[19] suggested that water moving at the speed of most storm waves would make navigation impossible.

He went on to clarify that how big the waves become depends on three things — the speed of the wind, the duration (or how long the wind blows), and the fetch (the distance of open water over which the wind is blowing). He suggested that it is the gradient of the waves, rather than the height alone, that causes problems.

Waves, measured from trough to crest, estimated to be 35 feet or even more in the 1913 storm, coming in rapid succession, suggested in groups of threes, would indicate steep gradients on Lake Huron whipped up by the weaving northwest–northeast raging tempest.[20] There is little doubt that such conditions, combined with the accumulations of tons of heavy wet snow and ice on decks and superstructures, led to the demise of virtually all ships caught offshore in this storm.

No matter how it has been described, or how it was forecast, it was clearly 16 hours of the worst hell ever experienced on Lake Huron and her sister lakes. It was truly a white hurricane, the likes of which has never been seen before or since. Wrote the Lake Carriers' Association in its Annual Report for 1913: "The storm threw a great pall on lake shipping and practically demoralized lake trade for the balance of the season … the lessons of the storm, however, will not be lost."[21]

May the guardian spirits of the sea ever protect us from such wrath!

CHAPTER 7

The Carnage of the Storm

Now cometh the hour that turneth back desire
from seamen bold, and melteth every heart
when from sweet friends and home they must retire.
And the new pilgrim feels the selfsame smart
when on his hearing tolled bells implore
the day which dying from him doth depart.
— Dante, from *The Divine Comedy*

Body Count

Dwight Boyer portrays the most dramatic description of the first
indications of disaster in an account from his book *True Tales of the
Great Lakes*. He tells us, yet again, but in such vivid and descriptive
terms, of farmer Robert Turnbull's trek along the lakeshore to appraise
the erosion damage done to his property:

> There in the wraiths of the fog a quarter mile offshore,
> he perceived the hair-raising sight of a man beckoning
> to him. It was James Glenn, the homesick Scot from

the *Wexford*, his upraised arms frozen stiff, and seemingly waving, as his body, supported by a life preserver, bobbed up and down in the surf. It was almost as if he had at long last found a friendly shore and was motioning his shipmates to follow. And follow him they did — cook Wilmott who had thoughtfully brought along his collection of patent medicine brochure; wheelsman Gordon; chief engineer Scott; second mate Brooks; assistant engineer Lougheed; watchman Allan Dodson and cousins Murdoch and Donald McDonald, all wandering ashore there on the Turnbull farm where the beach was white with the *Wexford*'s grain. One of the vessel's lifeboats had drifted in too, but it had obviously not been used by the crew.[1]

It is apparent that most of the bodies washed ashore from the *Wexford* were found between St. Joseph and Kettle Point, November 10th and 11th, 1913. There are also vague reports about additional bodies being found in the Point Edward area, but I have been unable to locate any actual documentation. Folklore tells us that the mouldered remains of many sailors, washed up along the shorelines months after the storm, were quietly and respectfully removed by farmers and others whose property was adjacent to the shoreline, and buried in unmarked graves along the banks of the lake between Sarnia and Point Clark. Four bodies with life jackets marked WEXFORD and one body with a life jacket marked LONDON washed up five miles south of St. Joseph, below the farm of Robert Turnbull. There are reports of two additional bodies being found in the next day or two. These bodies were taken to Zurich for identification. Five of the seven bodies found near St. Joseph were identified, according to the November 13 edition of *The London Free Press*. Yet only the names of four were listed in *The Collingwood Bulletin* of November 20, 1913: James Glenn, James Scott, Murdock [*sic*] Macdonald [*sic*], and Archie Brooks.

At Kettle Point, seven bodies were picked up, one of them said to be Captain Bruce Cameron of the *Wexford*, alleged to have foundered

10 to 15 miles southwest of Goderich. "In the pockets of one man, who was evidently the captain, was the shipping bill of the boat, and from his description it is clear that he is Bruce Cameron of Collingwood."[2] Captain W.J. Bassett, owner, stated that the last word the company received from Captain Cameron was Saturday, the 8th, at 12:45 p.m., suggesting that his arrival at Goderich might be delayed because of fog he was encountering in the St. Marys River.

Reports have been made of additional bodies washed up near Grand Bend and at Bayfield and, from other ships, north of Goderich. These bodies, unidentified, are said to be buried in unmarked graves in the Grand Bend cemetery. Bodies, severely mutilated, were said to be washed up at the southern neck of the lake along the Point Edward shoreline, according to a letter from Reverend Haslip, earlier cited.

All of this does not explain the pile of *Wexford* life jackets piled outside the back doors of the Brophey Funeral Home in Goderich. Were there several bodies from the foundering vessel that washed ashore between Goderich and Bayfield? Was the carnage from the storm of such massive proportion that not all of the findings were reported in the newspapers of the time? There was much confusion. One editor reported, at the conclusion of a front-page story, that there was so much information and such contrary statements that it was hard to know what to believe.

There were very disturbing reports in *The Port Huron Times-Herald* of Wednesday, November 12, 1913, just three days after the storm, under the headline, "Bodies of Dead Washed On Shore Near Port Frank [*sic*] Are Robbed by Vultures …" An accompanying editorial stated, "Added to the horror of the wrecks is the work of the ghouls along the Canadian shore. Pockets of dead men have been found sticking out with every evidence which might lead to their identity lost. The greed for gold destroyed all human instincts."[3] Folklore suggests that, as the law enforcement agencies closed in on the supposed culprits, life jackets that had been removed as corpses were violated were replaced, not always on the correct body, perhaps leading to confusion in the identity process. There is a very well-known and still persistent mystery about the strange and unexplained exchange of life jackets between crew members of the *Regina* and the *Price* near the foot of Lake Huron. Under the title "Ghouls Are Busy," *The Evening News*

Lifejackets at Brophey Funeral Home stacked outside the back door of the mortuary conveyed the image of death on the lake in all of its forlorn horror. Surprisingly, none of these life belts seems to have survived. The original photograph is part of a collection at Bowling Green State University, Ohio. Courtesy of Huron County Museum and Historic Gaol.

of Sault Ste. Marie (November 13, page 1) stated: "It is reported here that ghouls are busy and Canadian and American governments have instructed [authorities] to take drastic measures to prevent their ghastly work."

As part of the several inquests, the local coroners established inquiries to investigate the "cause of death" for the perished sailors. Invariably, the hearings began with depositions taken to describe the corpses found, sometimes in intricate and gruesome detail. At the Goderich inquiry, Coroner Archibald Cross Hunter took affidavits from several witnesses to confirm the identification of bodies found in the Goderich area. Former justice of the peace Karen Sturdy, a local resident and marine heritage enthusiast, made a copy of the transcript of the proceedings available to me. She has spent many hours trying to interpret those sections of the document which were illegibly copied many years ago.

Table 3: Table of Losses from Lake Carriers' Association Annual Report 1913 (page 154).

Name of Vessel	Over-All Ft.	Keel Ft.	Beam Ft.	Depth Ft.	Gross Tonnage	Net Tonnage	When Built	OWNER
*Str. *L.C. Waldo*	472	462	48-2	28	4,400	8,610	1896	Ruby Transp. Co. Ltd., L.C. Waldo, Mgr., Detroit, Michigan.
Str. *Chas S. Price*	624	604	64	30	6,322	4,001	1910	Mahoning Steamship Co., M.A. Hanna & Co., Mgrs., Cleveland, Ohio.
Str. *Isaac M. Scott*	624	604	54	30	6,372	4,840	1909	Virginia Steamship Co., M.A. Hanna & Co., Mgrs., Cleveland, Ohio.
*Str. *H.M. Hanna Jr.*	500	480	54	30	5,905	4,413	1908	The Hanna Transit Co., W.C. Richardson & Co, Mgrs., Cleveland, Ohio.
Str. *H.B. Smith*	545	525	55	31	6,631	5,229	1906	Acme Transit Co., Hawgood & Co, Cleveland, Ohio.
Str. *James Carruthers*	550	529	58	31	7,862	5,606	1913	St. Lawrence & Chicago Steam Nav. Co. Ltd., Toronto, Ontario.
Str. *Wexford*	270	250	40-1	16-7	2,104	1,340	1883	Western Steamship Co. Ltd., 72 Bay St., Toronto, Ontario.
Str. *Regina*	269	249-3	42 ½	23	1,956	1,280	1907	Merchants Mutual Line, Toronto, Ontario.
Str. *Leafield*	269	249	35-3	16-6	1,453	1,176	1892	Algoma Central Steamship Line, Sault Ste. Marie, Ontario.
*Str. *Major*	303	283	41	22	1,864	1,491	1889	Cleveland Steamship Co., John Mitchell, Mgr., Cleveland, Ohio.
Str. *John A. McGean*	452	432	52	28	5,100	3,777	1908	Pioneer Steamship Co., Hutchinson & Co., Mgrs., Cleveland, Ohio.
*Str. *Matoa*	310	290	40	25	2,311	1,836	1890	Pittsburg Steamship Co., Cleveland, Ohio.
Str. *Argus*	436	416	50	28	4,707	3,380	1903	Interlake Steamship Co., Cleveland, Ohio.
Str. *Hydrus*	436	416	50	28	4,713	3,384	1903	Interlake Steamship Co., Cleveland, Ohio.
*Str. *Louisiana*	287	267	39	21	1,929	1,383	1887	Thompson Steamship Co., J.R. Davock, Mgr., Cleveland, Ohio.
*Str. *Turret Chief*	273	253	44	19-7	1,881	1,197	1896	Canadian Lake & Ocean Nav. Co., Toronto, Ontario.
Bge. *Plymouth*	225	213	35	13	1,881	1,197	1854	McKinnon & Scott, Menominee, Michigan.
Lightship No. 82	105	89	32	12 ½	180	...	1912	Light House Bureau.
Bge. *Halsted*	191	171	32	12 ½	496	472	1873	Soper Lumber Co., W.E. Holmes & Co, Mgrs., Chicago, Illinois.

*Constructive Total Losses

Knevitt Naftel (elsewhere spelled Knyvet)[4] of the Township of Goderich swore the following statement related to the body of Thomas Stone,[5] for whom the inquiry was called, and two others found on the beach beyond the bluff and below his farm.

From the transcripts of the inquiry, pages 1 and 2, we learn that

> At 1:30 p.m. on Wednesday, November 12, I saw in the lake what I considered to be a life raft. It landed on the beach and I cut three bodies off and pulled them ashore. The lifebelts and raft were marked "Str. *John A. McGean.*" I notified Coroner Hunter, who with the Chief of Police examined the bodies.
>
> One body had papers addressed to Geo. L. Smith — no money — two small keys, body well clothed, blue suit — cloth top buttoned shoes — overcoat with long stripe, from Buffalo clothier. Age probably 25 or 30 years — 160 [pounds], 5[feet] 6[inches], clean-shaven — dark hair.
>
> Second Body: Str. *McGean* belt, oil skin and rubber boots, weight about 155 — Height 5[feet] 10[inches] — clean shaven — about 24 or 27 years — clothes from Buffalo clothier. Lake Seaman's Card named John Owen — Unable to make out place where he lived — had $1 American money — open face gold watch with bronze fob — watch stopped at 1:25 — Hair brownish.
>
> Third Body: Stout about 5[feet] 8[inches] 165 [pounds] — clean-shaven, long dark hair — Blue clothes made by Shulman of Buffalo, a sweater coat with fawn lining and corduroy trousers over blue trousers — several letters and post cards addressed to Thomas Stone — open-face gold watch with pearl fob — with monogram on back of watch — stopped at about 1:25 — $81.00 in American bills and $2.00 in silver and small pen knife. Had new pair of tan laced shoes. Wind was blowing from Southwest.

A Thomas Davis, and Lionel George (but known as "G.L.")[6] Parsons, superintendent for the Goderich Elevator, corroborated these observations. Parsons added sufficient additional detail to confirm that Thomas Stone was a Native. He carried a letter from the Sarnia Reserve, addressed to the deceased as "brother," as well as another from the courthouse in Owen Sound. There is no comment about the information contained in the letter. Stone's watch must have been admired, however. It was an "open face gold watch with a leather guard and shell fob, with DETROIT stamped on it — Monogram — apparently T.S. on back of watch.[7]

Parsons also offered his comments about the storm in his deposition, shown on pages 2 and 3 of the transcript:

> A storm commenced about 12:30 p.m. on Sunday, the 9th of November and continued with the wind very high, increasing all night. Wind apparently from the North. We expected the *Wexford* from our information to be here Sunday morning about daylight. Also expected the *Empress* of Fort William about same time. Heard no signals from vessels outside. I heard that Frank Bingham and Harry Stowe heard signals. Fred Shepherd was at the dock in afternoon of Sunday — Do not think lifesaving crew could have gone out Sunday night or Monday. Fog whistle did not blow until ten or eleven at night. I don't think a vessel could see lights owing to the storm. The only reliance would be sound. The present horn is inadequate. The sound if heard would assist in helping [vessels] in to the harbour…. Powerful whistles are placed at dangerous points [of land].

Most of the *Wexford* bodies, as recovered along the lakeshore nearby, and as already mentioned, were identified and addressed in the Blake Inquest conducted by a Doctor Campbell, of Hensall. As the corpses were recovered, they were lined up along the main street boardwalk, likely in front of the mortuary, to rest there until they could be accommodated in a more respectful setting indoors. An avid but unidentified local photographer took graphic black and white photographs of these remains. The images were never presented at the local inquests, it seems. The bodies of the young men are shown in contorted and pathetic positions, fixed in those postures by the rigor mortis imposed by being partially frozen. Medical examination confirmed that these sailors died from exposure, possibly on the open decks of their ship, on rafts, or as they clung perilously to flotsam from the foundering. It is said that they did not drown.

The full set of the original photographs seems to have disappeared. One set of copies is in the hands of the descendants of the undertaker; another rests in the collection of a deceased marine historian and retired mariner, Ron Pennington, in care of his widow, Lenna, a resident of the town of Goderich. Efforts are being made to acquire a set for placement in the National Archives in Ottawa or with the Marine Museum in Kingston.

Flotsam from the Storm

Most of the flotsam and jetsam from the 1913 November storm would surely find its way to the east coast shoreline of Lake Huron. The landfall, with the prevailing fall and winter northwest winds, would lie in the cradle formed by the "grand bend," commencing south of Bayfield and running southward in two great loops to the terminus of the lake at Point Edward.

To get a sense of how it really looks, one can drive away from the shore in an easterly direction, at Bayfield, to the concession road that runs parallel to Highway 21, south to Zurich. Inland, the elevation increases to the level of the probable lakeshore beach of the prehistoric shoreline (some 15,000 years ago). From this height, one can actually see the "grand bend" as it works its way south and west past the village of Grand Bend, reaching out to Port Franks and Kettle Point, then sweeping beyond to run almost due west toward Point Edward, near the lake's southerly extreme. It resembles, from this vantage point, the crook of an outstretched palm, from the tip of the index finger to the thumb.

The current flows slowly southward along this shore. Its speed will vary anywhere from 0.5 to 1.5 or even 2 knots per hour. In periods of gentle calm, the offshore southerly flow is also known to swirl inshore to the east and reverse its direction along the beach below the sandy dunes of this area. In these areas in the days, weeks, and months following November 9, 1913, the beaches were littered with sad reminders of the tragic loss of life and shipping from that devastating storm. Each storm brought new evidence of the tragic events.

Flotsam along the Huron shoreline. "First came the bodies ... then the barrels, the boxes, the shattered deck structures of strong timbers torn and shorn cleanly from sturdy decks to which they were securely bolted. There were lifeboats, foodstuffs, litter and paraphernalia of all descriptions." Original is from the Historical Collection of the Great Lakes, Bowling Green State University, Ohio. Courtesy of Huron County Museum and Historic Gaol.

First to arrive were the bodies — most wearing life vests, some of which bore the stencilled names of vessels that could not withstand the tempest's fury. Then came the barrels, the boxes, and the shattered deck structures — strong timbers torn and shorn cleanly from sturdy decks to which they were securely bolted. There were lifeboats, foodstuffs, litter, and paraphernalia of all descriptions. Along some portions of the shore, the beach was "white" with the grain from cargo holds, washed overboard and swept to shore as ships' hatches ripped open, whilst the great ships wallowed in the mighty troughs of the rampaging sea.

It was here that the contorted shapes of death washed into sandy pincers along the shoreline. The bodies of sailors, arms outstretched, legs bent as though kneeling to seek protection behind a bulwark onboard before being swept away by the icy spray. Some bobbed as gently as corks in the periods of calm that followed. Others were partially buried as shorelines were reshaped by the pounding waves. Still others were swept away from shore again as shifting winds carried the frozen cadavers to depths beyond recovery.

It was here that paddles and oars, masts and booms, chairs and cabinetry arrived in total disarray and mad confusion. Origins were mixed. An oar found by Paul Cleve, a farmer who lived some five miles south of Bayfield, said to be from the *Wexford*, has survived to this day and is currently in the collection of marine-heritage enthusiast Phil Gemeinhardt. While the flotsam of the *Carruthers* was tossed up largely north of Goderich, by Point Clark, the *McGean* scattered her cargo from Goderich to Grand Bend, and the *Wexford* from Black's Point and St. Joseph to Point Edward. Yet the souvenirs of her destruction were spread much farther along the shorelines than previously believed. There is growing credence that a large portion of the centre pilothouse from the *Wexford* crashed ashore on huge breakers at the Hick's farm, west of the Cut Line Road, south of Black's Point, beyond Naftel's Creek.

It was here that Leonard Hicks retrieved a clock said to be mounted on a board, perhaps from the pilothouse or the engine room, and carrying markings from the same chandlery that supplied the *Wexford* as she was being built in Sunderland in 1883. It was a brassy glint in the ice that attracted his eye. The device was retrieved and stored away quietly, lest some official wanted this shipwreck treasure as part of an inquiry or other such investigation. As mentioned earlier, according to the late Captain Roy Munday, the clock was removed from its mounting board along with some sort of steam valve or whistle, and used by young

Maurice, the son of Leonard, as a toy hoop to turn around the barnyard with a rod.

Also, as noted earlier, a *Wexford* life jacket was recovered, found hanging in the lower limbs of a tree above the lake bank at the back of a farm at Lot 6, Lake Range West, about three kilometres south of the current village of Bayfield. Not thought to be of any value, it hung for years in the driving shed on the farm of Harry Talbot, latterly owned by his son Edward "Len," until it was sold in 1987, at which time the preserver was discarded and burned. What value might an old and mouldy flotation jacket hold?

While one lifeboat was found north of St. Joseph and examined by Bassett, the owner of the *Wexford*, another washed up — along with a second life vessel from the *Regina* — in that great crook of shoreline at the southern end of Lake Huron, near Point Edward. Turned upside down, these abandoned lifeboats, dragged over the bank and hidden behind the barn, made excellent pigsties. And as such they met their pitiful, most shameful demise on the ammoniated grange of the ancestors of Reverend Edward C. Haslip, who recalls this memory from his grandfather's farm. "Much wreckage came ashore," he wrote in an undated letter sent to me in early 2002, "So naturally people recovered much of it ..."

Recovered, carried away, and reused!

CHAPTER 8

The Aftermath:
Consequences Abound

Down came the storm, and smote amain
The vessel in its strength;
She shuddered and paused, like a frighted steed,
Then leaped her cable's length.

The breakers were right beneath her bows,
She drifted a dreary wreck,
And a whooping billow swept the crew
Like icicles from her deck.
— Henry Wadsworth Longfellow, from *Wreck of the Hesperus*

On November 14, 1913, the *Detroit Free Press* included an account from a Port Huron correspondent that set the tone for the events that followed the storm:

> The chapters of the greatest tragedy of the great lakes are now being written. It is a story of successive tragedies without a parallel in fresh water maritime annals. Each hour, in fact, each message that comes clacking over the

wires adds to the horror of the situation, and when the end mark is written there will be a momentary loss to the shipping of the lakes that will run into the millions. This loss, however, is not to be compared to the loss of the gallant crews of the missing steamers who have gone to their death and whose bodies now rest between the waves or are tossed up upon the barren shores, awaiting the anxious eyes of searchers.... Standing out in bold relief in this story of death and disaster, which embraces a radius of 90 miles from Goderich to Sarnia and Harbor Beach to Port Huron, are at least 8 steamers which are among the missing. There is every reason to believe that they have gone to the bottom.

There were several inquests. In spite of the appeals of the *Wexford's* owner to consolidate the inquests in one location, or at the least to coordinate them, such did not occur. In fact, a separate investigation and inquiry seemed to take place in every community where bodies were found or taken for possible identification.

With respect to reparation for the widows and children of drowned sailors, there was to be none from government sources. Workers' Compensation had not yet been established. The Dominion Government acceded to the sum of $25,000 to support a Canadian fund. The province of Ontario added $10,000. The Canadian Mercantile Marine Association, the Dominion Marine Association, and the local hometown communities combined resources to raise funds. Donations were received, and donors were recognized by name and amount donated in the local newspapers. Funds accumulated reasonably quickly to meet and even exceed the overall $100,000 goal that had been set. Collections at memorial church services were set aside for the disaster relief fund. Special events were held.

In Goderich, all was not mournful. Local community leaders would sometimes let their hair down to entertain their fellow citizens as a means of raising money. At one such theatre event, G.L. Parsons, of the Goderich Elevators, sang a satirical and comic song, "Toper Murray," no doubt a parody about little Tobermory at the head of the Bruce Peninsula. Harry Sturdy, another well-known local, offered his vocal talents with an offering of "Down in Dear Old New Orleans" to raise a few more dollars for the fund.[1] As of December 4, about three weeks after the first news of the tragedies had emerged, $546.78 had been collected in the Goderich area. A benefit concert held at the Collingwood Opera House raised $33.18. The total of $926.35 was acknowledged for that community in *The Collingwood Bulletin* report of December 18, 1913. The overall total of funds collected by early December had passed the $50,000 mark according to reports from the Dominion Marine Association, issued by treasurer H.H. Gildersleeve of Toronto.[2]

A Lakes Disaster Fund, established by the American Lake Carriers' Association, also solicited donations along the shoreline communities on both sides of the lake. Spontaneous events, such as one held in Cleveland, Ohio, raised surprisingly large amounts of money. In the *Annual Report* for the Carriers' Association it was reported that claims had been paid in the total amount of $18,245.60 to 132 members enrolled in the Welfare Plan. By today's standards, the one-time, lump-sum amounts seem paltry. Seventy-five dollars was paid to the beneficiary of an ordinary seaman, $100 for a watchman, wheelsman, or fireman, $150 for a steward, $250 for a first mate or second engineer, $400 for a chief engineer, and $500 for a master. The Carriers' Association took great pains to elaborate how it provided additional funds, where necessary, when money was not otherwise available. Also,

> The bodies were then carefully prepared for burial and upon identification the relatives were again communicated with and orders obtained for disposal. All bodies were incased in good suitable caskets and either shipped to such destinations as ordered by the relatives, or, if buried locally, funeral services were held and the bodies placed in graves purchased especially for them, or in plots dedicated by the cities for this particular purpose.[3]

It is not clear what benefits may have been paid by owners whose sailors did not subscribe to the Carriers' Association or to other such Canadian groups. Owners did, however, contribute to funeral costs and wreaths in tribute to the dead.

Local opposition politicians blamed the Sir James P. Whitney government for failing to act on a Bill for Workman's Compensation at the last session of the Ontario legislature. Had it been approved, pensions would have been payable to survivors. Newton Wesley Rowell, Liberal opposition leader, bemoaned that, in many cases, widows and orphans and mothers were left without support as they could not claim compensation. "They have had a workmen's compensation law in England, even in poor backward Russia; they have one, in Spain, and in Manitoba, in Quebec, in New Brunswick, in Nova Scotia, in Australia, New Zealand and South Africa. Ontario is one large country under the British flag that has not such an act."[4] Rowell continued, "If they have no claim to compensation today, why? It is because the government did not put through that measure of workmen's compensation at the last session of the legislature."[5]

Rescue efforts were documented carefully by the Lake Carriers' Association and described in their report for 1913, beginning on page 28:

> The storm … destroyed all means of communication. For two or three days news of the disasters was very meagre. As soon, however, as the great havoc wrought by the storm was realized, the Lake Carriers' Association dispatched to the Canadian shore of Lake Huron a committee of captains with instructions to divide the shore into districts, employ all help necessary and establish a thorough patrol of the beach from Port Huron as far north as necessary. Headquarters were opened at Goderich, Ontario, where a telephone was installed and communication at once established with all points along the shore. This patrol system made a thorough search of the wreckage from the vessels and debris cast up by the storm, much of which was piled in tiers five to six feet deep at a distance 1,000 to 1,500 feet from the normal shore

line. It was found necessary to extend the patrols system north to the head of the peninsula projecting between Lake Huron and Georgian Bay.[6] Yet so thoroughly was this duty performed that every foot of the shoreline was thoroughly examined, and every body, which was washed ashore, was recovered. The beach patrol was reinforced by the employment of tugs and motorboats to search for bodies floating in the lake. The Revenue Cutters of the United States and Canada were also pressed into service to patrol the open waters of the lake.

The committee of captains was supplied with a sufficient number of copies of the crew lists of the lost vessels, together with descriptions of the men, which are included in the registration of each. Telegrams were at once sent

This image of a recovered body, though not from the 1913 storm, represents the pitiful drama that repeated itself time and time again as victims were recovered from the lakes. This event, a drowning, undated and attributed to the SS Clair Lully, *is one of those sad times.*
Courtesy of the Huron County Museum and Historic Gaol, 91-5, neg. #5.

to the relatives and friends of the men aboard these vessels and detailed descriptions, including distinguishing
marks, and in many cases photographs, were received,
and at once communicated by wire to the searching committee. As soon as a body was recovered it was taken to
the nearest town and compared with the description....
The Telegraph Companies extended to the Association
the free use of their wires for all messages pertaining to
the rescue work. The Lake Carriers' Association offered a
reward of $25 for the recovery of each body,[7] and notice
of it was posted in all towns and settlements bordering
upon the Canadian shore of the lake, as well as upon the
islands in the northern portion of Lake Huron.

Too much praise cannot be given to the public officials and citizens of Canada along the shore of Lake
Huron for their untiring efforts and assistance in the
work of recovery. Special acknowledgment is made of the
assistance rendered by the Honourable Edward Norman
Lewis, Member of Parliament, at Goderich, Ontario, the
coroners in the various cities and towns, and the ministers of all denominations. Much credit is due, also, to the
Rescue Committee of the Association, which consisted
of Captains E.O. Whitney, (chairman), C.E. Bowen, F.E.
Wiener, and T.A. Ferguson, for their efficient work in the
recovery and identification and care of the bodies.

The navigation season for Canadian traffic closed on
December 15 as the result of ice conditions at the Soo.[8]

Political Controversy Following the Storm

The Member of Parliament for West Huron, E.N. Lewis of Goderich,
brought several issues related to the 1913 storm to the attention of the
House of Commons on January 23, 1914. He raised complaints following

a speech from the throne, as a member of the government of Robert Laird Borden, prime minister at the time.

Lewis began his comments by documenting the importance of waterway traffic and transportation on the inland waterways, particularly Lake Huron. He suggested that the authorities must pay greater attention to the needs of vessels carrying in excess of 100 billion tons of cargo — a figure four times greater than that carried annually through the Suez Canal. He recounted the storm: "On the 9th of last November, Sunday evening, while the people on shore were at church, there occurred on the Great Lakes a catastrophe absolutely appalling, the greatest that ever happened either on the ocean or on the lakes affecting Canada or the United States. The gale that arose at that time wiped out of existence fourteen great steel steamships, eight of them disappearing absolutely, not a soul aboard being left to tell the tale. The loss was 205 [*sic* — probably misprint — 250] stalwart young men."9

He went on to document the vessels and their nature, and the loss of their crew by exposure rather than drowning. "These boats, Sir, could have been saved. I say so here from the evidence that was given at the inquest — not a soul need have been drowned, had we been advanced in our aids to navigation. They have on the ocean a wireless call, I believe SOS, which gives notice when a boat is in distress, but this is an entirely different proposition. There is no boat in the world that could have lived or effected a rescue in that sea at that time with the heavy snowstorm that then prevailed."10

Lewis went on to point out the physical deficiencies in the Port of Goderich harbour:

> Nothing could better illustrate the danger of the approach to Goderich harbour in a northwest gale than the fact that since the tragedy of November three steamers on three different occasions had attempted to enter that port in a northwest gale but had to put back to the open water. I contend that had the port, which I represent, and which for the last ten years, the Government of this country have [*sic*] designated a port of refuge,

and have [*sic*] been trying to make a port of refuge, had that port been a foul weather port instead of a fair weather port, and had there been a wireless station with a hurricane call, there was not one of those boats that could not have been in shelter inside of three hours. As a basis for that opinion, I give you the record as produced at the inquest of the weather bureau in the city of Toronto. On Friday morning, the 7th of November, the weather bureau sent out to the stations a warning that there was a strong northwest gale coming. The stations of all the upper lakes put up signals to that effect so that every captain had warning. That was on Friday the 7th. That storm continued through the 7th, and through the night of the 7th and on the 8th, but abated on the evening of the 8th. In the morning of the 9th of November the barometer on all the ships went up; the northwest storm signal was still up, but the storm had abated and the *Kaministiquia* left Goderich for Fort William at seven o'clock on the morning of the 9th of November. At half past ten o'clock she met the *Wexford* thirty-five miles northwest of Goderich bound for that port, but that boat and her crew were never seen afterwards. At 10:40 … on the evening of the 8th of November, the weather bureau in Toronto, according to the evidence, once in Toronto, had distinct information and evidence that there was a northwest hurricane approaching. They were asked why they had not sent out that notice. They said that the telegraph lines were not working. They were asked why they did not use the telephone. I think, Sir, that on one or two occasions since then I have seen telephone messages sent to the lighthouse after the telegraph service was closed, to bring word of a storm.

We have at Goderich the highest point on the whole of the shore of 200 odd miles; it is 120 feet above the water. To the north and south of the town the shore declines. I have asked that we should have a wireless telegraph station there. Even with the harbour entrance protected as I hope it will be, there should be still this extra call, because of late years the captains have not placed much credence in the weather bureau reports.[11]

So, according to Lewis and others, the existence of a wireless station at Goderich — and presumably at other strategic locations along the lakes — would have allowed the transmission of hurricane warning information to the masters at risk, and they would have been able to seek shelter in time. Further, had the Goderich breakwalls been extended, with a wider opening, a safe refuge, easier to enter during a blow, might have been provided.

During the Goderich Inquest, many ships' officers spoke of the unsafe conditions at Goderich Harbour. Among these was Captain Edward Robinson of the *G.R. Crowe*, son of the lightkeeper, who testified that Goderich was not a harbour of refuge at all, but could be made as safe as any of the ports on Lake Erie. Captain Frank Johnstone of the freighter *S.N. Parent* agreed, suggesting that the harbour as such was useless. Captain W.J. Bassett repeatedly advised the inquest officials that the harbour was being built and improved in a piecemeal fashion. "It was taking the government ten years to do what should have been done in one," a newspaper article declared.[12] The sentiment was echoed and re-echoed that since it was the only port on the east side of Lake Huron, and a significant location for the receipt of cargo from the head of the lakes, it should be a priority for improvements. Lewis also reiterated this plea in his House of Commons address, where he spoke as a member of the government side. His quest for improvements to the navigation aid system and harbours of refuge was supported by members of the Opposition as noted in remarks from John Sinclair, MP from the riding of Guysboro in the Maritimes.

The question of wireless radios was a controversial issue[13] with ships' masters. It is apparent that the masters themselves did not want this equipment. The Dominion Marine Association had filed objections to any government initiative to compel vessels to carry wireless equipment.

The cost was seen to be too great for the benefit received. Radios were seen also as a means of prying on ships' captains by the owners. The skippers on these lakers protected their privacy and would have to suffer the insult of constant contact and intrusive supervision by the vessel owners. In recent decades, the same issues, surrounding the introduction of computerized wireless communication and the installation of GPS and its related tracking devices, have been discussed. There was no longer any privacy. The owners could track every movement — and they expected updates on an ongoing basis.

The value of wireless contact for weather information and other safety issues was not yet seen as important. Skippers took pride in their grand history of survival on these lakes, even in the extreme conditions of the past.

CHAPTER 9

The Goderich Inquest

O captain! my captain! rise up and hear the bells;
Rise up — for you the flag is flung — for you the bugle
trills
For you bouquets and ribbon'd wreaths — for you the
shores a-crowding;
From fearful trip, the victor ship, comes in with
object won:
Exult, O shores, and ring, O bells!
But I, with silent tread,
Walk the spot my captain lies,
Fallen cold and dead.
    — Walt Whitman, from *O Captain! My Captain!*

General observations in this section have been taken from the newspaper records in *The Signal* and *The Star*, editions as published in November and December, 1913, with citations as noted. The original inquest documents are thought to have been lost in a fire that destroyed the Huron County Courthouse located on The Square in Goderich on February 26, 1954. The copies used for research for this book are comprised of some 160 photocopied pages, many of which are largely illegible, with page numbers missing. The source of these copies was the Crown Attorney's Office in Goderich in the 1970s, but the actual location of the original documentation remains unclear. Sharilyn Glazier, of the Huron County Crown Office, searched the local records base in September of 2009, finding only poor quality photocopies that originated in the 1970s. Folklore persists in the assertion that the original records were lost, along with a large number of other significant county records, in the 1954 courthouse fire.

In any event, I have tried to document the evidence taken from the hearings with care, and have made every effort to provide the correct source information. In some cases, it has been necessary to resort to the newspaper reports of the day. Efforts to locate the records from the Blake and Thedford inquests are ongoing, with current searches focused on the Crown Offices at Lambton County.

Dr. Archibald Cross Hunter, Coroner of the Goderich Inquest, November 1913. Hunter ensured that all voices were heard and that the inquiry was conducted in a prompt and efficient manner. However, he seemed to allow great latitude in the breadth and extent of questioning of the witnesses, even when it was apparent to some that scapegoats were being sought. Courtesy of the Huron County Museum and Historic Gaol, A950-1922-001.

Crown Attorney Charles A. Seager was in his 70s at the time of the Goderich Inquest in November 1913. He was relentless in his pursuit of logical explanations of the horrific tragedies encountered in the Great Storm.
Courtesy of the Huron County Museum and Historic Gaol, N000.3090.

Coroner Archibald Cross Hunter presided at each sitting, with evidence taken by former clerk of the peace, then-crown attorney, the elderly Charles A. Seager, in his 70th year. A Mr. J.L. Killoran represented the Canadian Mercantile Marine Association. Captain Edward Orson Whitney, chairman of the Lake Carriers' Association, was also present. In the words of knowledgeable local historian Peter Sturdy, who has written extensively about the Goderich Harbour and reported on matters related to the Great Storm, "In a situation where most of the witnesses were primarily concerned about coming out clean as opposed to coming clean, the perennial Canadian alibi emerged: 'it was not in my jurisdiction.'"[1]

The Evidence

On the first day of the inquest, Coroner Hunter called John D. Kelly, chief engineer of the Water Works and the Electric Light Plant located at the dock, as the first witness. Kelly went to the docks at two o'clock on the day of the storm, after church. He claims it was not blowing very much at that time, but the wind was rising. It was raining very hard and there was not yet snow. He left the power plant between four and five in the afternoon, at which time the rain had changed to snow. He offered the opinion that a vessel would be quite able to secure the harbour. When Kelly returned, at about eight o'clock, he did not recall hearing the fog whistle. He recounted that the wind was blowing very hard, and he returned home. He retired, but was up at 11:00 when the lights went out for a short while. At that time he could hear the fog whistle — and continued to hear it throughout the night.

Now, strangely enough, Mr. Kelly had the responsibility for blowing the whistle. His memory, therefore, seems more than a little vague. It must be noted, though, that his visits that day were only to check how things were going while other staff members were on shift. A man by the name of Harry Stowe carried the early shift that day, followed by Dan McLeod, who was there until four in the afternoon, and finally Mr. W.H. Bullard, on shift from four until midnight on that fateful November 9.

Bullard was not authorized to start the fog whistle himself, but rather when instructed by the lighthouse keeper, posted at the top of the hill. And, of course, there was no telephone connection between the lighthouse and the waterworks to identify when the fog signal should commence. He could, however, shut the signal down when the fog was seen to be clearing. Moreover, the signal was not inspected regularly — only when a request to do so was passed along to the lightkeeper, and thence to Ottawa, where the final authority was vested for supervising how the navigation aids were to be maintained and operated. It also became clear in the questioning that there was no contact between the lighthouse keeper of the day, Captain Robinson, and Kelly. It became evident that Kelly never took the initiative to activate the signal unless the lightkeeper or some other outsider suggested it.

Questioning also revealed that the fog whistle was of little value, in any respect, as it was quite a weak signal. As Kelly stated, "I do not think it would be heard farther than the breakwater. It is not loud."[2] The signal in question was situated on the roof of the waterworks building. Kelly indicated that it had not been used very much in recent years. He suggested that if it had been located at the opening of the piers, as it had been for the last 85 or more years, it may have been more useful. The signal seems to have been moved inshore with the opening of the new waterworks, as a convenience for access to the steam power required for its operation.

Thirty-year-old captain Reginald Bassett, skipper of the steamer *McKee*, was the next witness. He was questioned about the *Wexford*, the vessel expected at the harbour early on November 9. The first series of questions related to Bassett's experience on the *Wexford* as first and second mate over a six-year period. He confirmed that she had two new boilers in her since coming to the lakes, and felt that she had good water ballasts, which were often filled during a storm. He also confirmed that she had never leaked while he was aboard.

Questions were raised about the condition of her wheel. When asked about whether he had ever heard anything about her losing part of her propeller, he stated, "The last time I saw her, she was putting a flange on." (The issue of throwing blades/flanges was one of several safety issues.) That was about mid-October, three weeks before the storm, while she was in Goderich Harbour. Bassett claimed there was nothing wrong with her propeller. He recounted that she had actually made successful round-trip passages with only two, and on one occasion, with only three of the four blades in place.

He was questioned about whether he left the *Wexford* for safety reasons. His response was, "I always considered the *Wexford* one of the safest boats. She was built in the old country, and I always felt safe on the *Wexford*."

Had he heard anything about her movements at this time?

"I was upbound on Sunday night and figured on meeting her around De Tour."

Question: "Supposing she was thirty miles northwest of Goderich at ten o'clock in the morning, when would she arrive here?"

Bassett's response: "Well, we always figured the *Wexford* loaded would run ten miles an hour if the weather was fair, and she should make the ten miles good. She would no doubt make nine or ten miles unless something went wrong. With a fair wind she would make it good at nine or ten miles an hour. She always did when I was with her ..."

The reading of Bassett's answers suggests something about his manner of response that seemed to communicate a degree of anxious uncertainty.

Question: "Well it was not forty miles — I understand thirty?"

Bassett: "Thirty miles — she should be here in three hours. If she was seen at ten o'clock, she should have been here at one o'clock, unless something had gone wrong."

Question: "How severe do you think it [the storm] was?"

Bassett: "I never remembered having heard it blow so much. It was the worst storm I have known for years." He went on to relate that it was "snowing and blowing" — and that it "started from the Southwest and changed around to the Northwest. In Lake Superior, it was from North to Northeast."[3]

Further questions were raised about the *Wexford*. The matter of concern was whether the *Wexford* had been aground. It appears that Bassett commented on her being aground once in the six years he was aboard. He had seen her also in dry dock at Collingwood where it is presumed she was having plates repaired. Dialogue also confirmed that the *Wexford* was aground in the late summer of 1913, in the Soo (St. Marys) River, under command of Captain Playter. The witnesses could not identify whether repairs were required. Some newspaper reports suggest that up to 40 plates needed to be replaced and that part of her cargo was lost, becoming wet from the leakage after she went aground. According to Bassett, she had lost 16,000 bushels. Persistent questioning also determined that the *Wexford* had run into a pier at some time. No location was given, nor was any definitive statement about damage. Bassett clarified, "All boats do that more or less in trying to land."

Questioning then shifted to the safety equipment aboard the *Wexford*. Bassett clarified that he was the master of the steamer *McKee* and could not speak for the *Wexford*. He did indicate that, while he was mate on

Wexford *in dry dock at Collingwood. The ship seemed to undergo a number of hull repairs after various mishaps. It is not clear as to what repairs were being undertaken at this time. On one occasion it is known that her stack was removed, either for repair or replacement. I have often wondered if that problem, whatever it was, had anything to do with the stack being lost at the time of her foundering.* Courtesy of Ron Beaupre.

the *Wexford*, there were 21 life belts (life jackets) aboard the last time he was on. She carried two lifeboats. No mention was ever made of the fact that she carried four lifeboats at separate stations when she first arrived on the Great Lakes, and before her refitting at Collingwood. When asked about inspections — for the life belts — he replied, "They were done when I was on because I done it myself. I carried them out and piled them up for inspection." He also verified that "The Government inspector comes in the spring before allowing you to sail and he inspects them. He counts them and looks at them."[4] At one point during the proceedings, a cork-filled life jacket, in poor condition, was shown as an exhibit. It was plunged into a large tub of water. Observers agreed that it still had plenty of flotation in spite of the holes in its canvas cover and a small iron nail driven into one section of the cork.

Bassett was quizzed about the knowledge of the late captain, Bruce Cameron. He was asked why the previous captain resigned, and why the captain before that left the ship. (He had died.)

Captain Playter, as we have seen from other sources, gave up his post on sick leave. This departure occurred just after the grounding on Lime Island, south of the Soo. One has to ask whether the shipowners challenged his competence at the time. It may have been the culminating event in a series of bad luck incidents for Playter. The results of the research are not clear. The questions about his suitability for continuing in the role of captain must have been around. The questioning at the inquest seems to have had some underlying concerns related to the way the ship had been handled, her misfortunes, and her repair history prior to Captain Bruce Cameron taking command.

In a final, pointed question on that topic, Bassett was asked, "From your knowledge, can you say that any captain left the *Wexford* because he considered her unseaworthy?"

"No," was his definitive and blunt answer, "Because she has only had four captains." She was on the lakes from 1903 to 1913, a 10-year period.

The mystery of the *Wexford*'s disappearance was raised. "Have you any theory as to what would have happened to the *Wexford* coming to Goderich within a short distance from the harbour, without wind or sea, and the bodies were found between twenty to twenty-one miles from here? Do you think she met with an accident?" The younger Bassett refused to speculate.

At another moment in the hearing, his father, Captain W.J. Bassett, conjectured that there might have been some sort of tidal wave that swept down the length of Lake Huron, citing the observation that the clocks and watches of most sailors whose bodies were found had stopped about the same time.[5] The phenomenon of such a great rogue wave has never been observed or reported and is thought to be highly unlikely by experienced masters such as Captain Bud, my good friend, now retired, who would concur with the reports of the "three sisters" — three great, steep, and sometimes very dangerous waves occurring in succession, but never of a great "tidal wave" sweeping down the lake.

It was then posed that the *Wexford* was off the harbour at three o'clock. Would she be able to make harbour?

"Of course, I don't know what the weather was here," declared Bassett, "I would never try to come in here with a north or southwest wind. It would be taking a chance coming in. I probably would have come in and had a look and would have turned around and gone back. At least, that is what I always do, and I suppose he would do the same."

Question: "Where would you go back to?"

Bassett retorted, "Sand Beach [now called Harbor Beach]. That is where we would head if we could not get in here."[6] When the younger Bassett was recalled, he stated that he was off Goderich four or five miles with the *McKee*, but because he could not see land, due to the snowfall, he had turned and headed to Sand Beach and, unable to make that port, took refuge in the St. Clair River at Sarnia.

The next witness was a Mr. A.M. McInnes, an engineer with only two months experience sailing on the *Wexford*.[7] The questions raised concern about the ship going aground, about her safety equipment, and whether there were drills or inspections with respect to safety matters. While the witness did not seem competent to reply to many of these questions, Crown Attorney Seager was relentless in his pursuit of answers. He tried to prove several points:

- That little attention was paid to safety on these steamers.
- That damage to safety equipment, including lifeboats, was not repaired.
- That the engine might have broken down.
- That she might have been helped if she could still carry sail — as in her ocean-going days.
- That sea anchors may have prevented her from foundering.
- That the crew knew very little about "pulling an oar" — should they have tried to make shore in a lifeboat.

In a bizarre set of innuendoes, Dr. Hunter quizzed Engineer McInnes about a scenario in which, if the engine broke down, the engineer would leave the boat, knowing the vessel would soon perish. The line of questioning was based on the fact that the bodies of the engineer and the second engineer of the steamer *McGean* had been found, as had the chief engineer of the *Wexford*. McInnes simply stated that "He would not leave the boat."[8]

Lighthouse keeper Captain William Robinson, a skipper of 40 years experience, was the next to testify. He was asked to produce his weather records for the period, and he did so. He was questioned about the conditions on the 9th and the morning of the 10th.[9]

The weather signals were first put up on Friday the 7th. Captain Robinson explained that he normally kept a record every two hours. He recounted that the storm reached its limit at Goderich through the early morning hours on Monday (the 10th) where he calculated the wind to be "I think between sixty and seventy miles an hour."

He suggested the wind speeds were constant on the 9th until at least 8:00 p.m. "It increased up to ten o'clock and at two o'clock it was sixty miles an hour." Robinson clarified that these records were not from any instrument but from "my own judgement from my experience of the weather."

"So you cannot say positively," challenged the Crown.

"I can guess very close," responded Robinson.

In a relentless sequence of questions, Seager queried Robinson about the details of the weather, and sought to clarify the exact sequence of changes in the wind and sea conditions. It seemed as if he wanted to prove that there were breaks in the weather that would have permitted a seasoned master to enter the port safely.

"Of course, you must remember that a boat ten miles out in the lake is getting more wind than we are," responded the retired captain, in an apparent comment to defend the actions of any master caught off Goderich is such trying and marginal conditions.[10]

The questioning of the lightkeeper then shifted to whether the foghorn was blown that day. The testimony seemed to confirm the evidence given earlier by the superintendent of the water plant, that it did not start until ten or eleven o'clock, but seemed to blow all night thereafter. Robinson also confirmed that "You would not hear this fog horn very far — I don't think you would hear it any further than the end of the pier."

Robinson also spoke of having a very busy night. "It is a bad light and I had to go outside to keep the snow off the glass ... about every fifteen or twenty minutes." He confirmed that once the storm started he had to stay with the light to keep it operating and visible. He defended his action in not going down the hill to instruct that the horn be sounded, saying, "I know Mr. Campbell (the previous lightkeeper) used to go down and I followed up his instructions and used to go down and I kept it up until 1912 and when the inspector [from Ottawa] was here, I asked him to get a phone, as I found I could not run up and down that hill."

"Is it a high hill?" questioned the Crown.

"Yes, about 120 feet, and he [the Ottawa inspector?] says that the Town of Goderich maintains that thing. 'You have nothing to do with it,' said Mr. Peter Harty, the Inspector of Lighthouses."

Regardless, it was Robinson's feeling that blowing the foghorn would have done no good. "If you had all the foghorns on the lake, you could not have done any good," he stated. He concluded in later testimony, as had earlier witnesses, that "a foghorn should be located on the end of the breakwall, where it might be heard."[11]

According to the town clerk, Loftus Lin Knox (the longest-serving clerk in Goderich), the marine and fisheries department in Ottawa had offered to install a new fog whistle if the town would furnish the steam to blow it, as early as 1889. The offer had been taken up, but the new whistle was installed at the waterworks building, far away from the shore. Interestingly, there is no mention of the whistle at the Goderich Elevator Company being blown over an extended period on the Sunday afternoon of the storm, as claimed by Goderich area resident George Parsons, the elderly son of Superintendent G.L. Parsons.

Crown Attorney Seager attempted to question Robinson about possible defects in the *Wexford*; however, the lightkeeper had had no experience on such iron freighters, having been a schooner captain. Seager then pursued questions parallel to those raised with an earlier witness, seeking answers about safety equipment, the condition of lifeboats, and safety drills aboard the *Wexford*. The line of questioning seems to seek confirmation of rumours that suggested the *Wexford* was ill-equipped and did not follow the good seamanship regimen of lifeboat drills and other basic safety practices.

Seager was obviously unhappy with Captain Robinson's comments in these areas. He ended his questioning with a terse "You haven't any experience," and called the next witness.

John W. Taylor, a ship's engineer with the Western Canada Flour Mills, was the next called to the stand. He recounted his 26 years of work on various freighters, and was questioned about the integrity of the construction and possible deficiencies of a number of boats — the *McGean*, the *Carruthers*, and the *Wexford*, in particular. Seager seemed anxious to identify whether they were under-powered, compared with their tonnage and length.

Taylor responded, saying that "those that I have had experience with, I think, have ample power to carry them — that is, the boat will go through the Welland Canal."[12]

Seager: "But have they power which would enable them to control the vessel other than in fair wind conditions?"

Taylor: "I have been out on the lake and handled them in a moderate gale."

Seager went on to query whether very long vessels such as the *Carruthers* would have "power enough?"

Taylor: "I think so." He elaborated that she should have power in proportion to her length, and suggested that he thought she did. In regard to suggestions made that the lost vessels should have had more power, he stated, "It would apt to get beyond control if you drive the engine too hard in a high sea."

Seager briefly continued to pursue the question of whether these boats were suitably powered to cope with extreme heavy weather, and, in the absence of any definitive clarification, switched his line of questioning to whether the inventory of safety equipment and its condition was up to snuff. He tried to intimate that boats were ill-equipped. Taylor conceded that some vessels may have had shortcomings with respect to their lifeboats and the safety equipment stored aboard.

Taylor was speaking about the vessel *Fairmont*, and further suggested that the life belts were not a means of saving a man's life in bad weather. He recounted a situation where he travelled one full season without access to a life jacket in his quarters, saying, "There was not any in my room or in the second engineer's or the oiler's, but we [usually] get them, but I was one season without. I could not say how many."

The questioning then switched to the loads carried by vessels in the fall of the year. Taylor pointed out, "I believe that captains are very careful about loading. I would prefer to be onboard with a full load ... there would be less tendency for the cargo to shift."

Taylor was one witness who did not seem reluctant to offer an opinion. Seager pursued his questioning of the witness in an effort that seemed to try to identify fault with the equipment on the ships that foundered, the judgment and decisions of the captains, and the nature and extent of engine power, once again. He also pursued Taylor's opinions about whether captains ignored the warnings of the weather office and disregarded storm warnings that had been raised at Goderich and other ports. Taylor suggested that storm warnings alone would not keep a captain in port, saying, "the Captain follows his barometer in going out and staying in and found it right." He finally conceded that, in view of the warnings issued for high gales from the north with snow, he would not be justified in taking a vessel out, saying, "No, not in the face of such warnings as that; I think a man should use a certain amount of judgement."

Rather than recognize that the vessels on the lake during the storm had been caught unaware, their barometric readings showing an unusual but temporary rise in the pressure, Seager abandoned this line of questioning and went on to examine the witness with respect to lifeboat drills, trying to confirm that the *Wexford* might have had deficiencies with its life-saving equipment and that the crew were poorly trained in such matters.

Captain Steven of the *Kaministiquia* confirmed the details with respect to his sighting of the *Wexford*: "at about a quarter past ten, Sunday morning ... about fifteen miles above Point Clark. That would be northwest a little.... She was going along all right." He confirmed that they were six or seven miles apart. Steven went on to elaborate that the *Wexford* would be in the thick of the storm by the time she reached her destination, and that "Goderich was no harbour to get in in bad weather.[13] It was only a question of money to make Goderich a harbor of refuge." He considered the breakwall "to be of no use when a northwest wind was blowing."[14]

187

In his testimony, Captain Patrick D. McCarthy of the *Turret Cape* indicated that "There was no harbor on the lake I could enter in a bad snowstorm.... Under the conditions it was safest to make for the [St. Clair] river. Goderich is not a safe harbor to enter during a storm. It was not properly equipped. There were many things which should be done.... The government has spent so much money, it would be folly to go other places to make a good harbor. The breakwall should be completed now and the opening between the piers made wider. The main light on the hill should be made into a red and white flashlight to distinguish it from the town lights."

When asked about the fog signal, McCarthy responded, "It's no good at all."

"When I see the improvements made all over the lakes, there seems to be very little done here for the amount of business which is done here," concluded the captain.[15]

Captain Edward Robinson of the steamer *G.R. Crowe* (son of lighthouse keeper Captain William Robinson) testified that Goderich was not in any sense a harbour of refuge, but that he thought it could be made as good as the ports on Lake Erie. Captain Frank Johnstone of the steamer *S.N. Parent* said that Goderich was not a harbour of refuge at all. In the current condition, he thought the harbour there was useless. When questioned by the crown attorney as to whether one might get into the harbour in a storm, McCarthy's answer was, "Yes, if you were fool enough to try it."[16]

The superintendent of the Goderich Elevator and Transit Company, G.L. Parsons, verified that Goderich was a busy port, standing second in gross receipts and first in domestic traffic of all ports on the Upper Lakes. And Captain Frank Scott[17] of the steamer *Collingwood* suggested that the loss of so many ships was not due to any fault with their design or construction, but rather with the overwhelming seas that most likely crushed their cabins and swept them off, allowing the hulls to fill with water and sink.[18]

Findings and Recommendations

The Goderich inquiry, although conducted to determine the circumstances regarding the death of one Thomas Stone, the Native Canadian whose body washed to shore near Goderich from the ill-fated *John A. McGean*, recounts many details related to the steamer *Wexford* and circumstances related to her disappearance the night of November 9, 1913.

The findings of this inquest were reported in the December 18, 1913, edition of *The Signal*, published in Goderich, Ontario, under the headline "Jury's Verdict Asks for Government Probe." All quotations are from that lengthy third-page news report.

In summary, the inquiry heard from five key witnesses, and a number of others, in five separate sessions. It began November 13, 1913, with additional sessions held the 21st and 24th of November, followed by two more sessions held on December 1st and 13th. The jury was comprised of Messrs. John W. Salkeld (foreman), William T. Jennings, Isaac Salkeld, Harry Salkeld, Robert Andrews, George Andrews, Robert McLlwain, and Chris Johnston. The family ties among the three Salkelds and also the two Andrews serving on the jury are not given. It would be curious if these men were closely related.

The inquest adjourned at 3:30 p.m. on Saturday December 13. The jury took but two and a half hours to bring in its verdict. In his charge to the jury, Coroner Hunter summed up the evidence presented and reminded jurors that they were called to find out how and by what means Thomas Stone, fireman on the *McGean*, came to his death. He affirmed that he felt the crown attorney had put all possible evidence before the jury. It was clear, he suggested, that while Goderich Harbour was seen as a port of refuge, all the mariners examined as witnesses did not consider it such. He expressed the opinion that wireless telegraphy would be a useful tool, and offered regret that Canadian shipowners did not keep better tab on the crew list, citing that only five bodies were identified out of 17 recovered from Canadian vessels. (It is clear that more than five bodies were actually identified from the *Wexford* alone.)

The jury offered recommendations that extended well beyond the matter of the untimely demise of Thomas Stone.

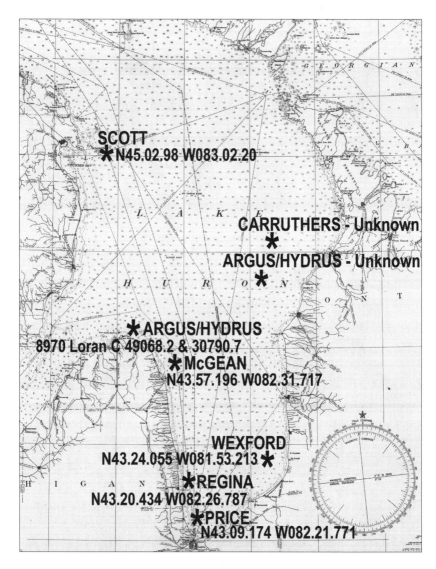

Location of Vessels Totally Lost on
Lake Huron in the Great Storm of 1913.

Conclusions

In addition to the 160-page set of proceedings for the inquest, the findings are summarized in a three-page attachment that outlines key observations and calls for changes to be made to Goderich Harbour. The jury concluded that Thomas Stone did indeed drown in Lake Huron as the result of the foundering of the freighter *John A. McGean* in an unusually strong November storm. The primary intent of the inquest was to confirm his cause of death. However, the findings seemed to focus on the efforts of several vessels that tried to make refuge at Goderich Harbour. The report was not entirely accurate, stating, for example, that "the loss of lives was 191[19] and in property $2,500,000."

The jurors reviewed the departure times and locations for ships bound for Goderich and other Lake Huron ports. Their report summarized the severe weather observations and the storm signal postings from November 7th and the following lull in the storm and the peculiar fact that "early on the morning of the 9th of November, the barometer was rising, indicating clearing weather."[20] The report went on to conclude that, with the false security of thinking that better weather was coming, "Captain Stephen of the steel freighter *Kaministiquia* left Goderich harbour upward bound, on the morning of the 9th of November, meeting the *Wexford* about 10:30 the same morning about 30 miles northwest of Goderich making good weather."

Other vessels also disregarded the storm signals that had been posted and decided to rely on their own barometric observations.

Unfortunately, according to representatives of the Meteorological Department at Toronto who testified that "it was well known to that department at 8:30 p.m. on the 8th of November that a storm of unusual velocity was about to reach Lake Huron almost immediately, but no intimation of this was sent out, reliance being placed on the continued display of the storm signal put up on the 7th and continued up as above stated." Had there been wireless available on these ships, or if notice had been provided by telephone, perhaps these ships would not have departed, the jurors concluded.

The jury went on to suggest, in the strongest terms, with respect to the Goderich Harbour,

> that if completed and equipped as a harbor of refuge, as are all such harbors in the United States ports, some of the said vessels might have found safety in it.
>
> Considering the vast amount of lake traffic along this part of Lake Huron exceeding (as we are informed) that elsewhere on any part of the Great Lakes; and that Goderich is the second largest grain receiving port on the upper lakes; and considering all the circumstances appearing before us, we strongly recommend and believe that the Government should without delay and, at any cost, complete and equip the Goderich harbor as a real harbor of refuge; by fully completing the breakwall now begun; second, by installing up-to-date lights and a fog signal at the entrance of the breakwall, the present fog whistle being utterly inadequate in character, in equipment, being improperly placed and of no value whatsoever; third, by dredging to the necessary depth the outside basin formed by the breakwall so that ships may have some sea room after the stress of entering to manoeuvre and steady themselves before trying to enter the piers.
>
> Without these necessary additions, Goderich harbor will not withstand the expenditure on it already made as a harbor of refuge, will continue to be no real harbor of refuge affording necessary shelter for shipping ... or available as a refuge to shipping in any ordinary heavy weather from which vessels are accustomed to seek shelter.

It was a damning condemnation of the government for acting in a piecemeal fashion about its commitment of some 40 years ago to rebuild this harbour and equip it as a harbour of refuge. In fact, the jury called for a full commission of enquiry to review the entire situation, including "the questions of construction, power, equipment, inspection, loading manning and life-saving appliances on lake freighters." The jurors bemoaned the evidence presented that one freighter had approached the harbour and stood off, not being able to make entry, and left to seek protection elsewhere at an American port.[21]

Given the impossible task of determining how many crew were actually lost, the jury also recommended that immediate steps be taken to require shipowners to keep more complete and accurate crew records. For the *Wexford*, for example, the owners were only able to produce a payroll report from the previous month.

Following the storm and its consequences, a number of changes were made to lights and to navigation aids at Goderich Harbour. Extensive work was undertaken at the Goderich lighthouse. The cupola and lantern were removed, the tower base was raised, and a new cupola and light were installed. According to Jan Hawley, former co-chair of the Goderich Marine Heritage Committee, "Under Government supervision, Mr. B[enjamin] C. Munnings pulled down the residential part of the lighthouse and built the lamp room five feet higher to provide the proper lighting. In 1914, electricity was installed and a new light was erected."[22] The proper lighting including a revolving "flashlight," as it was called at that time. It was housed in a new, more functional cupola.

The adjacent and attached buildings comprising the lightkeeper's residence and work sheds were removed and relocated easterly to the property next door, to be used for many years as summer cottages, known locally as the "Craigie Cottages." They were painted dark green, perhaps to disguise their former use as components of the lighthouse structure. The lighthouse itself has remained largely unchanged to the present day. Brighter lights and an automated timer were added eventually, of course, obviating the need for a full-time lightkeeper. The operation of the lighthouse, no longer critical to navigation because of sophisticated electronic GPS equipment used on all commercial vessels and most pleasure craft, has been transferred to the town of Goderich from the federal government authorities who held responsibility for its operation when it was an important aid to navigation along the Lake Huron shore. In the fall of 2009, a major restoration of the lighthouse, now about to be designated as an official historic site, was undertaken to repair the lime mortar pointing of the limestone and slate blocks, to renew the whitewash coating, and to repaint the faded red cupola, replete with its ornate copper finial atop. The structure had been ignored for years, with some officials fearing that the building should not be touched for fear of excessive levels of poisonous lead in the paint used to coat the limestone blocks and the metal of the rails and lantern structure. It was eventually determined that this fear was unfounded.

Changes were made to the fog-warning system. In 1914, an electrically operated foghorn, allegedly the most powerful in Canada, was installed in a cement tower on the inner end of the north breakwater. In this location it could bring the warning sound of the horn to the closest point possible to warn approaching vessels of the harbour opening. It was tested in an official opening ceremony by Mr. Lewis, the local MP. The warning system was activated from a small shack on the south pier, connected to the actual horn by a submarine cable. In 1952, a decision was made to relocate the foghorn to the end of the south breakwall. New navigation lights were installed at the breakwaters, and the range lights, with the inner range, located on a tower at Snug Harbour, were the subject of ongoing improvements. Regardless of these changes, the opening between the breakwalls was not made any wider, nor were the outer ends of the walls extended in any significant manner to provide full protection to the inner harbour entrance between the two piers that extended into the lake.

In one ill-fated proposal, first raised around 1904, the concept of extending the breakwalls right to the shoreline, enclosing the river mouth and reaching the southern shore below the extension of Britannia Road, was recommended. Such a new harbour, as would have been created along the present beach areas, would have allowed the construction of a series of piers where lakers could come and go with relative ease, in total protection from the elements. Access to the inner harbour would have been retained for traffic requiring dockage at the grain elevators or the flour mill. The proposal was never realized, but was highly touted at the time Goderich was in competition for a military base that was eventually built in the eastern end of the province of Ontario and became known as Camp Petawawa.[23]

This aerial view of Ship Island was probably taken from the top of the nearby grain elevators. Originally used as a postcard, it shows a myriad of activity near the end of the Marlton Shipyard activities, probably in the 1920s. The island had accumulated nearly a 100-year-span of shipbuilding work. Very large sailing ships were built here and launched on side-launch skids. In its final decline, the site was used by "Big" Bill Forrest for the construction of dredges and scows for his marine construction business. Forrest lost possession of the island in the 1930s following a successful ownership suit by the province of Ontario, one that he most certainly would have won today. Later court rulings have confirmed that a province cannot own land within a federal harbour.
Courtesy of the Paul Carroll Collection.

Another small change in the harbour was the creation of a small tunnel near the inner end of the harbour, near Ship Island, to permit the passage of water to and from the harbour and the Maitland River. This installation, along with a "checkwater" at the main inner harbour entrance were supposed to assist with a reduction in the surge of waves experienced in that area during periods of high winds. It is not clear that either had much positive impact on solving the problem. The tunnel also allowed safe passage for small boats, usually rowboats or canoes, to travel to and from the river without having to travel into the lake in challenging

weather conditions. As a youngster, I recall using this tunnel in my harbourfront adventures as my buddy Larry Atfield and I "sailed" our rowboats (borrowed from fisherman Ab Leonard, who lived on the "island"[24]
at Snug Harbour by the current site of the salt mine) to conduct "piracy"
and other important activities at the abandoned shipbuilding site.

There was never a formal enquiry to examine the deficiencies at
Goderich Harbour in any systematic fashion. Its evolution has continued, according to some, in a somewhat piecemeal fashion. It still offers
challenges to mariners who want to enter the harbour in periods of
inclement weather. Large freighters, even those equipped with sophisticated and powerful horizontal bow and stern thrusters, can be seen
today, waiting for waves and weather to settle or in periods of high winds,
when passage through the narrow breakwall opening would be treacherous even with the support of small MacDonald Marine tugboats from
the harbour that help to turn the large and unwieldy vessels.

Work continues today. The Goderich Port Management Corporation,
on behalf of the town, devises improvements in the protective barriers

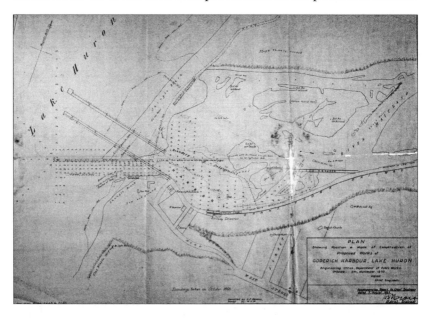

Proposed Improvements to Goderich Harbour, *circa* 1868–70.

at the mouth of the two piers and executes plans for new installations to improve the function of the aging breakwalls.

The controversy over Goderich Harbour as a safe port of entry and as a harbour of refuge actually started as early as 1832, shortly after the river mouth was converted from a natural harbour by dredging it out. Two wooden piers were constructed in that era by the Canada Company to create some protection for an entrance channel. These piers, which pointed in a southwesterly direction and would now cross the southerly portions of the main harbour beach, compounded a silting problem at the mouth of the river. The entrance to the harbour was constantly being blocked by sandbars.[25] Dramatic changes could occur even after one big storm. In 1832 the harbour was blocked by one such storm, shutting down all navigation. There was economic turmoil in the young community as ships could neither enter nor leave the harbour. The Canada Company was so frustrated in its efforts to maintain the harbour, given the need for slow and politically sensitive approvals by the Executive Council for Upper Canada, far removed in York, that it threatened to abandon its harbour development plans if the government could not see its way clear to authorize new works without bureaucratic delays. With much political pressure from local business, the door was opened to a hastily drawn 25-year lease, which authorized the Canada Company to undertake works to open the harbour, maintain a navigable channel, and to construct wharves and appurtenances.

This action led to the formation of a more formal 99-year lease and grant of land by an Act of Parliament in 1837. Yet controversy continued. Ultimately, the Canada Company abandoned its efforts by selling everything, lock, stock, and barrel, to the Buffalo and Lake Huron Railway, which took over the Harbour Lands in agreements signed between 1859 and final Parliament ratification in 1865.

A scathing report was published in *Smith's Canada* around 1852, and referenced in *The Goderich Star*, August 30, 1928, at the time of the centennial of the Huron Tract, under the subheading "Something Rotten in the State of Denmark, Says *Smith's Canada*, or Goderich Would Have Made More Progress." The ensuing article takes the position that Goderich would have become a place of considerable importance if it had "been properly fostered and encouraged by the Canada Company." With respect to the harbour,

> Piers were run out some years since at the mouth of the Maitland in order to make a harbour and some sixteen thousand pounds were expended on the work, but so little care has been taken to keep the piers in repair that they at present seem in a very dilapidated state. The cribs at the ends of the piers are nearly covered with water and appear to be almost destroyed. Indeed judging from the present appearances there must be considerable danger of the vessel attempting to enter the harbor on a dark night running foul of the piers. A lighthouse was built some five or six years ago, but being placed on the top of the cliff, the light shows above and beyond the harbor, so that although the light will guide a mariner at a distance on the lake to the mouth of the river, it gives him no light when there to enable him to see the entrance.
>
> On the whole, as the district town of a large district, the headquarters of the Canada Company, and the only shipping port for many miles of coast, the place has made but slow progress. It is evident that there must be "something rotten in the state of Denmark."[26]

Folks in Goderich tended to be a little bit sensitive about criticism of their beloved harbour. Witness the editorial comments in the columns of a leading page story in the *Huron Signal*, dated November 24, 1853. The comments are in response to a widely reported mishap that included the phrase (also quoted) "… it is a very difficult harbour to make at all times":

> The above, which has been extensively copied by Provincial Journals, has evidently been put into circulation for the purpose of damaging Goderich Harbor in public estimation, and probably with the view of raising

the character of those of other places. We have no objection that our friends at Southampton or the advocates of the ports and places on the Georgian Bay should take every *honorable* and *fair* [italics included in article] means of bringing their respective ports into notice, but we decidedly object to allow the petty jealousies of those parties, by such a contemptible distortion of facts, to stigmatize our harbor with impunity. Indeed the gross culpability of such conduct is too apparent and is deserving of the severest censure, although we are sorry to say that this is not the only instance in which a mere shadow of a pretext has been used to gain credence for slanders so dangerous.

The article goes on at length for three more full paragraphs to decry the vicious rumour-mongering about the faults at Goderich Harbour.

In 1868 a vicious spring freshet washed through the harbour, ripping out upriver breakwaters and carrying much of the then four-acre Ship Island into the harbour basin, also blocking shipping. This time the railway company refused to spend the necessary emergency funds to clean up the mess, and the Dominion Government was required to intervene by declaring the Goderich Harbour to be an official "harbour of refuge," thus enabling the expenditure of federal funds to undertake major reparations. It was in this period that the existing north and south piers were constructed, and the river mouth was diverted northward to its present artificial opening.

Two breakwalls were finally constructed after several failed attempts in the early 1900s, with success accomplished by Bill Forrest and Bill Bermingham[27] using local tugs and dredges. These breakwalls were extended to their present configuration at that time over about a 10-year period. However, dredging problems have persisted. Witness the litany of annual expenditures in the Department of Public Works and Government Services Canada "History Book," kept at the offices of the Ontario headquarters of the Department of Public Works (DPW), Toronto. The record for Goderich covers 1835 through the 1970s. The most commonly repeated expenditure is for dredging.

The team of Bill Forrest (left)and Spike Bermingham undertook many marine projects along the Lake Huron shoreline, including the construction of the breakwalls at Goderich Harbour after several unsuccessful attempts by other contractors. It is said that Forrest provided the "brawn" while Bermingham provided the "brains" for the operations. The portrait on the right is the younger Bill Bermingham during his military career. The photograph first appeared, circa *1908, as part of an annual report for the Bermingham Construction Company at a major anniversary of its founding.*
Courtesy of the Paul Carroll Collection.

Goderich may be the busiest port on the Canadian side of Lake Huron, as it plays host to domestic and international traffic for salt, grains, and other special products, but it remains an ongoing challenge for access by mariners in periods of stormy weather.

CHAPTER 10

Searching for the *Wexford*

There are some of them who have left a name,
So that men declare their praise.
And there are some who have no memorial,
who have perished as though they had not lived;
they have become as though they had not been born
and so have their children after them.
— Ecclesiasticus 44:8–9, used for the Feast of All Saints
(November 1).

The Elusive Shipwreck: Found again! And again!

There are many stories about the discovery of the *Wexford* shipwreck. Most of these tales are in the form of hearsay or folklore, for which any documentation is difficult, if not impossible to pin down. Rumours of her discovery recur throughout the decades following her tragic loss. There are several maps published in local histories that show her resting in numerous underwater graves. Even contemporary accounts tend to confuse the location. A recent book places her at Port Franks, south of Grand Bend, instead of her actual location offshore at St. Joseph, between Bayfield and Grand Bend.

The first known, detailed account of her underwater whereabouts came from the skipper of the *Mariska*, who reported, convincingly, that she lay 15 miles northwest by north of Point Clark, and 16¾ miles northwest of Kincardine. The skipper claims he sighted her masts in a trough in a great summer storm, August 24, 1918, and he knew for certain that these masts were the exact configuration for the *Wexford*, a vessel he claimed to know well.[1] A further sighting in this area was never made.

Key members of the search crew are reviewing the details on the first Klein scanner image taken of the Wexford *shipwreck. Left to right: Bob Carey, survey licence-holder; David L. Trotter, surveyor; Jan Hawley, Marine Heritage Committee organizer; and, Paul Carroll, author.*
Courtesy of the Paul Carroll Collection.

In general, there have been three geographic areas identified for her supposed whereabouts. According to some, she was thought to be located north and west of Goderich — anywhere from three to seven miles offshore, in 75 feet of water. There has also been convincing information about her loss off Black's Point, about five miles south and three miles offshore in 75 to 100 feet of water. Finally, as was reported to be

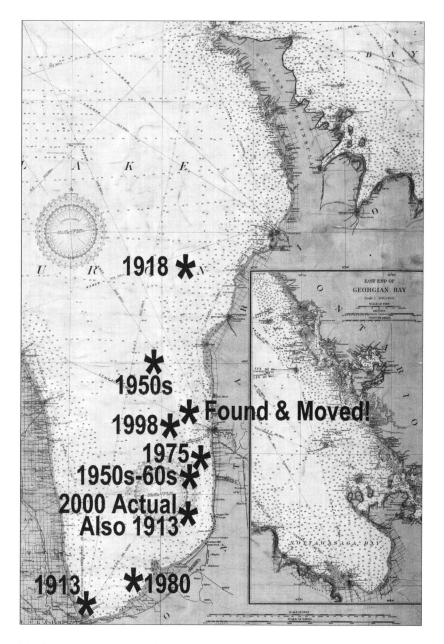

Various Locations Where the *Wexford* Has Been "Found!"

her point of loss in the newspapers of the day in 1913, she was expected to be found in the waters of southern Lake Huron in the Grand Bend/St. Joseph area. There was also speculation that she would be found in other, less touted locations.

The most bizarre story about her whereabouts, from Ontario diver Pat Murphy, shows her sunk originally just north of the Goderich harbour entrance, on a shoal,[2] where supposedly she foundered after hitting the bottom in a trough between the 30-foot waves encountered in the Great Storm. For documentation, the authors of this tale cite life jackets found at Goderich within 10 hours of hearing the distress signals — claiming there is no way they could float against the wind and come ashore at the Goderich location. There were life jackets marked *Wexford* in Goderich — having been removed from corpses transported there to the local Brophey Bros. Mortuary on West Street. Yet, I have not yet seen any documentation for such items found on their own along the shoreline in the immediate Goderich area. As mentioned earlier, only one abandoned life jacket was noted as found in a tree south of Bayfield. Furthermore, Murphy claims that the *Wexford* was towed from its original location by a salvage tug to a spot "out of sight of prying eyes." He also claims that "explosive cutting" had been done on the wreckage "where the most profitable cargo would have been stored," and that, in his estimation, "towing a vessel of the *Wexford's* size would be entirely within the realm of reality."[3]

The most credible discovery and salvage effort was reported in several newspapers in the fall of 1975. The story had also been published in *Inland Seas*, the quarterly journal of the Great Lakes Historical Society, in the summer of 1975. It addresses a claim that the wreck of the *Wexford* had been found by Captain Robert Wilson of Goderich and diver/historian Bill Humphries of Mooretown, near Sarnia. The article identifies the location as "just north of Goderich Harbour" and being the culmination of three years of research by Wilson and Humphries "which included numerous personal contacts, letters and telephone calls."[4]

The article, originally published in *The Goderich Signal-Star* on April 10, 1975, claimed that the finders had "received permission from the federal government under Section X of the Canada Shipping Act" to salvage the wreck, and "hope to make their first dive as soon as the ice clears," which was thought to be in late April. The actually salvage operation was to begin in May. The members of the salvage dive team were named. Artifacts retrieved from the ship were to be placed in the care of the Huron County Museum, the Moore Township Museum, and the Knox Presbyterian Church in Goderich, where an annual Mariners' Service has been held.

Ten years ago, personal contact was made with all known and available survivors of the 1975 salvage expedition as reported in the Sarnia and Goderich papers. Of the six participants named in the news articles, Bill Humphries and Captain Robert Wilson (a Great Lakes pilot from Sarnia, and later Goderich) have died. And to this day, no surviving family members have been identified from whom to seek corroborating information. Jim Macdonald has not yet been found.

Les Begarnie of Sarnia recounts that he walked the beach at Black's Point, south of Goderich, in the late fall of 1975, with Bill Humphries, to confirm land-based orientation points for Bill's later charter airplane flight over the water off the point. Les claims Bill *saw* a dark shadow in the outline of a shipwreck, but he never did dive on any possible site with Bill. He also claims that Bill never did any actual search work south of Black's Point. In a follow-up visit to view photographs owned by Les, and to read a manuscript by the late Bill Humphries, Les then made reference to remembering claims by fishermen that they had found a wreck in the Black's Point area. I have heard the same rumours directly from mariners, including the late Jim Bridle and the late Robert McGraw, both of the town of Goderich, and contemporaries of mine. Bridle asserted the existence of a wreck some "six miles south of the entrance to Goderich Harbour, some three miles offshore."[5] Yet, longtime commercial fisherman Ed Siddall of Goderich told me that, although he had long heard stories about these supposed shipwrecks in the area, he had never experienced contact with any of these in his many decades of fishing on the lake.

Lawrence Brander of Bright's Grove has only vague recollections of his diving with Bill — under the bridge in the St. Clair River, and in the "North," presumably Georgian Bay. He has no recollections about any major find or any work being done near Goderich. Mike Hughes of Corunna, Ontario, planned to go with Bill to see his "find," but it never panned out. He knew about Bill's claim to have found a wreck, but weather always interfered with his efforts to accompany Bill on any such dives. While the newspaper reports were not a hoax, it is apparent that many of Bill's claims were premature. They were incorrect assumptions. There is no evidence to support the claim that the *Wexford* actually had been found and that salvage plans were underway.

Subsequent side-scan work in the Black's Point area, conducted by the Marine Heritage Committee and continued after the summer of 2000, has not yet found any indication of wreckage from a large vessel. The only apparent artifact appears to be a length of heavy chain, stretched out along the bottom for over 150 feet in some 90 feet of water. The survey work continues, from the 50-foot depth shoreward, searching for a smaller wreck or pieces of debris that may give credence to some of Bill Humphries's claims. Contact with the Huron County Museum, the Lambton Museum, and the Mooretown Museum confirm that they have no artifacts from the *Wexford*, nor do they appear to have any archival material from the 1975 episodes — other than copies of the news articles at the Mooretown Museum where Bill was a volunteer supporter.[6]

Commercial fishermen provided other reports that she had been found in the 1914–18 period. It was claimed that she was in relatively shallow water, lying on her side. Locations are not specified.

According to Reverend Edward C. Haslip, in a letter to the author,

> in the spring of 1980 a plane pilot told divers at Point Edward he [had] seen a ship in clear water one and one-half miles offshore in the area where Kettle Point fishermen set their nets. This area was near Gustin Grove[7] and Hillsboro Beach.[8] The pilot explained that he had seen the *Wexford*. At that time the lake had been calm for 8 days, so any ship lying in 40 feet of water that was clear and a sandy bottom as exists in that area should be reasonably sure that a ship is there.[9]

The pilot's report was certainly credible. Mr. Haslip may have recalled the location incorrectly, as the wreck was ultimately found in that general location, but farther offshore and much farther north. In the same letter, Haslip also cites the story, as noted earlier, about a mysterious wreck being located three miles offshore and six miles south of Goderich, a story similar to that told by others in the Goderich area. The *Lake Log Chips* magazine of March 27, 1987, printed this information, "*Diving Times* reports the *Wexford* has been found off Goderich."

In the late 1980s there is a story passed along by veteran shipwreck hunter Bob Carey, about a diver who walked into a scuba shop in London, describing his recent dive on the *Wexford*. Dark ship-shaped shadows have supposedly been sighted many times by aircraft flying over

Mike and Georgann Wachter, Erie Wrecks *authors, are best known as shipwreck hunters from Lake Erie. They operate a company called Corporate Impact in Avon Lake, Ohio, and spent considerable time photographing the* Wexford *wreck in 2000–01.*
Courtesy of Mike Wachter.

the Goderich area waterfront, particularly offshore from the local Sky Harbour Airport. These were alleged to be the outline of the *Wexford* by some. As well, fishermen report "zinging" large objects with contemporary fish finders — but no locations have ever been provided.

According to Jim Stayer, a diver and charter operator from Lexington, Michigan, "Since 1989, several of us had permits to go into Canadian waters and look for it. At one point we were only a half-mile from it."[10] And according to a J. Clary, an American research group claimed that

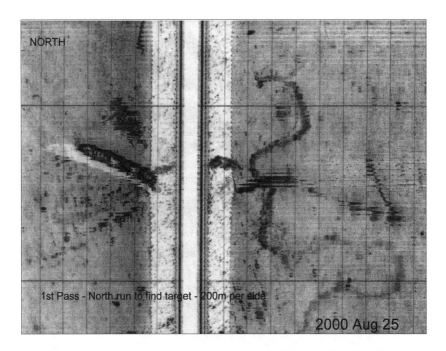

Side-scan outline of the wreck. The image shows the "first pass" outline of the Wexford *wreck as recorded by David L. Trotter, Undersea Research Associates. The white line down the centre of the page represents the space immediately under the hull of the search vessel. The images left and right represent those seen by the sonar scanner on both sides of the hull, respectively, some 75 feet below on the bottom. The white "shadow" along the hull, left side, is a "null" response in the vertical area hidden by the hull sitting upright on the bottom. The curved snake-like line on the right side is actually a false echo, which does not represent anything on the lakebed in that location.*
Photo of original side-scan tracing by Paul Carroll.

they located the *Wexford* during the summer of 1998 off Goderich. They supposedly profiled a wreck and planned to dive on it in 1999 to confirm that it was the *Wexford*.

Wexford finally gave up her hiding place, definitively, in mid-August of the year 2000. As reported in *The London Evening Free Press* of November 12, 1913, she was "Wrecked off St. Joseph, Ont., 23 probably dead." The same edition, it should be noted, also declared that she is "believed to have foundered about 10 to 15 miles southwest of Goderich harbour." And there she lay — quietly resting offshore from St. Joseph, in the original location where she was said to have foundered in early November of 1913.

It was Don Chalmers, an avid sailor and angler, who found her, quite accidentally, with a fish finder, while Great Lakes wreck expert David L. Trotter worked on the tug *Danel Mac* with members of the Goderich Marine Heritage Committee at the site off Black's Point. Quite a coincidence!

Don Chalmers, Bob Carey, and SOS member friend Brent Bamford completed the confirmation dive on August 25, 2000. Trotter was there the next day, along with the author, Jan Hawley from the Maitland Valley Marina, and Jack Riddell, a boater from the Maitland Inlet Marina, to complete the side-scan sonar analysis of the wreck and the site around it.

Finally, after 87 years, many futile searches, and numerous false reports, the elusive shipwreck had been found.

CHAPTER 11

The Wreck Today

Eternal rest grant unto them, O Lord;
and let perpetual light shine upon them.
May they rest in peace.
Amen.
— Roman Catholic Mass, from the Seven Days of Prayer for
the Souls in Purgatory.

First Approaches to the *Wexford*

There was no question about it.[1]

She knew we were coming. She knew that her secrets, tightly guarded for more than four generations, were soon to be disclosed. The solitude and the private dignity preserved in the enigma of her final resting place presently would be cast away.

The first intrusion came just about a week before, on August 15, 2000. An errant angler, Don Chalmers, trolling for salmon, struck her amidships with a downrigger cannonball. He then passed over her several more times. The image on his simple fish finder showed a dramatic aberration in the lake bottom. This was not a problem with his machine. Nor was it geological in nature.

There was an aura that stirred anew within her shattered holds. A tremor seemed to emanate from deep inside her. The sonic beam of a fish finder was a recent experience. She sensed that new electronic presence only for the last dozen years. It was troubling — and seemed to foreshadow the impending end of her privacy.

She knew we were coming. Somehow she had acquired the power to intervene in our slow but steady progress toward her resting place.

It was August 26. We steamed along in the 40-foot tug *Danel Mac*, a converted fishing boat. She would do about nine knots. It was a quiet afternoon, sunny. The lake was smooth with low rollers under a light breeze.

Jan Hawley, the excited co-chair of the recently formed Marine Heritage Committee, was trying out her hand at the wheel. It was a modified hydraulic rig, somewhat archaic, and with a great deal of play in the helm. If one wasn't careful, one could slip in the small puddles of Dexron fluid that accumulated on the wheelhouse floor. A dribble was added with each hard turn. Jan's task was to steer a straight track, following the GPS course line to our coordinates for the *Wexford*. It was a good experience, and success would mean one more pair of hands to take a shift when it was time later to "mow the lawn"[2] following direction from Dave Trotter, the side-scan expert from Undersea Research Associates. It would be boring work — back and forth; back and forth.

After the initial site survey of the *Wexford* wreck, we would work to establish a sonar base line north to Goderich. The Heritage Committee would be asked to finance the subsequent systematic survey — over the next several years — of the entire lakefront area. There were more wrecks than this to be found. In fact, two big ones still remained from the 1913 Great Storm.

We were headed south from our initial search site off Black's Point to conduct the first side-scan fieldwork over the *Wexford* wreck site.

Three divers had confirmed her presence yesterday. A second vessel, a small centre pilot runabout, the *Rumrunner*, a Shamrock design with an inboard engine, was set to assist us. She was to be towed to Grand Bend in the half hour trip from Goderich, and to be used as a base for the scuba dive team, to set markers and perform other underwater tasks to assist in the preliminary sonar grid survey being taken from the equipment onboard the *Danel Mac*.

David Trotter was an old hand at wreck-finding. Word has it that he has discovered more shipwrecks on the Great Lakes than any other aficionado. And although he had not actually discovered this one, he would be in on the ground floor with the rest of us who had pursued the mystery of the missing *Wexford* for so many years.

We carried Dave's "fish," a two-metre stainless-steel torpedo, full of electronic guts and suspended on twin cables some 10 metres below our

Shipwreck hunter David Trotter (right), assisted by Robin Wilson (left), and Paul Schaus (centre), getting ready to launch the electronic fish that "sees" sonar images and reports them to the Klein receiver/ printer onboard.
Photo by Paul Carroll.

hull, feeding sonar reflections to electromagnetic sensitive paper on endless rolls in the cabin/work area of the tug. Two cables held her in place: one stainless harness to ensure we didn't lose the brute; the other a vinyl-sheathed umbilical nerve cord that sent data to the processor above for translation into images on heat-sensitive paper. They showed, in stark silhouette, any significant objects lying on the bottom. We were reading echoes some 75 feet below us.

She intervened.

Within one nautical mile of the site, we suddenly lost all reference points on our GPS. There was no reason. The screen just went blank. Jan, still at the wheel, panicked just a little. "How can I find the way?" We had to reboot the machine twice, but finally found our position again. We resumed our heading, reducing speed as we approached the underwater target. It is not normal that we should have had to reboot the GPS twice in quick succession. Just a coincidence, of course!

The only sound was the quiet and steady throb of the diesel. No one spoke. All eyes were fixed on the sounding equipment, watching the slowly unrolling image of the lake floor below us. At the wheel, Jan spun the hydraulic wheel just enough to find the target.

Beep ... beep ... beep ... Just a mere 0.1 nautical miles to the target. Suddenly, a sharp electrical snap — the crackle of a short circuit! The wires leading from Dave's high amperage bank of 6-volt batteries had somehow fouled. In a single puff of acrid smoke, the scanner stalled. The images ceased.

"Holy s--t!" I proclaimed. My usual expletive did not resolve the problem.

But Dave's quick hand — or foot — flipped the smoking cables in time to avoid the two heavy, copper, multi-strand wires welding themselves together. He saved the costly sonar unit from instant self-destruction. And the images, albeit reluctantly, returned to the ever so slowly turning rolls of scanner film.

There was no sign of Keith Homan's runabout, the *Rumrunner*. He should have been on site long before we reached the scene. Keith and his companion divers, Bob Carey, Brent Bamford, and Paul Schaus, should have completed their first dive and be resting aboard, awaiting their first surface interval before helping us to place the markers for the side-scan grid work.

She did not want to be ravaged. She would not accept this intrusion quietly.

Keith had his own problems. The *Rumrunner* had been docked at the Homan Inlet Marina. The trailer had not been used since spring. Keith backed his SUV into the long summer grass to connect the trailer ball to his hitch. He disturbed a nest of bees. In the flailing and yelling that followed he was only stung two or three times.

Why Keith? His allergic reaction was far from being fatal, but each time it was getting worse. It sure put a damper on the start to an exciting day. After the proper treatment, there was still considerable discomfort, but the divers, following this first delay, eventually set out on their way.

Another strange coincidence.

Tires? The trailer tires were new — well, almost new. The damned thing hadn't been used that much before. Somewhere past Bayfield, almost directly inshore from the wreck site, one tire belched and burst. The trailer careened dangerously, the rubber collapsed. Of course, there was no spare — another hour.

She would not suffer this intrusion.

As Brent Bamford descended, finally, into the blue-green water, he peered below. From the darkening depths of turquoise green, the *Wexford* revealed herself beneath him. It was eerie. The visibility was high. She almost glowed; especially from inside her open holds. In fact, he said, "She seemed to shimmer, moving ever so slightly. She had a ghostly white lustre issuing from inside her holds."

It was as though, finally, she was forced to forfeit her soul. Dr. Paul Padfield, a local optometrist with a passion for scuba diving, who dove on her later, was struck by the deep spiritual reverence he felt as he explored her. Except in those early survey dives, no one else has offered any sensations of her gentle throes.

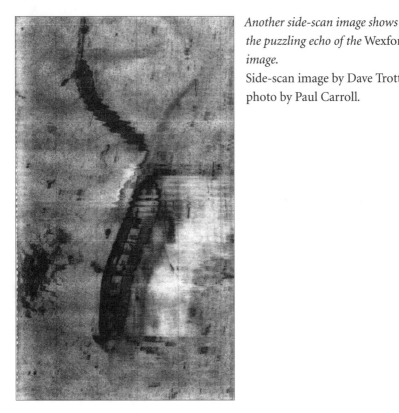

Another side-scan image shows the puzzling echo of the Wexford *image.*
Side-scan image by Dave Trotter; photo by Paul Carroll.

The scanner pen went wild. You could hear the static click as the first stark black images appeared on the scanner above. There was no longer any doubt. This was a centre pilothouse vessel, seeming to match almost exactly the reputed dimensions of the long-missing ship. We stood in silent amazement as we watched her profile emerge. She lay almost east and west; sitting upright on the sandy bottom. There was little evidence of a debris field.

The *Wexford* had truly — and at long last — been found.

As She Sits Today

During the summer of 2001 a comprehensive archaeological survey was conducted on the *Wexford* wreck. Under the supervision of Peter Englebert, *the* Ontario government marine archaeologist,[3] a team of area divers with special marine heritage training worked to record the current state of this vessel and to quantify her artifacts. Numerous dives were made in the summer months. A summary report was prepared by the survey licence-holder, Bob Carey.

He wrote a general overview of the condition of the wreck, as found in his report of March 22, 2001, submitted to the Ontario Ministry of Culture:

> The *Wexford* lies at the bottom of Lake Huron approximately 14 [kilometres] West of St. Joseph. Exact coordinates are (Latitude) 43° 24.06' (Longitude) 81° 53.30' The depth to the bottom is 24 [metres]. The *Wexford* pilothouse decking is approximately 18 [metres] ... below the surface. The lake bottom is flat, blue clay silt. The underwater visibility and current vary. Visibility has been from 1.5 [metres] to 18 [metres]. The current

As She Sits Today, *a painting of the* Wexford *wreck as she lies on the bottom of Lake Huron. Her easy sport-dive depth attracts thousands of curious divers each summer, but alas, it also exposes her to malicious damage and the theft of her precious artifacts.*
Courtesy of Robert McGreevy, artist.

has varied from nil to noticeable, estimated at 2 knots....
Immediately upon the discovery the *Wexford*'s location
became quite well known. Our priority was to document
the "as found" state of the *Wexford* before recreational
divers disturbed the site. We felt the best way to do this
in the limited time available was through underwater
photography and video recording. Approximately seven
hours of video and 36 still photographs were collected.

The *Wexford* is sitting upright generally encrusted
with approximately seven to ten [centimetres] of zebra
mussel growth. Most wooden structures, such as the
pilothouse and spars, are gone at deck level. The hull
appears intact; the rudder is missing and has not been
located. The bow is pointing toward the shore — east.
It appears that the hull has settled approximately two
to three [metres] into the silt. The hold has over 1.5
[metres] of silt. The propeller is mainly buried in silt,
but appears intact.[4] The starboard lifeboat davit and
block are intact. The chadburn throttle is in the forward
$\frac{1}{8}$ position. Boilers are intact and the coal fire doors are
closed. The bow anchors are stowed. The bow deck-
ing supporting the bow anchor windlass has collapsed
somewhat. It appears that the bow decking is held from
further collapse by the bow anchor chains to the bow
windlass. Most rail stanchions are intact. Most portholes are intact and the glass in place.

As noted, her masts or spars were gone. If they survived her foundering, some historians feel that they would have been stripped away in
periods where the thickness of the winter ice cover reached down from
the surface, encapsulating them and tearing them away from the deck as
the ice fields shifted. According to one authority, there are records of ice
scours on the bottom of the lakes as far down as 75 feet.[5]

One of the divers, Dan Thomas,[6] offered his own observations following the diving activity. These observations were recorded in dive

notes sent to me October 8, 2001: "Swimming along the port side I could see how much damage was done as there was no wheelhouse, masts or stacks. Notice was also taken of portholes in the hull … how some were open, some were closed; others had cracked glass or were missing altogether. Zebra mussels encrusted the frames, which made it difficult to see if they were still there."

The challenge for the surveyors would be to assess which damage occurred during the storm and at the time of her foundering. How much of the current deterioration was the result of nearly 90 years of sitting on the bottom of Lake Huron in relatively shallow water. It was clear that local commercial anglers must have known this wreck.[7] She would have been an underwater hazard to avoid.

Said Thomas, "Fishing nets in abundance hang all over her, some modern — some older — perhaps from the 1950s or 60s. There are old fisherman around still, I'm sure, who must have wondered if there was something out of the ordinary on the lake bottom." Dan is the first diver to suggest that her current state shows major destruction. His comments suggest that the ship was badly weakened in her fight with the elements. He states, "Something else that struck me was how steel deck plating could be torn like paper. Some sections of the main deck, from the bow to the stern, are in varying degrees of collapse with some sections having fallen in. These include the aft hatch, hatch coaming, and surrounding deck, having fallen forward. Also, the foredeck and windlass is held in place by only the two attached anchor chains with anchors pulled tightly into their hawse pipes." And again, according to Thomas, "Railings, or lack of them, on some areas made me wonder how a section could be mangled or missing, but elsewhere left nearly untouched. The stern railing is bent slightly inward on the starboard quarter but does stand vertical."

I have read accounts of ice damage during early winter storms on Lake Huron, where the ice buildup during a voyage was such to rip the rails from their stanchions and to carry fixed pieces of equipment overboard. Thomas observed that "the steering gear on the aft deck seemed to be turned hard to one side. However, silt, mussels, and lack of specific attention on my part make me think that a couple of dives could be done to sketch and

The underwater remains of the Wexford *are encrusted with layers of zebra mussels. Shown here: (top left) the steering mechanism, the remains of the stern-deck mechanism, turned hard over; (top right) the deckhouse; (bottom left) below decks, the tween deck space; (bottom right) the engine top.*
Photos by Mike Wachter.

dimension this area if such a sketch does not exist already." One has to wonder whether, in desperation, Captain Bruce Cameron, having lost all or part of his pilothouse, including the main steering station, was forced to make the treacherous passage across the decks[8] to try to take charge of his ship at the stern-steering station at some point during the storm. Such effort would have been in vain. His loss of steerage would be attributed to the fact that the rudder had been torn from its shoe and its post.

The divers observed an unusual brass plate bolted to the deck. According to Thomas, "It appears to be cast with what looks to be a compass rose and clock face in a fair amount of detail. I'm very interested to know what it is and what it represents."[9]

Everyone offers a theory as to how she went down. Dan Thomas is no different. "The orientation of the vessel to shore (bow/east), along with the fact that the rudder is gone, may suggest she was caught in a trough of the northerly wind driven storm after managing to turn to the east."

The side-scan work completed by David Trotter did not seem to reveal a significant debris field. He did recommend that divers survey the areas adjacent to the wreck, particularly to its north side. This work still remains to be done. An indication of the kind of problem that can occur when work unfolds in other than the most desirable order follows. In the words of Dan Thomas, "After the mooring block was set (dropped) in place, about 30 feet from the bow of the *Wexford* on its port side, Bob and I dropped down the chain to attach a dummy line from the block to the wreck. When the block came into view, it appeared the block had landed on top of a part of the wreckage. This piece is relatively small. Some of the debris field may be closer than we think." Even if the formal survey work has been finally completed, it is apparent that more work remains to be done. I am not aware of any systematic records being devised to inventory a debris field, following an orderly survey of the areas around the wreck.

One of the early divers on the wreck was Paul Schaus, a dive instructor and graduate of the Nautical Archaeology Society (NAS) 1 Program in marine archaeology. His observations provide some additional information about the wreck. He weaves his own conclusions into the mix.[10] On his first dive, Paul witnessed the same eerie glow inside the hull that was also reported by Brent Bamford, who along with Don Chalmers, Bob Carey, and Keith Homan made the discovery confirmation dive on August 26, the day after the wreck had been found. "There was a white film within the hull," he wrote. "It looked like a milky cloud, just floating there."[11] Paul also confirmed the existence of something hanging over the hull, with fish nets tangled on it. Will it ever be confirmed to be a section of the now missing masts? He continues:

> I started at the bow; both anchors were present. I was surprised that they were not dropped to ride out the storm. There is a lot of machinery and winches still present. The midship railing is missing but the posts are still there. No railing was seen either side amidships. At the bow, I looked through a hatchway and could see a ladder going two

decks below. In the bow, the first deck damage is inward as well. The stern section has also taken a beating. There is much disarray. At the stern, the port side railing was missing. The stern deck and cabin area were collapsed. There was evidence of some kind of trauma. Stuff was sitting on various angles. On the deck the steering quadrant was still in place, the lower section seemed to be like a pie wedge, with handles still intact. Others were missing.

Near amidships I saw machinery that appeared to have been tossed around — big gears — were they winches or windlasses of some sort? I did see a piece of iron rail or beam. Was it structure or cargo? Needs to be measured — about 6–7 inches height — profile like a rail but needs to be checked.

Most of the funnel was missing — jagged break all around — not as wide in diameter as expected for a vessel this size. I saw one davit on the starboard side — one cabin [amidships] seems intact — looked in doorway — much silt, did not enter — wooden door, knocked over into hull…. Fishing nets were present, but not as much as I've seen on some of the wrecks off Long Point.

Both boilers were completely intact with doors shut. I was told that this means the boilers were cold at the time of the sinking. If the Captain lost power, why didn't he drop anchor to keep the bow facing the waves?[12] Although I do feel he may have lost power, I think that the waves he was facing were so high that dropping anchor would have been of no use.[13]

There was considerable evidence of the amenities required for life aboard ship:

In one cabin, midships, there were two toilets side by side, but no privacy divider wall to separate them. On the starboard side, also at midship, I saw a dresser with top drawer missing and a wardrobe with door open. There was coal piled up to the missing drawer. I suspect the ship leaned enough for the coal to be piled there since boilers are on the next deck down. This must mean at some point the ship had leaned very far to the starboard side.

There were many broken and intact dishes on port side near stern. All were white. There were a few glass porthole plates, also near some dishes. On my third dive, I came across a green wine bottle. The bottle was embossed with the name Pernod Fils. Although it was still corked, there were seeds in the bottom of the bottle. In one spot, I saw a white iron bench. The end was quite ornate. It looked like it had been painted? Near the stern, I saw a broken plate edge sticking out of the silt. It showed a 2-inch sliver of white with bluish porcelain — no other markings. Approaching amidships from the stern a porcelain fixture — toilet or sink — towered above the current deck, held up by its drainpipe.[14]

Paul was part of an early dive team of three who, before the rules got clarified, removed three artifacts from the *Wexford* — according to him and others, for safekeeping. This incident, described elsewhere, led to a full-blown police investigation. No charges were laid; the artifacts have since become the property of the Huron County Museum and Historic Gaol, Goderich, where they form part of a Great Storm exhibit that has toured museums across Ontario. The outcome seems to have done little to protect other precious artifacts, which some visitors have decided are better suited elsewhere, in private hands, away from the wreck.

Dr. Paul Padfield, a Goderich optometrist, completed the first survey sketch of the *Wexford* wreck. A variation of his drawing was devised by Peter Englebert to assist a team of volunteers in the recording of survey observations. The surface survey of the deck was finished in the summer of 2001, the report for which was filed as an official survey report with the Ontario Ministry of Culture.

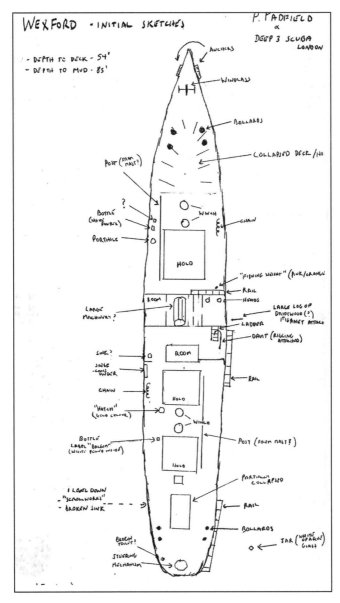

Sketch plan by Paul Padfield. This is the first drawing created to illustrate the location of key components of the wreck requiring further investigation. Such drawings are actually made underwater, with pencils that scribe on plastic tablets or create drawing on waterproof paper.
Courtesy of Paul Padfield.

The critical issues relate to separating what happened during the storm and the ship's foundering from the effects of long-term decay as the vessel sat on the bottom. There will continue to be many differing opinions. All we can do is research the options with care and reach our own conclusions.

Perhaps the most radical opinions have been offered by Patrick Murphy, who suggested in discussion board exchanges on several occasions during the survey that the *Wexford* had been extensively salvaged at an earlier date — and moved to its current resting place. In a document dated October 5, 2000, he wrote,

> The most surprising thing to find was the complete lack of any cargo or debris. The engine, without [its] cover, the many open hatches — actually, completely removed hatches. Even the hatch covers couldn't be found. They would have survived in some form. This is clear evidence that the ship has been extensively salvaged many years ago.... The current was surprisingly strong. I figured it to be about 1.5 knots. A most surprising thing was there was no high and low side of sand. The ship almost appears to have been dragged to this spot from some other location.... I think it was dragged to [its] current spot and looted.

He goes on: "The very lightly built uprights have not been bent. In a storm that would have removed the cladding these would have bent," suggesting a salvage effort. Murphy continued to express the opinion that the *Wexford* had been moved and extensively salvaged in comments written in notes to various people, including two to Don Chalmers sent on May 31, 2001.

The presence of the current is not surprising. It is consistent with the lakeshore characteristics in southern Lake Huron. It adds credence to the theory that the hull drifted awash, to its current resting place from a point further north, and settled gently in the St. Joseph area. Such events would also explain the absence of any significant debris field around the wreck.

On November 12, 2000, divers Peter Askew and Ray Hunt completed a detailed inventory of the 30 portholes along and around the complete hull, below deck level, ascertaining their condition and noting that several were found to be open and at least one was completely missing. (It must have been a chilly dive; the water was noted to be only 44 degrees Fahrenheit.)

The official survey report contains detailed notes and measurement drawings completed by divers Ray Hunt and Walter Cunha on June 12, 2001. These notes and drawings, along with others prepared by Don Chalmers, Paul Padfield, and Paul's son, John, on the same date and on June 13, provide absolute corroboration with original plans acquired from

A porcelain-covered bowl recovered from the Wexford.
Courtesy of Huron County Museum and Historic Gaol, a Virtual Museum image 0841.

the Maritime Museum in Kingston that this ship is indeed the *Wexford*. In a sketch dated June 13, 2001, by Don Chalmers and Peter Englebert, the extent of collapse of the main spar deck and the tween deck, behind the forward windlass, to and along the starboard side of the forward cargo hold, is shown. A pencilled note adjacent to the sketch, "What a mess — both decks have collapsed," attests to the extent of the damage.

There were numerous small artifacts found throughout the wreck when it was first visited in the fall of 2000. These included numerous items of pottery — a crock, cups, dishes, a small nappy bowl, and many broken shards. There were beer bottles and a wine bottle, as noted earlier, marked Pernod Fils — still corked and containing a dark-coloured fluid, probably the original contents. There were pieces of silverware, spoons, a sink, toilet bowl pieces, doorknobs, door hinges, filigree ironwork for lamps, and perhaps a bench, a Victrola, porthole glass replacements, a rubber boot, canvas pieces in the stern hold, and numerous other pieces of broken machinery. Most observers suggest that the presence of so many objects would indicate that the wreck has been largely untouched over the years.

Undoubtedly, there are hundreds of additional items buried in the more than two-metre "quicksand" of silt resting inside the hull. It is not yet clear whether this silt is mud or the decayed "compost" of the cargo of grain — some of which was said to have coloured the beaches along the Turnbull farm white in the days following the storm. To clarify whether the wreck actually carried any steel rails at the time of her loss, the silt within the hull should be probed in several places. (We need to remember that the manager captain, W.J. Bassett of the Western Steamship Company, said that she did *not* carry any package freight or deck cargo while she was in that company's ownership.)

The debris field has not yet been surveyed. Visibility often presents a problem at the site. It varies from excellent to very poor. In late November 2001, Bob Carey reported that artifacts were disappearing. Each dive seemed to reveal more items missing. In addition, natural factors appear to be creating a degree of deterioration of the wreck. How much is quite uncertain. There is still a gentle, almost imperceptible movement of parts of the wreck perceived by some, perhaps attesting to her frail condition, activated by the sometimes strong underwater currents that wash by.

It is a popular site, with many divers visiting the wreck each year. In spite of its location — almost 10 miles offshore — by the summer of 2003, dive charters were visiting the *Wexford* shipwreck on a daily basis throughout the diving season. Visitors from Grand Bend, as well as Lexington and Port Sanilac, Michigan, seemed to be most common. A few vessels ventured south from Goderich and Bayfield, and a few more made the voyage north from the Sarnia–Port Huron area. It has been suggested that over five thousand divers visited the site in the year 2003.

The site is still the most intact wreck available in this area and is a perfect sport-level dive. The decks are at about a 50-foot depth, while the sandy bottom is just 75 feet down. Diving around the hull and across the decks is safe; however, only experienced divers, with a definite escape plan, should enter the hull.

CHAPTER 12

The Plunder of the *Wexford* Wreck

Within the rising vapor, wretched
souls of the drowned seamen embrace
my spirit as we ascend from the cold
depths of eternal strife.
> — Casey Wise, from his poem "Vapor Rising"

It did not take long for the artifacts to start disappearing. Several errors were made at the time of the discovery. While the wild enthusiasm about publicizing the find can be understood, it was surely a mistake that the first physical contact with the wreck was called in to the media, apparently by cellphone, before the dive gear was dry. In just a few hours, the discovery and location of this long sought-after wreck, was widely known across the Great Lakes' region. Interest was intense. So many wreck hunters had tried, over so many years, to find this Great Storm relic. The location, if not the fact of its discovery, would better have remained confidential for a period of time. A systematic plan had not been devised to complete a detailed survey of the wreck in short order. Such was necessary, at least to record the existence and location of the many artifacts reported by those early divers who visited the site.

This is not to suggest that the wreck would not have been pillaged regardless of such a survey, but at least there would have been an accurate inventory of what it contained. Although the pure historian might want to see everything left intact and in the exact place it was found, the experience of the losses of the *Wexford* artifacts should have taught us otherwise. It remains a policy of the government of Ontario[1] that a shipwreck must remain untouched. No artifacts should be removed. Such also is the position of the highly respected organization, Save Ontario Shipwrecks. It is a noble aim, but has proved to be rather senseless for those items that could be safely removed and relocated to an appropriate repository in a marine museum display, where they can be protected indefinitely. Perhaps the many items that have disappeared could have been saved for future generations to enjoy. Do we not routinely remove artifacts from land-based archaeological survey sites for cleaning, restoration, and reconfiguration as may be possible, for study and further research, for preservation and public display?

Consider the following panic calls and comments, which began just a few weeks after the untimely announcement of the discovery. As Bob Carey quietly stated after two years, in a December 20, 2003, note to me, "Maybe Joe Durand has much more foresight than I originally thought." Durand discovered the fully intact wreck of a large dredge somewhere off Bayfield, alleged to be in 90 feet of water, with its spuds and bucket still in place. The wreck had foundered in the mid-1930s during a fierce storm. Joe has protected the location to this day. Although much effort has gone into trying to locate the underwater treasure, its hiding place has been maintained. There is little doubt that it has remained intact. Any artifacts of interest, or having some historic value, will still be in place. It is hoped that he will disclose the location eventually to some qualified and authentic survey team to conduct the needed underwater survey and create a permanent record of this wreck and its history. The wreckage of the *Wexford* should have been thus protected until its documentation and scientific study could be completed. Further, its moveable artifacts should have been catalogued and removed for placement and display in the Huron County Museum. In the words of Brent Bamford, a heritage supporter and one of the first divers on the *Wexford* wreck, "It offends us that others are doing such damage and showing such little respect — not only for the wreck — but for the families of those sailors whose descendants are only one generation removed. "Grandpa's watch" would be much more likely to be enjoyed for years to come, by countless numbers of citizens and family, in a museum, rather than in some diver's contraband collection to be enjoyed by one or two — and then thrown out with the garbage when that diver passes on. It is a real shame!"

The following partial record of the concerns and comments relayed to me after the first disappearances of artifacts speak for themselves. The reader can be the judge as to who and what is right or wrong.

November 1, 2000, in a note from Bob Carey: "The bottles and china items on the deck in Paul Padfield's sketches were not there on Sunday Oct. 22 either."

November 9, 2000, from Bob Carey:

Just to keep you posted, sometimes it is better not to know, but I felt I should share this with you. The Stayers run a charter out of Lexington. Takes them less than an hour to reach the *Wexford*! He has over five hours of digital video now. He is totally appalled at the amount of items going missing. Each time he dives the *Wexford* he finds some more things are gone or moved. He feels someone is stockpiling artifacts in an area by the stern.

I honestly don't have any idea who is doing this. Any divers with Ian [MacAdam][2] always report. Plus I know most of the divers he takes out and can't believe they are involved in anything like this. Stayer says when they are there, the *Hurd*[3] usually circles them, maybe the *Hurd* has records of someone there other than Ian and the Stayers. The Stayers have a reputation of being purists and would leave anybody in the water they catch even touching an artifact. The Stayers have placed a mooring line on her, so the location is now old news.

Who is plundering her?

April 17, 2001, in a note from Dave Trotter, owner of Undersea Research Associates: "Twenty years of wreck discovery and diving has taught me one thing. Control the knowledge of what is going on until you are ready to release it. Once that genie is out of the lamp, it can never be put back in."

September 7, 2001, a comment posted on a message board maintained by Great Lakes Shipwreck Research Group by Bob Carey: "Dove on Saturday morning about 4 weeks ago, 2 mugs on a bench plank, as we left a dive boat arrived. Dove the next day 1 mug gone. Pitcher surveyed last year by prop gone."

April 19, 2001, in a discussion and note from a diver who's asked to remain anonymous:

> According to a staff member of the St. Clair Shores Library, and a member of the Association of Great Lakes History, and volunteer at Dawson Museum, Belle Isle Detroit — a middle man attempted to sell "brass keys" on behalf of a diver — keys said to be from the *Wexford*. These items had been incorrectly cleaned, polished, and lacquered. This event occurred at an antique shop between the lakeshore area, Lexington, and the Thumb at the head of Saginaw Bay. The staff member was said to be angry and frustrated at the theft.

The incident was to be reported to the Michigan Department of Natural Resources.

A Canadian pleasure boater from London recently told me about a visit he and his wife paid to Lexington, Michigan, a few years ago. There was a small museum on the main street, with many exhibits from Lake Huron shipwrecks. There were many artifacts on display. A number of these were purported to be from the *Wexford*, illegally removed from the Canadian wreck site, of course.

July 6, 2003, in a note from Don Chalmers: "Terry Kovacevic, the local Grand Bend dive charterer ... reports finding baskets and pails of objects from the wreck laying on the deck of the ship ready for salvage, on two different occasions."

In that same July, the wording of a plaque proposed to be placed by the Grand Bend Friends of the *Wexford* group was presented:

SS WEXFORD 1883–1913: 250' x 40' x 24' STEEL PACKAGE FREIGHTER A CASUALTY OF THE "GREAT STORM" NOVEMBER 9, 1913. UNDERWATER SURVEY BEING CONDUCTED UNDER LICENCE ISSUED BY THE PROVINCE OF ONTARIO No ITEM SHALL BE REMOVED OR RECOVERED FROM A SHIPWRECK IN ONTARIO. PERSONS DISTURBING ARTI-FACTS ARE SUBJECT TO POLICE INVESTIGATION AND PROSECUTION. DO NOT DISTURB. ARTIFACTS ARE UNDER SURVEY. THE LOCATION AND POSITION OF ARTIFACTS IS PARAMOUNT TO THE SUCCESSFUL SURVEY AND INTERPRETATION OF THE ARCHEOLOGICAL SITE. SURVEILLANCE OF THIS SITE BY "GRAND BEND FRIENDS OF THE WEXFORD".

July 6, 2003, a decision by a meeting of Huron Shores SOS as communicated in an email message to interested persons: "At last week's meeting of the SOS group it was moved, seconded, and 'Carried': 'That Claus Breede, then-curator of the Huron County Museum, be asked to take the lead with the Lambton and the Bruce County Museums, SOS, and the Friends of *Wexford*, to acquire permission from the Ministry of Culture to retrieve fragile and other artifacts "at risk" from the shipwreck *Wexford*, for appropriate and protected Museum storage.'"[4]

August 25, 2003, in a suggestion made by Paul Padfield to Dave Schelken, chair of the Huron Shores SOS and posted on a public notice board:

The issue of the artifacts on the ship keeps "resurfacing." We all know that every time we dive the wreck things have been moved and likely many things have possibly been removed. Although I know this is contrary to a lot of thinking, and currently against the law, I think we need to give serious consideration to some better way to preserve these things. Either we gather them up and put in a museum (or some other local display that the public AND divers could see — perhaps somewhere in Grand Bend?) or we somehow put them in a secure display cage or case directly on the ship. The cage method on the *Sweepstakes* at Tobermory might be an option, for example, somewhere on the ship one could erect some bars and place the artifacts within the cage.

In any event, something has to be done or everything will eventually be lost.

December 9, 2003, in a bulk, message board note from Tim Legate, an Ontario diver:

In a perfect world, society would care deeply about its heritage and would actively seek knowledge and preserve all cultural remains. Unfortunately, ours is somewhat short of perfect, leading to the fact that choices need to be made based on priorities that are different from one person to the next.

I would argue that SOS's aims of promoting a knowledge and understanding of our marine heritage, along with preserving the cultural remains devolves from just such a choice. I would further submit that the "knowledge" is probably the generally higher priority. Thus archaeologists justify the dismantling and destruction of sites in order to do the research on them — tempered with the ethical standard of leaving a greater or lesser portion of a site undisturbed against the possibility of better techniques in the future.

It would seem to me that here in Ontario, our society (as embodied by our elected officials and their departments) has placed value on preservation and ownership, rather than knowledge. As evidence, I point to the total lack of funding available for archaeological field research — what has been done to study the *Atlantic*[5] since the court case has been settled? Great find — fabulous potential — no action — it's getting trashed — too bad, so sad. What of the *Hamilton/Scourge*,[6] etc.?

A final word, subject to confirmation by a current dive on the wreck, came from Bob Carey, in an August 25, 2009, note sent to the author as the final manuscript was being completed. His words reflected a sense of desperation:

A light Wexford *is approaching port to be loaded. The steam plume at her bow is from her forward windlass being fired up in preparation for docking.* Courtesy of Sault Ste. Marie Museum.

All the rumours I am hearing from divers recently on her are bad. Rumours are she is being savagely pillaged. Thousands of divers are visiting her yearly; more if the Lake would cooperate. Rumours are her brass fire hose nozzle is gone, Victrola is gone (I saw it go from the Captain's cabin to the deck in 2002), block and tackle in the chain locker is gone, and it was huge. The tool room door in the engine room was forced open; who knows what was stolen from here? The Crew quarters in the bow have been penetrated; no reports other than divers have gone in the cabin. List is endless. I dearly hope the block is still hanging from the lifeboat davit.

So lies our *Wexford*, slowly, but most certainly, being stripped of her treasures. The situation has not changed, nor has any new legislation been formulated in the 10 years since her discovery that would protect her collections. It is clear that her many artifacts, numbering in the hundreds at the least, will eventually be "lost." Whether they are stolen in dribs and drabs by naive divers who sense that the removal of one small piece of detritus can do no harm, or whether they are systematically removed and sold for profit, or pillaged for some other nefarious reason, this wreck will be denuded. Her frail hulk, too, with the coming decades of acidic, polluted Great Lakes water,[7] will crumble and decay. In the fullness of time, she will be no more.

Remembering the *Wexford*

On November 11, 2000, a solemn gathering stood quietly at the Cobourg Street harbour lookout to honour the memory of the sailors lost on the ship *Wexford* and other vessels that foundered in the Great Storm. The timing was set to commemorate the discovery of the *Wexford*'s final resting place off St. Joseph. A wreath was placed at the base of the metal post supporting the province of Ontario heritage plaque commemorating the Great Storm of 1913. A candle was lit for each of the crew.

Thirty years earlier, the booming deep voice of the late Professor James Scott, author and historian, echoed over a placid Lake Huron on August 3, 1969, when the memorial plaque to The Great Storm was unveiled by Harold Turner, president of the Huron County Historical Society at the time, assisted by the Honourable Charles McNaughton, minister of highways, MPP Murray Gaunt from northern Huron County, and Mayor Frank Mills for the town of Goderich. Lion's Club leader Clayton Edwards chaired the program.

As a new — and very young — member of the town council, I stood, spellbound by Jim Scott's emotional account of the tragedy unleashed by this savage storm. He spoke passionately about the many — sometimes ugly, other times placid — moods of our Lady, the lake, Huron. He recounted the rising terror of the daylight hours on November 9, 1913,

This classic shot of the Wexford *shows her steaming along, fully loaded, on her way to a lower lakes destination.*
Courtesy of the Paul Carroll Collection.

as sailors and their ships in peril sought refuge from the growing tempest. He speculated about the raging nightmare and the fear of certain death that must have tormented the men and women aboard the 23 ships out there that day — fears intensified by the screaming gales in the blackness of the nighttime hours. He helped us to remember in such an articulate manner, and as this plaque was unveiled, he offered solemn tribute to the heroic mariners, every one of whom was lost in that tragic storm.

We must continue to pay tribute and to remember the crew of the lost ship *Wexford* and her many sisters on which sailors have perished from the earliest days of our habitation along these shores.

The 90th Anniversary of the Great Storm: Maitland Cemetery, Goderich

Memorial Remarks by Paul Carroll, at the "Sailors" plot, November 8, 2003:

> In honouring the memory of mariners who died in the Great Storm of November 1913, we are also reminded

238

of those others who have perished over many generations in work and toil on ships that plied our lakes.

Today, in the year 2003, ninety years after this great tragedy, we have little understanding of the importance of our Lady, Lake Huron, and how her placid masquerade could instantly be transformed into a treacherous throughway for hundreds of ships and thousands of mariners who plied her numerous routes. In every small port, there were fishermen who supplied fresh food to their communities, deckhands who served on package schooners, captains on tugs, crew members on passenger sidewheelers, and officers and hands on large, steam-driven freighters such as those lost in this great storm.

Nor do we appreciate the number of times other "great storms" have wrecked havoc upon the waters of the Great Lakes, resulting in the loss of ships and lives of the men and the women who work as crew aboard these vessels. Lake Huron has claimed more than one quarter of all the victims recorded as lost in our marine histories. And it is storms and great tempests such as the Great Storm of 1913 that have claimed well more than half of all ships lost.

Lakeshore families in our community: the MacDonalds, the Glens, the MacAulays, the Leonards, the Grahams, the Robinsons, and many others, can point to shipwreck sites or graveyards where relatives rest, having lost their lives at sea.... One has only to walk amongst the gravestones in the older part of this Maitland Cemetery to see the significance of Lake Huron in the lives of so many of our early maritime families.

The final tally from this great storm shows thirteen vessels totally lost, eight of them (*Charles S. Price, Isaac M. Scott, James Carruthers, Wexford, Regina, John A. McGean, Hydrus,* and *Argus*) on Huron; two (*H.B. Smith* and *Leafield*) on Superior; two (the barges *Plymouth* and *Halsted*) on Michigan; and one (*Lightship No. 82*) on Erie. Estimates for lives lost range between 235 and 250. Six more vessels were written off as constructive total losses, and no less than twenty-one others were stranded and damaged.

In the days and weeks that followed this storm, families of missing mariners travelled from community to community in pursuit of lost sons, husbands, fathers, and a number of mothers, too.

While most could be identified and taken home for religious rites and burial, a few, such as these here interred, were left unclaimed. The large procession from the Brophey funeral home to this very site is an image indelibly stamped in our minds. Even as we are removed from this event, to the third or fourth generation, we know this image — and it reminds us of the fickle nature of our lake.

It would have been difficult to avoid this tragedy. The fierce November gales were viewed as being just a "part of the job." The last run of the season was always as late as it could be made — and it was in this perilous month of November that the most horrendous consequences have been meted out.

Let us especially remember these un-named mariners who served and died.

Let us also remember all of those who have served on the sea: in peace, for commerce, and in war, to protect our freedom.

It is fitting to gather here each year and pay brief tribute to mariners lost — May this remembrance keep us mindful for all those who have worked for us upon the waters of the lakes and seas.

For many years, the tradition of organizing a graveside memorial service has been continued. The late Ron Pennington, a mariner for some thirty-three years and an avid marine historian, initiated the tradition and maintained it zealously for many years. Upon his death, John Doherty, mariner for some eighteen years and longstanding member of Goderich Town Council, undertook to carry the tradition forward until his death earlier this year. We are honoured to ask the widows of Ron and John — Lenna Pennington and Ann Doherty — to come forward at this time to place a wreath to honour these and all mariners lost at sea.

A bell will toll five times — to honour each of the mariners interred below.

The Annual Mariners' Service

The tradition of an annual Mariners' Service continues. A special service, including thematic presentations and displays, is scheduled each year at Knox Presbyterian Church in Goderich. The remembrance is now held in February each year, according to Fran McLean, a member of the planning committee for the contemporary services: "My understanding of the date chosen is that the official opening of the shipping season is March 1, and, therefore, the Sunday before is the special time to offer prayers for those about to embark on the new spring season on the lakes and celebrate our marine heritage — the Blessing of the Fleet."

According to the program published for the 95th annual service held February 22, 2009, "While the Mariners' Service is still intended as a service of recognition for those who make their living on the waters and a service of thanksgiving for the blessings we receive for the use of the lakes for both commerce and recreation, it is also a memorial service, not only for those who lost their lives in 1913, but for all those who have lost their lives on the waters since then."

"There was a time," according to Glen I. Gardiner, a local historian and activist in the commemoration of marine history, "when you could not go down a street in Goderich without passing by the home of a mariner. In the early days, all of the persons who assisted at the Mariners'

Service, including the ushers, were connected with the lake or the sea in some way. My, how times have changed; but we carry on the tradition."[1]

Organizers for the 100th Anniversary Service are already thinking about special plans to commemorate the centenary of this horrific storm.

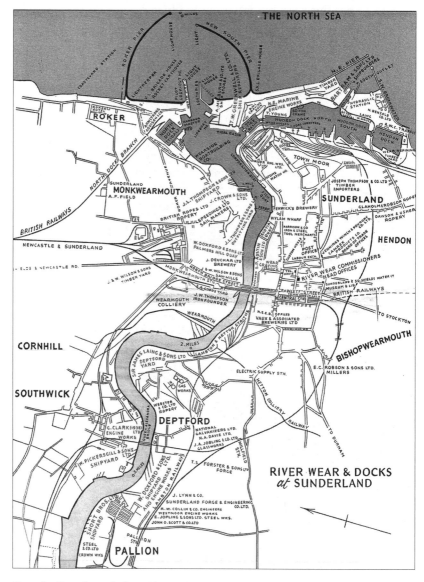

Sunderland and the River Wear:
"The Largest Shipbuilding Town in the World."

APPENDIX A

"Discovery of the *Wexford*" by David Bannister, Friends of the *Wexford*, September 2000

The *Wexford*, an ocean-going packet freighter, was built at Sunderland, England in 1883. The Western Steamship Company of Toronto acquired her for use on the Great Lakes in 1903. At 250 feet long, with a beam of 40 feet, she was smaller and slower than the typical laker of the time, and of a different, but very seaworthy design. Her main deckhouse was located centrally, compared to fore and aft on most lake freighters.

Loaded with grain in Fort William, Lake Superior, the *Wexford* left the dock on November 7, 1913, and sailed into the greatest storm ever recorded on the Great Lakes. She was last seen by another ship shortly before noon on November 9, down bound approximately 30 miles north of Goderich. At about 2:00 that afternoon, a Goderich resident heard a ship's whistle offshore, but visibility was severely limited by snow and the hurricane-force wind and wave conditions. The whistle has generally been thought to be the *Wexford*'s.

Nineteen ships were totally destroyed in the Great Storm of 1913, and at least that many were stranded on the rugged reefs and shorelines of the Lakes. Dozens more suffered severe damage. The *Wexford* was one of 12 ships that were lost with their entire crew. Eight of these were last seen in southern Lake Huron, where violent North and Northeast winds left freighters with no safe port of refuge during the four-day storm. Without

The Doxford Shipyards, Sunderland. "X" marks the spot where the Wexford *was born, at the Doxford yards along the River Wear, Sunderland, in northeast England. William Doxford and Sons Limited, originally established in 1840, was the greatest shipyard establishment in Sunderland. At the time of the* Wexford *there were five berths laid down for the construction of ships. Doxford built little coasting vessels until the 1860s when he turned his efforts to steam and the iron hull. The company was eventually succeeded by the famed Pallion Shipyard, which survives to the current day. Photo originally published in* Where Ships Are Born *(1946), 78.* Courtesy of Owen Delve.

radio communications and with limited navigational equipment, these ships had to fend for themselves in unbelievably harsh weather conditions. The fact that the *Wexford* made it as far as she did is testimony to the tenacity of her crew and their belief in her seaworthiness.

In hurricane conditions, the Great Lakes are among the most formidable waters in the world. Because of their relatively shallow depth and restricted size, waves are steeper, closer together, and more dangerous than those found in the open ocean under similar weather conditions. Captains of ships, which survived the storm, reported waves of 30 feet or more. Stacked up like slabs of concrete, the waves roared down on the freighters with devastating force, sweeping away hatches, wheelhouses, and equipment mounted on the decks, and battering bulkheads in until they burst. Driving wind and snow reduced visibility to a few feet, and ice buildup made the already sluggish boats top-heavy.

Throughout the entire duration of the storm, engineers had to man the throttles in the engine room, reducing speed as the propellers cleared the tops of waves and raced in the air, then throttling up to maintain headway as the screws bit deep into the next following wave. If the engine raced, propeller shafts could be damaged or destroyed. If there was not sufficient power applied when the propellers were submerged, the ship might turn broadside in the troughs, exposing its full length to the fury of the wind and waves. Either situation could be lethal for the ship, and likely was for many. With the loss of their deckhouse, many crews were forced to steer with the exposed aft emergency backup steering gear, if any.

No one knows what happened to the *Wexford* on November 9, 1913, except that she went down with all hands. She certainly lost her deckhouse and funnel along with all of her hatch covers. Following seas may have entered the hatches, and unhindered by cargo bulkheads,[1] gradually filled her up, extinguishing her steam engines and robbing her of the ability to manoeuvre.

As the storm subsided, frozen bodies of crewmembers from the *Wexford* and other lost ships began to wash up along the Ontario shoreline from Goderich to Port Franks. None could tell the tale of the last hours of the *Wexford*. She was thought to be on the bottom of Lake Huron somewhere off the coast between Goderich and Bayfield. Over the 87 years since she was lost, many have searched for her. The search intensified out of Goderich when a group of dedicated volunteers employed the latest technology, including side-scanning sonar to find the wreck. Still it eluded them.

The Discovery

Fate and circumstances must have conspired to bring the *Wexford* to light in the summer of 2000. In August, Don Chalmers, a retired Ford Talbotville line supervisor, spent quite a lot of time fishing out of Grand Bend on his 26-foot sailing Folk Boat, *Odysseus*. Don's boat is outfitted with GPS and a fish finder to help him locate the ideal fishing grounds and the right depth for his downrigger. In previous years, Don had had pretty good luck fishing, bringing home some beautiful salmon and lake trout for summer barbeques. The spring and summer of 2000 had generally been unproductive though.

As it happens, Don is also a diver and a long-time friend of Bob Carey, who headed up the Goderich *Wexford* expedition. Through Bob, Don knew about the search for the *Wexford* and some of its history. Early on the morning of August 15, 2000, Don was out on Lake Huron about eight-and-a-half miles west northwest of Grand Bend, fish finder on, downrigger out at about a 65-foot depth, slowly steaming along looking for salmon. The depth sounder showed 75 feet of smooth, flat bottom, typical for the area.

Suddenly, the fish finder showed a depth reduction to about 60 feet continuing for some distance, then back to 75 feet. Curious, Don backed the *Odysseus* over the object and accidentally caught his fishing gear on it. After retrieving his line, he made several passes over the site and determined that the object was at least 200 feet long, fairly wide, and really interesting. He thought of the *Wexford*. It looked like this could be a shipwreck. He might have caught "The Big One."

Don marked the location on his navigation display for future reference and returned to shore. Later, he asked a long-time fishing buddy and co-worker, Ron Haynes, to come out to the site with him for a second opinion. Ron, also a diver, was uncertain about the underwater formation, but the two agreed to dive on the site as soon as calm conditions prevailed and they could get back out. It would be fun to go diving again. It had been some time since they had last dived on the many known Great Lakes wrecks.

Rough weather set in for some time, and it was not until August 25 that conditions were right. The day before Don and Ron were to go, Don called Bob Carey and said, "I think I know where the *Wexford* is. We're checking it out tomorrow. Do you want to come?"

Bob knew it wasn't the *Wexford*. It was common knowledge the ship was somewhere off the coast between Goderich and Bayfield. But a week's worth of work with a United States expert and side-scanning sonar had so far been a frustrating exercise, so why not? He agreed to come along, and brought one of his *Wexford* expedition team members, Brent Bamford, along with him.

As the dive team descended over the site, a ship that could only be the *Wexford* emerged out of the clear waters, 60 feet below. Its distinctive ocean-going profile, with the remnants of its centre deckhouse still evident, was like a signature for the ship, calling out for recognition at long last. The divers were ecstatic, and although they were keen to view the wreck in its entirety, they also couldn't wait to get the news to the topside world. They headed back to shore, preparing for a *Wexford* champagne party in Goderich and notification of all proper authorities.

Notify the media!

After 87 years of waiting in silence, the *Wexford* was found, sitting upright in 75 feet of water, beautifully preserved. A lifeboat davit still stands upright on her port side, with a block [pulley] delicately suspended from it, the lifeboat missing, possibly launched or torn from its davits in the dying moments of the packet freighter's 30-year existence. Her anchors are stowed in the hawse pipes on her bow, ready for deployment to keep her off a lee shore, if needed. Her bow windlass still holds the anchor chain at ready, but they are sinking under their own weight into the stem of the ship. The hold, likely full of grain as well as water when the ship went down, now holds only water.

Divers can swim the full length of two (upper) decks, thanks to the absence of bulkheads, which might have saved the *Wexford*, or merely prolonged her death. Zebra mussels cover every exterior surface of the ship, but none are evident inside the holds. These crustaceans, foreign to the Great Lakes, cling to every man-made surface in them. Yet, even as they threaten underwater structures, they preserve them and their presence creates a clarity of the water that is beautiful as well as useful for underwater exploration. At 75 feet, the *Wexford* is a perfect depth for recreational diving. When conditions are clear, there is a beautiful jux-taposition of colour, from the brilliant aqua blue-green of Lake Huron's water, to the gold-rust colours of the wreck's surviving surfaces.

The Present

By any measure, the *Wexford* is a beautiful wreck, or "marine heritage site," in the currently fashionable vernacular. It is clearly owned by the Ontario government, Ministry of Citizenship, Culture and Recreation, who have proved their claim to wrecks within Canadian/Ontario territo-rial waters through high-profile international court cases, most notably with the United States steamer *Atlantic* in Ontario's Lake Erie waters.

The Ministry of Citizenship, Culture and Recreation has issued a licence to the Goderich group to survey, map, and catalogue the site. Until this is completed, and mooring buoys are installed at the site to prevent damage from anchors, they have requested that no diving tourism devel-opment take place. Peter Englebert, the ministry's marine heritage archae-ologist, has stated that the province has limited ability to prevent diving on the *Wexford*, and would expect divers to voluntarily practise good con-servation. (It is illegal to tamper with the wreck or to remove artifacts.)

Summary

The *Wexford* discovery provides us with a golden opportunity to diversify our tourism, offering into a more complete package, which will appeal to a wider market. It also provides an opportunity to educate residents, students, tourists, and others on the rich marine heritage that is part of the fabric of the region. It brings a part of our history to life.

We are very fortunate to have in the wreck's finder, Don Chalmers, a person who is committed to ... a conservation ethic for the *Wexford*. His leadership and contribution will continue to be recognized.

APPENDIX B

A Letter to the Minister of Culture, Province of Ontario

The Honourable David Tsubouchi
Ministry of Culture
12th Floor, Ferguson Block
77 Wellesley Street West
Toronto, Ontario
M7A 1N2

30 July, 2003–07–30
By Fax: 416–327–3790

Dear Mr. Minister

Over the past several years a number of issues in the area of heritage preservation and museum services have been developing that need some urgent attention. As a professional Museologist practicing in Ontario for the past thirty-five years I have seen huge changes in the Province's approach to a number of issues. Some of these have been very positive and some not so positive.

All of us, in the field, were thrilled when the Ministry established its conservation lab, and extremely disappointed when that lab closed. The closing of this lab meant the discontinuation of very valuable resource to the community museums of Ontario. The need for the service is critical as is the advice offered by the now discontinued conservator the Ministry used to have on staff.

Are there any plans to re-instate this service, including the position of conservator, and if not, why not?

When the Heritage Act was proclaimed, this was seen as a major step in the right direction and a good place to start from. We felt betrayed when the first review, some ten years later, was abandoned after a huge and very expensive amount of work was done, not only by Ministry staff but by many members of the heritage community. It was encouraging to see the Act dusted off for review a second time and disappointing to see the speed and superficial way in which this second review was undertaken. The sense of urgency developed by the Ministry prevented many of us from taking a meaningful role in this process. The changes were detrimental to a number of areas of heritage conservation and weakened further an already weak Act.

Is a comprehensive review, equal in scope to the one done in the early 1980s planned, and if not, why not?

We are now faced with a new series of issues I would like to bring to your attention. I have been asked to address these by a number of individuals and organizations in our local marine heritage community, of which I am an active member.

This year we saw the retirement of your Marine Archaeologist, Peter Englebert, and I am under the understanding that he has not yet been replaced. This is a major concern to many of us interested in the preservation of the archaeological resources currently resting on the bottom of our Great Lakes. In addition I understand that Ms Kathi McAimsh, Mariner Heritage Administrator, has also left her position and I further understand that she too has not been replaced.

Are we to see the delays in filling these positions as the phasing out of this division within the Ministry (much like we saw the abandonment of the conservation lab and its associated services and staff)? If not, when can we expect to see the two positions filled?

The Huron County Museum is currently traveling an exhibition on the Great Storm of 1913 (opened for a six month tour at the ROM [Royal Ontario Museum] in the fall of 2001 and currently booked for the next four years across the province and northern U.S.A.). This exhibit is drawing attention to the many sailors and ships that were lost on the Great Lakes during this single event. One of these ships lost is the *Wexford*, discovered by divers off the shores of Huron County, in 2000. A licence for surveying the ship has been issued by the Ministry which prevents the removal of artifacts from the ship, a restriction that, in theory is correct, but in practice does not work. Many objects have been removed from this ship illegally and to date only three of these have been recovered by the Ministry (two of which are on loan to the Huron County Museum).

We are aware of continued looting of this important underwater site and are powerless to do anything about it. I have heard reports from divers visiting the site that objects have been observed in baskets resting on the lake bottom ready for removal. Being honest divers and aware of their legal limitations, these divers have left them there and when returned to the site, some days later the baskets have been removed, with their content. We need the legal tools and practical solutions to address these types of issues and the ability to take remedial action.

Will the Ministry give us the legal tools to remove those objects before they are all lost to looters and allow us to place them with a designated depository such as the Huron County Museum?

This then raises the next issue which speaks to a formal system of depositories for archaeological materials recovered under licence. The Huron County Museum currently houses two major archaeological collections excavated with a licence issued under the Heritage Act.

Mr. David Newlands (at the time of the work, employed with the Royal Ontario Museum) excavated two late 19th [century] pottery sites, one at Egmondville and a second at Holmesville, both here in the County of Huron. The Huron County Museum has, as a professional courtesy to Mr. Newlands, been holding this material, on behalf of the people of Ontario. This is an appropriate location for the two collections and we are pleased to have them. It is a valuable resource not only from the standpoint of the research they facilitate, but the collection also provides a substantial asset in the area of public interpretation and exhibition. As I noted early in this letter, we are also in possession of two of the three *Wexford* objects recovered by the Ministry after their illegal removal from the ship. The Museum would welcome the opportunity to be designated as the official depository for any future objects recovered from underwater sites and land excavations within our area.

A precedent has already been established by you in this matter. As objects recovered from the *Atlantic* have been placed in the care of the Port Dover Harbour Museum, it would appear that the concept of regional depositories is not a new initiative. Any such depository should, by its very nature not only include the objects from the excavation but copies of all field notes, research data, photographs and reports.

Would you be willing to designate the Huron County Museum as the official depository for archaeological materials recovered in or around Huron County, including the objects recovered from underwater sites such as the WEXFORD?

The final issue I would like to raise is dealing with the training currently in place of volunteers engaged in underwater research/archaeology under licence in this province. A training system has been adopted from the Nautical Archaeology Society (NAS) based in Great Britain. It is very difficult to become an instructor for this course, which is needed by sports divers to qualify (NAS Level I and Level II) to work on archaeological sites. As a result there are far too few instructors to meet the demand of the diving community. The scarcity of instructors is in fact at the point where courses have had to be cancelled and work has been delayed, further endangering the objects being looted from the lake bottoms of this province.

We need a program to train the instructors that is tailored for Ontario needs and provides solutions that are suitable for this province. There is enough expertise available in Ontario to develop our own program. We need to access those individuals and increase the number of instructors available throughout the province. With over thirty years of diving experience and having worked on underwater sites in Ontario, the Caribbean, Bermuda, and Atlantic Canada, I am willing to serve on a task force to establish the guidelines and a curriculum for such a program.

Is the Province prepared to develop a provincial solution which includes the development of qualified instructors to train sports divers not only to respect our underwater heritage, but to assist in its recovery?

In closing, I would like to thank you for your attention to these urgent matters. I do apologize for the length and breadth of this letter. There are many issues covered here, and many of them are of an urgent nature. I look forward to your response and hope we can work together in achieving a positive solution to these issues.

Yours truly,

[Original signed]

Claus Breede, BA, MPA.
Director, Huron County Museum

Legislation Affecting Marine Archaeological Sites

Marine archaeological sites in Ontario are governed by the terms of the Ontario Heritage Act and its Regulations. There has been much controversy about these laws and their impact on preserving our marine heritage environment. The basic tenet under dispute is that there is little point in declarations that say "hands off" and that you may not remove or alter artifacts, in the absence of any supervision and policing of such sites.

There are those that suggest that education will solve the problem. As a member of Save Ontario Shipwrecks (SOS), I would like to be able to endorse the organization's position that underwater marine heritage sites should be left entirely intact. As suggested to me by SOS president Brian Prince, "We believe in in-situ preservation and access dive sites for the enjoyment as well as low impact diving." Yes, we must educate the diving community. Yes, there will be many, and hopefully most, divers who respect the need to look and enjoy and not to touch. But there will always be those who choose to disregard the ethics and requirements of respect for heritage sites. The desecration of underwater heritage sites is well documented. It continues to be my own belief that fragile artifacts should be removed or protected in some physical manner. Conservation, and display, in an appropriate museum is best, in my opinion. I wish it could be otherwise, but the experience of the travesties committed on the *Wexford* has taught me otherwise.

The diving community in Ontario reacted loudly to a piece of draft legislation, Bill 13, 1999, *An Act to Preserve Ontario's Marine Heritage and Promote Tourism by Protecting Heritage Wrecks and Artifacts.* This legislation, if passed, would have severely restricted recreational diving on any marine heritage sites. Its requirements were so stringent, the purpose, statement of ownership and prohibitions are worth quoting here:

Purpose

1. The purpose of this Act is to enhance the protection and preservation of Ontario's marine heritage resources and to promote responsible exploration of marine heritage sites.

[Definitions omitted]

Ownership

3. The Crown in right of Ontario owns every heritage wreck and protected artifact.

Prohibitions

4. (1) No person shall engage in any of the following activities unless the person is specifically authorized to do so by the terms of a licence issued under Part VI of the Ontario Heritage Act:

1. Enter a heritage wreck, or cause an object to enter a heritage wreck.

2. Move part of a heritage wreck.

3. Remove silt or other naturally occurring substances in a marine heritage site.

4. Remove a protected artifact from a marine heritage site.

5. Damage a heritage wreck or a protected artifact.

6. Take any other action that alters or adversely affects, or is likely to alter or adversely affect a marine heritage site, a heritage wreck or a protected artifact.

7. Any other activity specified in regulation.

Exception

(2) Subsection (1) does not apply at such marine heritage sites as may be prescribed but only with respect to such activities at those sites as may be prescribed.

Seizure of property

(3) A person having the power and authority of a member of the Ontario Provincial Police Force may seize a vessel or equipment which the person believes is being used or has been used to contravene this Act.

There was a virtual uproar in the diving community in response to these proposals. The prohibitions would have introduced severe restrictions on access to the most interesting dive sites in the province. The proposed legislation died on the Order Paper.

Rigorous discussion about Ontario legislation has recurred since the publication of a discussion paper designed to strengthen the Ontario Heritage Act in 2002. This document[1] acknowledged that while the then current legislation might identify underwater heritage sites, it contained no tools to enforce protection of such sites. It suggested that marine sites be defined specifically in the Act; that is to say, that it be clearly stated that archaeological sites also included marine sites. It also suggested that it state clearly that altering an archaeological site and removing artifacts from a site are not permitted without a licence. There was also discussion about whether the government should be given power to protect a small number (It was estimated less than 10 percent) of fragile marine heritage sites, such as those containing human remains. These sites might merit additional protection, the paper suggested. I believe that no action has ever been taken in this regard.

Several years followed before any amendments to the Act were made. Changes were reported to be in place in the 2005–2006 changes the Act brought forward by Bill 60.

The following text represents the most relevant sections of the current (2009) Ontario Heritage Act as it applies to underwater marine heritage sites:

Licence, activity on archaeological sites:

48. (1) Subject to subsection (2), no person shall do any of the following unless the person applies to the Minister and is issued a licence under this Part that allows the person to carry out the activity in question:

1. Carry out archaeological fieldwork.

2. Knowing that a site is a marine or other archaeological site, within the meaning of the regulations,

alter the site or remove an artifact or any other physical evidence of past human use or activity from the site.

3. With respect to a marine archaeological site that is prescribed by regulation,

i. Dive within 500 metres of the site or within such other distance of the site as may be prescribed by regulation.

ii. Operate any type of submersible vehicle, including remotely operated vehicles, autonomous underwater vehicles, submarines or towed survey equipment such as side scan sonars or underwater cameras within 500 metres of the site or within such other distance of the site as may be prescribed by regulation. 2002, c. 18, Sched. F, s. 2 (27); 2005, c. 6, s. 35.’ Specific distances are prescribed banning access to the *Hamilton*, the *Scourge* and the *Edmund Fitzgerald*.

I am not aware of any *legislated* restrictions against access to any other underwater sites in Ontario. Further, according to Brian Prince, "At the Provincial level the Heritage Act amendments in 2005 are perfect. Better protection, bigger fines, only 3 sites requiring a permit not most sites as was feared by some. SOS was very involved with the consultation of these."[3]

I want to underscore the importance of the work of the SOS in preserving our underwater heritage and, especially, its tireless efforts to educate the diving community. The organization runs extensive education programs, conducts excellent public relations programs through participation in public events with displays, the provision of guest speakers, and the distribution of informative handouts. They also conduct very important formal education programs in partnership with the Nautical Archeology Society of the United Kingdom and encourage all divers who might visit underwater heritage sites to acquire this special certification.

Nonetheless, the unscrupulous activity of some divers seems to persist. The actions of just a few surely deny the general population of access to some of the most important and more intriguing records of our past.

According to Doug Taleski, Travel Sports, London, Ontario, who has dived the wreck numerous times, in response to an enquiry made by the author in the summer of 2009, "We dive it occasionally, [it] has become more encrusted, plundering continues, Americans are chartering to it, more than Canadians.... Too bad on that, as I had always thought and promoted a control point to register for diving it."

APPENDIX D

Shipwrecks Along the Huron Shoreline

The Canadian Shore of Lake Huron:
Kincardine and Point Clark to Grand Bend

The Canadian shore of southern Lake Huron, along the coast of Huron County, seems to be littered with shipwrecks. The best attestation seems to be from the reports of beachcombers who annually reported finding bits and pieces of timber, in single pieces or in large slab sections, that has evidently come from the hulls or rigging of ships. I am certain that other areas hide a similar, plentiful legacy on their adjacent lake beds. If David Swayze's fairly famous *Great Lakes Shipwrecks File* tells the tale, then there are thousands — as many as 16,000, I have heard — lost over time, starting from the time of LaSalle and his legendary *Griffon*. As a means of rather "proving the point," I thought it would be of interest to many readers to document, at least in part, an inventory of local shipwrecks.

Let us begin by addressing how one goes about documenting the existence of shipwrecks. As noted in the main text of this book, the key approach for the big finds is to conduct some sort of, hopefully systematic, side-scanning activity. It can be done with simple equipment, like the fish finder that Don Chalmers used on his sailboat when he accidentally found the *Wexford*; with a more sophisticated sonar "fish" from a company like Shark Marine that runs from a laptop computer and costs about five thousand dollars; or with a highly technical device, like a Klein scanner as used by David Trotter of Undersea Research Associates, or its contemporary, computerized derivation. Other systems involve the use of magnetometers that can "see" metal on the bottom or below the surface of a beach or a lake bed. There are now even highly advanced, multi-beam scanners that can "see" in three dimensions, and top-secret derivatives of magnetometers carried in the bellies of military aircraft that can discover hidden objects lying beneath the sea. (That would be a great way to find the *James Carruthers*, one of the two missing shipwrecks from the Great Storm, if anyone happens to have a good connection with an admiral or an air-force general!)

But you usually need a clue about where to start looking. And that's where the land-based research comes in. You can consult source documents in government shipwreck files, you can read old newspapers on the dates just following lake losses, you can examine stories from local histories, piece together evidence from news reports, or you can go to an electronic database, like the *Great Lakes Shipwreck File* maintained by David Swayze at *www.greatlakeshistory.homestead.com*, or use Brendon Baillod's dozens of links to databases on his Great Lakes Shipwreck research web page, *www.ship-wrecks.net*. You can also check out Walter Lewis at his Maritime History of the Great Lakes location, *www.maritimehistoryofthegreatlakes.ca*. Assuming you have a starting point, just go to the next step. Get out there, with persistence, and look for it!

The compilation of a list of wrecks along the Lake Huron shore, west of Huron County, has been devised from a review of many of the sources noted in the preceding paragraphs. In this area of lakeshore, and along the adjacent lake bed, a large number of wrecks can be found, or attributed to the activity at the mouth of the Maitland River — the original Goderich Harbour location — where marine activity commenced around 1828, when the first maps and charts of that area were made at the time of the establishment of the Huron Tract by the Canada Company. There are even old engravings from the mid-1800s that show local ship names, many of which were actually built in shipyards at this location. Similar observations may be made by examining early records for Kincardine, Point Clark (first known as Point Pine), Port Albert, Kingsbridge, Bayfield, St. Joseph, Grand Bend, Port Franks, and beyond to the south. All of these areas were either bustling marine communities with significant shipbuilding enterprise in the early years, or, as in the smaller communities like Port Albert or St. Joseph, at least some nominal activity. In these places, there remains no visible evidence of the commercial marine activity that took place nearly two centuries ago.

The oldest shipwreck found and documented on this section of lakeshore is resting at Southampton, reburied on the beach after her exhumation a few years ago for the purposes of documenting the wreck. It is the wreck of the *General Hunter*, a British Royal Navy brig, built in Amherstburg, Ontario, and active in the famous Battle of Lake Erie in 1813, when she was lost to the Americans. She later foundered in a storm off Southampton in 1816 when she sailed as a transport ship called the *Hunter*. It is noteworthy that all artifacts were removed from the wreck at the time of its excavation in 2004 and are now on display in the Bruce County Museum and Cultural Centre in Southampton. These artifacts have also travelled for display in other Ontario museums.

Some wrecks and wreckage can be definitively identified. Documentation is available and certain. For example, two wrecks in the Bayfield area, the *Malta* and the *Hyndman*, are known in absolute terms. The former, originating in 1855, was documented, wrecked in 1882 on November 11, its hull washing ashore a week or two later. It was salvaged for parts; it has been plundered of its equipment; its presence along the shoreline has been photographed for generations. Its rudder, which was about to disappear forever, has been ambitiously preserved, and now towers like a beacon as part of the entrance sign that beckons modern day boaters to the world famous Northcastle Marine Boatyards, where the prestigious Gozzard Yachts are now crafted by Ted and Jan Gozzard, their family members, and the boatyard team. And even though the remnants of the once-proud ship get buried by sand in years of high water, the wreckage always shows up again when the water levels recede and the sand is eroded away. The latter hulk, the *Hyndman*, was placed in its location and sunk. It was an ill-fated attempt to create a barrier against shoreline erosion, and its story, indeed its history, is well known.

In the 1970s the *Linda Hyndman* was moved from her moorage in Goderich Harbour (where she was being scuttled) by fisherman Ed Siddall, on behalf of Brigadier Morgan Smith, who wanted a sunken breakwater to protect Bayfield's eroding shoreline. She was dropped in just 11 feet of water, destined to be pulled ashore by bulldozer operator Garth Postill, but abandoned when the brigadier decided to open the cocks and scuttle her where she presently lies.

Other wrecks are not so well understood. Such is the case with the withering hulks of two schooners that have never been formally documented, and that present their ghostly outlines below the cliffs at Bluewater Beach, inshore just south of Goderich. There are no distinct markings; nothing unique seems to present itself. They remain as unknowns.

In the old "boneyard" for Goderich Harbour there are three distinguishable wrecks. One can surmise what they might be, but it is not absolute. The *Scotia*, the tug *Phillips*, and at least one other hulk, perhaps the remains of *Olga* or the burned-out *Tecumseth* (often spelled *Tecumseh*), rest there quietly, awaiting final documentation before they deteriorate and disappear. In this shallow-water graveyard, pieces often get torn loose from the security of their underwater tombs during the spring and fall tempests and are thrown ashore, sometimes carried back underwater in the next vicious storm; other times returned by conservation-conscious boaters and tug operators who want to preserve the watery specimens for as long as possible.

The Goderich "Boneyard" wrecks, as noted, not only include the vessels mentioned above, but also the *Rathbun*, cast upon the north pier in 1886, and the *Abercorn*, along with several other unidentified wrecks. The hulk of the burned out *Annamac* is now buried under the nearby Rotary Beach, where her hull washed up after she was set ablaze and scuttled many years ago after her time as a tug and tour boat at Goderich Harbour had ended. Many of these derelicts were towed to this final resting place by the tug *W.L. Forrest*, captained by "Big" Bill, the owner of the small dredging company that carried out harbour works in the lakeshore town.

Beginning with underwater survey work done by David Trotter for the town of Goderich in the year 2000, the survey of approximately 200 square kilometres of lake bottom has been conducted by the local Marine

Heritage Committee. A baseline for further work was established from the breakwater openings at Goderich, running south to the *Wexford* wreck site. Additional work has been conducted north of Goderich in the area known as the Homan Beach. A small portion of deeper water off Point Clark has also been surveyed in an unsuccessful effort to find the *Carruthers*. This work is continued on an annual basis by the Port of Goderich Marine Heritage Committee, some members of which are also part of the Huron Shores Save Ontario Shipwrecks chapter. With persistence, there will be additional big finds.

At the mouth of the Maitland River, the lake casts up mysterious remains from time to time. Many ships were lost in this area as they tried to make Goderich Harbour in countless severe storms. Among these were the *Rockaway* and the *Mary Watson* (1858). No one knows what evidence remains of these two ships. The wreckage lying offshore, known as the Labour Day Wreck, does not seem to be of that time period. The *Huron Signal* of November 24, 1853, points out a wreck of the *Anne* out of Kincardine, which became waterlogged and apparently sank offshore before it could reach the harbour. In 1868 the *Evening Star* capsized in a sudden squall five miles north and west of Goderich Harbour, but rested upside down and floated until the steamer *Clinton* could tow her home. A barge of unknown name went to pieces off Port Albert and sank. The year is unclear; perhaps a catastrophe from the first decade in the 1900s. On November 11, 1901, the steamer *India*, bound for Goderich, where she would leave her cargo of wheat, was accompanied by the disabled and abandoned schooner *Marine City*, which carried pulp wood. Both were required to anchor offshore, where they were battered by a gale. The steamer survived the overnight storm, but the schooner was never seen again.

A flat-bottomed fishing boat went down in March of 1902, carrying one man to his death, just north of Goderich Harbour, while said vessel was trying to retrieve some nets that might have been lost in a storm. There is, somewhere, the wreck of the *I.L. Quiney*, lost off Point Clark in 1902. In October 1907 the steamer *Lurline*, newly purchased by the Ontario government for service on Lake Huron, ran headlong into the hidden breakwater at Goderich Harbour, missing the new lights, which were hardly visible because it was not yet dark. Her skipper ran in on the old lines, and had not heard about the revised route established for safe entry to the harbour. She was broken up on the rocks in high winds over the next few days. To the north there were reports of a barge lost, carrying a load of Model "A" Fords en route from Detroit in the early decades of the 1900s.

The *Fashion*, a side-wheel steamer built in 1847 at Panghorn, Michigan, lies off Bayfield somewhere after her loss in 1856. Somewhere nearby also rests the *Nemesis*, built by the Marlton Yards in Goderich, 1868, and lost November 11, 1883. The *Lewis Hotchkiss*, 1870, a 210-foot barge, lies somewhere west of Goderich after her tow tug, the *Wales*, also foundered in late August or September of 1891. The *Nashua*, a propeller-driven 134-foot lumber hooker, lies off Bayfield after her demise in an October 1892 storm. Her barge in tow, the *C.C. Ryan* capsized and drifted ashore some four days later, her boiler, stern, and machinery gone.

The *Azov*, 1866, originally of Hamilton, skipped by a Captain McDonald, one of the famous maritime clans at Goderich, was lost off the Michigan shore in 1911, north and east of Point Aux Barques, and drifted to her resting spot at McGregor Point, north of Kincardine, after her captain, his wife and family, and the crew "rowed" home to Canada, not wanting to land in a foreign port. The vessel was "found" again in 1956 by Bruce MacDonald, a descendant (who spelled his surname differently than his ancestor), and Allan MacDonald, not a descendant of the original clan.

In the Point Clark, Kincardine area are the *J.S. Minor*, the *Fannie Campbell* (perhaps off Stokes Bay), the *D. Ferguson*, and the *Phenix*, among others; the names and details not recorded. The *Gilly*, a small lake-cargo freighter, first built as a schooner in 1913 in L'Anse-St-Jean, Quebec, was stranded and lost 12 miles north of Goderich in 1937 when her tow, the tug *Superior*, broke the cable; she foundered carrying 35,000 cedar posts. Captain Harold Ebel and crew were rescued by Bert MacDonald of the tug and "patrol" boat the *Annamac*, also mentioned earlier in this account.

Government *Dredge No. 1*, 1903, lost north of Bayfield in a June 1932 storm, discovered and partly salvaged at the time, was rediscovered in 1999 or 2000 by Joe Durand, who stills protects her hiding place. The *Argus* (or the *Hydrus*) and the *James Carruthers* are also out there somewhere, "whispering" to be found.

The search continues, as the list of wrecks discovered grows ever longer.

The "Plimsoll" Mark and "Well-deck" Ships

In the 1870s, the British Parliament heard grave concerns about the safety of ocean shipping from a number of members. Apparently, ship-hull design had not changed significantly, as large steam-powered engines had been added to hulls primarily designed for sailing vessels. The loss of cargo space for the installation of engines, boilers, and propeller shafts created an "off balance" in the distribution of weight as cargoes were added to these modified below-deck spaces. It was felt that such heavily loaded vessels were subject to capsize with the resultant loss of life, ship, and cargo.

The matter was debated fiercely in the House of Commons. Two principal members of parliament taking the lead roles in the campaign to improve ship safety were Samuel Plimsoll and William Gray. They were both members of a Parliamentary Load Line Committee that recommended that all ships be required to show a painted load line on the side of the hull, which would disappear underwater if a ship were to be overloaded. The markings, called the "Plimsoll Mark," were designed to allow for seasonal conditions and also for variations in the temperature of the water, factors that affected both flotation and safety. The use of the Plimsoll Mark became law in 1876, just seven years before the *Wexford* was built. The codes for the Plimsoll Mark vary for ocean and freshwater locations.

William Gray also became involved in the development of a new design for ships, to create a better balance for vessels than the traditional designs. He suggested a design, commonly called a "well-deck" design that raised the rear deck to increase the aft cargo-hold capacity, thus restoring a degree of balance to the distribution of weight over the entire vessel. One example of this design might be the *Wexford* as she was originally designed and launched in 1883, before she was converted to a flush-deck hull with the addition of her seven-foot spar deck in 1884. Another good example would be the salty *Leafield*, built in the same era.

There are many variations of the well-deck design. Terminology used to describe such vessels also varies and is sometimes a cause for confusion. What can be called a "centre-island" design, or a "cabin amidships" layout, or even a "centre pilothouse" design, may or may not also be well-deck vessels. The key distinguishing factor appears to be the break in the deck line, with fore and aft sections raised. The primary purpose appears to have been the creation of a safer and more seaworthy design.

According to a British Admiralty publication dated January 25, 1954, the *Manual of Seamanship, Volume III*, includes the following description of cargo ships:

> The earliest type of cargo steamer was a "flush decker," in which the openings above the engine and boiler rooms were surrounded by low casings fitted with skylights to admit light and air. Experience showed that this type of hull was dangerous, and so light superstructures extending from side to side of the ship were built around the machinery casings. A further development was the addition of a forecastle and poop, for improved seaworthiness, which in turn led to the well-know "three island" type of cargo vessel with forecastle, bridge, and poop superstructures, and before and abaft the bridge a well-deck protected by bulwarks and well-suited for the carriage of deck cargoes such as timber. Variations of the three-island type are the "shelter-deck" ship, in which all three superstructures are extended to form a continuous,

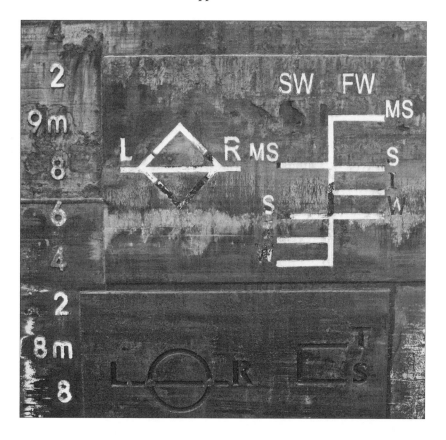

It is a requirement that all commercial cargo vessels show a load line as determine by the surveyors and insurers of the ship, according to the regulations in the country of registry. There are different load lines for freshwater and for salt-water use, as shown in the photograph of the Plimsoll markings for the Canadian Navigator *as she was seen loading salt in late October 2009, at the Compass Minerals Sifto Salt mine docks at Goderich Harbour. Look for the freshwater versus the salt-water markings. Look for the different load lines for summer, fall, or winter. Code for initials used: (MS) midsummer load line; (S) summer load line; (I) load line in intermediate seasons; (W) winter load line; (SW) salt water; and (FW) freshwater, markings apparently for special trips to Magdelan Islands or New Brunswick; (T) Tropical in oceans; (LR) Lloyd's Register. Symbols: Diamond is Great Lakes; Oval is Ocean.* Photo by Paul Carroll.

non-watertight superstructure from bow to stern, thus providing a sheltered stowage which is not included in the net or registered tonnage and is therefore exempt from harbour dues when no cargo is carried in the super-structure spaces; "well-deck" ships in which the poop is extended to join the bridge; and the "raised quarterdeck" ship in which the upper deck abaft the bridge superstruc-ture is raised a foot or so to provide more cargo space aft.

Poetical Tributes to Mariners

Poetical Address
Dedicated To
"The Mariners of Lake Huron" and read by
the Authoress of *Golden Leaves* at the
Marine Social Club held at their Club Room
on Monday evening, February 3rd, 1913.
Goderich, Ontario.

Ye Mariners of Lake Huron

Ye Mariners of Lake Huron,
Ye fear not wind or wave;
And ye are known all o'er the land,
For being so staunch and brave.

Ye never delay from duty,
Your courage is too strong;
But plough the waves right steadily,
With enlivening song.

No rain, no storm, no raging sea,
Holds you from dark'ning sky,
No lightning flash, no thunder loud,
Can daunt ye passing by.

Then save your strength, ye
    Mariners,
Perils lie on the deep;
And ever on the stormy sea,
A watchful vigil keep.

Some day "Old England" will call you,
For Service on the sea;
When "Fair Canada" gets ready,
"Queen of the Sea" to be.

Your hearts are pure as finest gold,
Molten by flames of love
Which bring you fame on sea and land,
And Gifts from God above.

— Eloise A. Skimming, Goderich, Ontario

1913 Great Storm Poem

The ninth day of November last
Will be remembered long.
The loss by storm on that day
Could not be told in song.

On that November morning
The wind and sleet and snow
Increased until the afternoon
The storm was fierce I know.

Not only on Lake Huron,
Lake Erie and St. Clair
And also Lake Superior
Each one received their share.

Their loss they will remember
But who could count the cost,
Two hundred and seventy sailors
And thirty ships were lost.

The strongest vessel on the lake,
Will never reach the shore.
The bravest sailors on the boats
Will see their friends no more.

Life boats and life preservers
Proved that day to no avail.
They were no use that stormy night
They could not stand the gale.

Some tried the life preservers,
No sailors need be told,
It's better to sink at once
Than to perish with the cold.

And after that eventful night,
For one full week or more
There have been many sailors found
All along Lake Huron's shore.

One of them a letter from,
His mother, far away,
Saying "You will be home at New Years
Can't I see you Christmas Day."

— Anonymous. *Courtesy of Huron County Museum and Historic Gaol, Record No. 106, 1913 Great Storm Virtual Museum Exhibit.*

For Those in Peril on the Sea
Melody — John Bacchus Dykes, 1861; Words — William Whiting, 1860

Eternal Father, strong to save,
Whose arm hath bound the
  restless wave,
Who bidd'st the mighty ocean deep
  its own appointed limits keep;
O hear us when we cry to Thee
For those in peril on the sea.

O Christ, Whose voice the waters
  heard
And hush'd their raging at Thy word,
Who walkest on the foaming deep
And calm amid the storm didst sleep
O hear us when we cry to Thee
For those in peril on the sea.

O Holy Spirit, Who didst brood
Upon the waters dark and rude,
And bid their angry tumult cease,
And give, for wild confusion, peace;
O hear us when we cry to Thee
For those in peril on the sea.

O Trinity of love and power,
Our brethren shield in danger's
  hour;
From rock and tempest, fire and foe,
Protect them wheresoe'er they go;
Thus evermore shall rise to Thee
Glad hymns of praise from land
  and sea.

Amen.

— William Whiting, 1825–1878

Acknowledgements

1. In a telephone call with the author, September 30, 2009.
2. Or should this be the *Hydrus*? The debate continues in some quarters as to whether the early 1970s wreck discovery off Grindstone City, Michigan, near Port Austin Reef, is actually the *Argus* as claimed. Shipwreck hunters like David L. Trotter would suggest that the true identity of that wreck has never been proven in definitive terms. The absence of coal in the wreck location, given that the *Argus* was carrying a cargo of coal, raises doubts in some minds. The *Hydrus* was carrying ore. So which shipwreck is actually missing? They were virtually identical in specifications, carrying the same length, and both built in 1903. They were partner ships operated by the Interlake Steamship Company, Cleveland.

Foreword

1. *www.numa.net*, accessed on October 2009. Founded in 1979 by Clive Cussler, the National Underwater and Marine Agency (NUMA) is a non-profit, volunteer foundation dedicated to preserving our maritime heritage through the discovery, archaeological survey, and conservation of shipwreck artifacts.

Prologue

1. Pie Island is on Lake Superior, near the present site of Thunder Bay.
2. The newer, larger freighters were loosely described as 730s. Their sizes varied. The *Edmund Fitzgerald* was actually 729 feet in length.
3. A gyrocompass, with its card suspended in liquid mercury, tended

to be more stable and perhaps more accurate because of the low-friction environment.

4. David G. Brown discusses the language of the sea at the end of his book *White Hurricane*, as listed in the bibliography. He cites one of the greatest differences as being the tradition by which ships are named. Ships are customarily assigned the female gender, being called *she*. Such is the custom of the sea. On the Great Lakes, however, bulk freighters are given masculine names. As Brown says, "The reason is a long-standing tradition to name vessels after executives or investors in the companies that own them. Quite often the ship and its namesake are active at the same time, which can lead to gender misunderstandings. So, in conversation, only the ship's last name is used and it is usually preceded by *the* to signify that the name refers to a vessel not a person." Other differences are quite simple. A "voyage" on the ocean is a "trip" on the Great Lakes. A "wheelsman" steers a ship on the Lakes; a "quartermaster" plays the same role on the oceans. A fluctuation in lake level is referred to as a "seiche" on the Great Lakes but is never called a "tide." On the lakes, a "chadburn," found on older ships, is the communications device used by the captain to signal the engine room for power changes requested. It is most often called a "telegraph" at sea. (The full name is engine order telegraph.)

The circumstance to which Roy referred was following a winter lay-up challenge at Goderich Harbour where a number of ships in winter storage broke loose. There were strong westerly winds but little ice in the harbour to help hold ships in place.

Introduction

1. "Compass correction" — normally called a deviation card.
2. Reprinted from *The Port Huron Times-Herald*, November 13, 1913, 1.
3. Lake Carriers' Association *Annual Report*, 1913, 152.
4. In his book, *Lake Huron*, Fred Landon devotes Chapter 18 to the Great Storm of 1913. The quotation is from page 325.
5. Dave Trotter in conversation with the author, August 2000.
6. As my friend, Captain C. "Bud" Robinson, a mariner with over 40 years of experience on the lakers, and hailing from a long line of

seafaring ancestors, said during his "edit" read of the manuscript, "Only the lost crew knows the real, or partial truth. The ship itself conceals the direct cause. She failed them, or did they fail her? For now, we have to depend on dead reckoning and hope we are in good water and close to our intended position."

"Wexford Found Off Grand Bend"

1. Bruce Cameron was born in 1889, September 4, thus making him only 24 years of age.
2. The issue of cargo carried on the *Wexford* during her final voyage has never been actually documented by examining the vessel log. Other than a single observation about an object that "might" have been a rail, or a piece of a rail, by one scuba diver exploring the wreckage, all evidence points to the reality that the *Wexford* carried a cargo of wheat on her last voyage. No actual steel rails have yet been found at the shipwreck site. The *Annual Report* of the Lake Carriers' Association, in a Table of Total Losses on page 154, also shows the *Wexford* cargo as "Steel Rails." This information is not consistent with other records and reports, including that of the owner, manager of the Western Steamship Company, Captain W.J. Bassett, who clarified at the Goderich Inquest that she had only carried bulk cargo while owned by the Western Steamship Company, mostly grain, with only two loads of ore.
3. Actually, David Trotter has found and documented more than 90 sites, as of September 2009. Most of these are shipwrecks, and few were aircraft remains.
4. The licence was in the name of Bob Carey.
5. The *James Carruthers*, a brand new 550-foot ship, just launched, was lost, but has never been found. The body of her captain was recovered near the Point Clark lighthouse. The remains of her crew were found along the shoreline to the south. Their shoes were lined with grain, according to marine historian Ron Beaupre, perhaps the sign of one last desperate act to shovel grain to try and right a badly listed ship with a shifted cargo. While much of its flotsam and jetsam washed up in the area between Point Clark and Goderich, recent rumours seem to indicate that the *Carruthers* itself may lie

northwest of Kincardine. There are unconfirmed reports that she has actually been found, and if so, her custodians have very wisely kept her location a secret until archaeological survey work has been completed fully. To add credence to that location, and perhaps the *Argus* nearby, the local folklore says that two ships were seen, hull down, one firing rockets, far offshore from Kincardine, the other trying to assist, in brief pauses between the blinding squalls at the height of the storm.

6. Bob Carey, as noted earlier by Cumming, was also a long time Ford employee, also working at the St. Thomas plant, a co-worker with Don Chalmers.

Chapter 1: Historical Perspectives: Great Britain to the Great Lakes

1. The order papers were acquired by Brent Bamford, after research to track down ship plans. According to Brent:

> The builders of the *Wexford*, William Doxford and Sons, went out of business decades ago. Mr. Phil Hall, a local historian at the Sunderland Public Library informed me that what limited records of the company remained are now housed at Tyne & Wear Archives and are now in the public domain. I contacted them and found that no existing plans for the *Wexford* were thought to be in existence locally. They did, however, have a "ships particulars" book from William Doxford, which included a longitudinal drawing as well as written specifications of the ship. The book was described as being much too large and fragile to be photocopied — but we could have an actual size photograph.... My understanding ... is that the "ships particulars" book was sort of a catalogue of the various basic designs that Doxford and Sons offered to prospective buyers. Those buyers would then sit down with the marine architects and engineers to "customize'

the basic design for their particular needs — hence all
the handwritten notes and insertions on the plan.

From correspondence, July 29 and September 20, 2009.

2. The flag for the Hudson line is red in colour with a white disc within
which is charged a red, upper case *H.*

3. Quotes are from the Order Papers.

4. The term fondly used by mariners for their captain.

5. In addition to the pencilled notes on the order sheets, which identify
that a "seven foot" spar deck was added, evidence at the 1914 inquest
hearings made reference to damage to the spar deck that would have
occurred during the storm that sank the *Wexford.*

6. Retired laker captain Bud Robinson offered the following information about spar decks in a dialogue with me in July 2009:

> The original main deck or uppermost continuous
> deck is sometimes incorrectly referred to as the "spar
> deck." Should it be needed, however, an additional
> deck can be added above the main deck, then this
> becomes the spar deck. It was usually constructed with
> lighter scantlings than the main deck, thus resulting
> in a lighter cargo-carrying capacity with the addi-
> tional weight added to the vessel. So this additional
> seven-foot spar deck fitted to the *Wexford* in 1884
> must have been constructed for the purpose of spe-
> cific light cargoes, bailed hay, cotton, people, or ani-
> mals, etc. Heavier cargoes, grain, steel etc. would be
> carried below the main deck constructed over heavier
> scantlings, webs, or beams. Today, ships such as the
> *Halifax* and the *Saguenay* (scrapped a few years ago),
> etc. had their main deck raised approximately five feet.
> Therefore the freeboard was increased and also their
> load lines. Perhaps this upper spar deck gave way to
> stress during the storm if lighter scantlings were used

when it was added. There was not much freeboard at 5 foot 8½ inches for weather conditions encountered.

After this spar deck was added, she became flush-decked with no raised fo'c'sle (bow deck) or raised poop deck aft. This would allow tons of green water to wash over her in heavy storms and ice to build up over her decks in late-season runs. A collapsed deck may have been the cause of her foundering.

I have read in some articles that she was loaded with steel rails. I believe that she was loaded with grain for Goderich, but did she also have some steel rails perhaps in the tween deck, below the spar but above her main deck? If heavier cargoes were loaded in this way, then her center of gravity would be raised considerably with the topside weight. The rails may have been loaded at her bottom to allow for this unstable condition. Cargo may have shifted. Guess only the dead will ever know.

The Western Steamship Company owner, at the Goderich Inquest, attested that she had never carried package freight or deck cargo, and only two cargoes of ore, during the time he had owned her.

Captain Bud's observation confirms my own suspicion that the collapse of spar deck, especially the forward section, as observed on the wreck today, was a critical factor in the loss of this ship. The hundreds of tons of ice (perhaps up to a thousand tons) that accumulated on the upper decks, played havoc with the viability of these vessels in the legendary storms of November. I also have wondered whether the spar deck was added also to increase the coal capacity of the bunkers because her new state-of-the-art engines consumed higher quantities of coal than anticipated, and whether it was found on the 1883 voyages that the ship's bulwarks were just too high, catching dangerous volumes of green water in ocean storm conditions encountered. It was not an uncommon practice to convert such "well-decked" vessels to "flush-deck" ships simply to increase their cargo capacity.

7. Dive notes submitted to the author, October 15, 2000.

8. The Lake Carriers' Association lists her at 270 feet in their after-storm records.
9. A brief account of Cromwell's venture into Ireland can be found at *www.irelandseye.com/aarticles/history/events/dates/cromwell.shtm*, under the title *The Curse of Cromwell,* accessed in August 2009.
10. The dates are inconsistent in various records. In a letter of reference for a crew member, William Deal, signed by Captain Sloggett, October 30, 1894, says that he travelled with Deal on the "S.S. *Wexford*" for two trips between Liverpool and the River Plati, Argentina. James Sloggett was obviously the ship's master at that time, or the date was wrong in his letter.
11. This is an extra boiler, sometimes used for special purposes, or while at shore when the main engines were down.
12. While it is really a separate story, shipowners often found it more economical to purchase older, used vessels, such as these and in this size range. These ships were often called "canallers." They were perfectly suited to a variety of uses, from carrying package freight to bulk cargo, and were the perfect size to suit the canal dimensions of the time, which allowed passage through the full extent of the Great Lakes. Readers wanting to explore the background related to this topic are urged to review a couple of relevant articles on canallers on the Great Lakes. One is by James Gilmore, and available at *www.maritimehistoryofthegreatlakes.ca/GreatLakes/Documents/Gilmore/default.ap*. The other is by Stephen Salmon, *British Competition: "Canadian" Great Lakes Vessels built in United Kingdom Shipyards 1854–1965: An Archival Checklist,* and can be found at *www.maritimehistoryofthegreatlakes.ca/Documents/Salmon_BritishCompetition*.
13. The note by the British vice-consul is found on page 8 of the Articles of Agreement for the transatlantic voyage to Canada. Information is recorded in Port of Montreal Articles of Agreement and Ship's Log, National Archives of Canada, Record Number R184–202–5–E, 1903.
14. Shillings rather than pence.
15. Port of Montreal Articles of Agreement and Ship's Log, Library and Archives Canada, Record Number R184–202–5–E, 1903.
16. *Ibid.*

17. *Ibid.*
18. "Father Point," or Ste. Anne-de-la-Pointe-au-Père, is a village in Rimouski County, Quebec, on the south shore of the St. Lawrence River.
19. *The Collingwood Bulletin*, January 21, 1904, 4.
20. A logbook of *Wexford* 1903 was thought to exist at the Library and Archives Canada, database RG12 DOT. However, this document is actually the 12-page "Agreement and Account of Crew" for her transatlantic sailing, authorized by the British consulate in Dunkirk, April 6, 1903, as referred to earlier. Logbooks are normally kept onboard, with carbon copies sent to the ship's office at the end of each loaded trip. The document found in Bruce Cameron's pocket may have been the copy of the final log entry.
21. *The Signal*, November 27, 1913, 1.
22. *Ibid.*
23. Lime Island lies west of St. Joseph Island in the St. Marys River. It is found alongside the main navigation route, which takes a dogleg turn to pass by Lime Island. It is not an easy passage during fog, but seems to be an area where an experienced skipper would not take any chances. The incident was also described in detail in *The Sault Ste. Marie Evening News* of August 18, 1913: "A large hole was torn in the hull and pumps are unable to keep the water under control. It is thought that much work will be required in order to place the boat in condition for travel."
24. Additional bracketed material in quote added by Mr. Ken McLeod.
25. The number of crew will be a point of confusion throughout this account. We just do not know for sure. I have accounted for 20 persons present onboard through my own review of newspaper records, but this is probably incomplete. We know that careful records were not always kept, and that passengers could join a ship informally, often as crew from another boat, usually on a return passage to the home port.
26. It was suggested that the scar on his ankle would be a useful clue in the positive identification of his body when it was eventually found.
27. Recounted in *The Owen Sound Sun Times*, November 9, 1963, 10, in an article by W.J. Carmichael, which appeared on the fiftieth anniversary of the Great Storm.

Chapter 2: The Skipper's Log

1. As I have reflected on my own record-keeping while on cruising passages with our own sailboat, these following thoughts are conjectured to be the kind of musings going through the mind of young Cameron as he proceeded on his first and fateful voyage as Master. As duress increased, he would have become occupied with the single task of minding the ship. On these stressful occasions, I have always found that I did not keep records beyond a certain point — and never returned to my log to complete the missing entries. They were challenging times better forgotten.
2. Captain Edward McConkey's diary is at the Huron County Museum, access number M983–20.2.
3. Letter accompanying diary, by Amy McConkey McKernan, June 1984.
4. The *Regina* was actually operated by Merchants Mutual Line, Toronto. Perhaps Interlake was a previous employer?
5. Amy McConkey McKerman, letter of June 1984.
6. *Ibid.*
7. *Ibid.*
8. *The Saturday News*, Collingwood, November 15, 1913, 1.

Chapter 3: The Final Voyage

1. *The Signal*, November 27, 1913, 1.
2. *Ibid.*, attributed to Captain Whitney at the inquest.
3. The records of the Lake Carriers' Association were donated to the Historical Collections of the Great Lakes, being held at the Bowling Green State University, Bowling Green, Ohio, in August 1985. Literary and property rights have been dedicated to the public and duplication is permitted for the purposes of preservation and scholarly research. A fully catalogued inventory is available for review at *www.bgsu.edu/colleges/library/cac/ms/page43230.html*, as of August 2009. In my own collection of records, I have copies of portions of the 1913 *Annual Report* as related to the November storm and its outcomes.
4. *Annual Report*, Lake Carriers' Association, 1913, 151.
5. A "lead line," literally, was a lump of lead on the end of a long line that was swung out over the side of a moving ship, in a long, forward

arc, and let fall to the bottom at the end of a measured line. Often the bottom of the lead was coated with grease or a sticky wax to pick up residue from the lake bed to confirm the nature of the bottom, another useful clue in determining a ship's position. The expression "swinging the lead" was sometimes used as a term for "goofing off," a reference to the boring and repetitive nature of the task of reading the bottom for the ship's master in this fashion.

6. Hay Lake, now called Nicolet Lake, lies just south of the Sault Locks.

7. *The Signal*, November 27, 1913, 1.

8. I am reminded so much of my uncle's hesitation to depart as he worried about that storm that brought his fearful rogue wave as described in the prologue.

9. *The Collingwood Bulletin*, November 20, 1913, 4. Captain Stephen had taken just a week to "drift down" to Port Huron, make Fort William, and then return to Goderich, "almost a record, considering the circumstances."
   "You're back from a watery grave. Praise God," said one woman.
   "After greeting a score of admirers the sturdy captain broke away with, 'Well, the snow was fierce, but we are still here.'"

10. In the DVD *Lake Fury: Final Run*, by Ric Mixter, Airworthy Productions, 2003.

11. Gordon Jamieson was a senior citizen crossing guard at Victoria Public School, Goderich, in the mid-1970s. He was about 12 years old at the time of the storm. He reported this observation to Ron Ritchie, a teacher there. It was relayed to me by Ron, in a note, September 5, 2000, upon news that the *Wexford* had finally been found.

12. Reported in *The Signal*, November 13, 1913, 1.

13. Reported in both *The Signal*, November 13, 1913, 1, and *The London Free Press*, November 17, 1913, 1.

14. *The London Free Press*, article dated November 15, 1913, 1. The general consensus seems to be that it was absolutely impossible to launch the lifeboats from the life boat station. Its location, at the inside end of the south harbour pier at Goderich, probably had it so inundated by storm waves crashing in along the beach, that the doors to the vessel storage area would not have been able to be opened anyway.

15. Goderich Inquest transcript note, as reported by *The Signal*, November 13, 1913, 1.
16. Somewhere in her final hours, the *Wexford* lost her rudder — completely. Only a short stub of the rudderpost protrudes from her shipwrecked hull. It could not, likely, be the item reported in the newspaper. It was presumed to be much too heavy and would most likely go straight to the bottom. There are circumstances, however, that could see a rudder washed ashore. Large, flat, heavy, and seemingly dense and immovable, waterlogged pieces of shipwrecks have been washed up along the Lake Huron shore many times, only to disappear again in the next storm.
17. Reported in *The Collingwood Bulletin*, November 13, 1913, 1.
18. Once again, the mystery of whether the *Argus* or the *Hydrus* lies offshore is raised. No bodies from the *Hydrus* are noted, yet the supposed hulk of the *Argus* is the shipwreck said to be lying far away, across the lake, near the Port Austin Reef. One might think that bodies from the closer ship would come ashore along the Kincardine shores. Which ship was actually sighted by the crew of the *G.C. Crawford* as it broke in two and sank?
19. Reported in *The London Free Press*, November 12, 1913, 1.
20. Reported in *The Collingwood Bulletin*, November 13, 1913, 1. Identified partly by presence of the boat's shipping bill in his pocket.
21. Robert Turnbull's visit to the lakeshore will be cited several times in this book. It is the most often recounted story in association with the *Wexford* in the Great Storm, and as such will appear in its many variations throughout this account.
22. *The Detroit News*, November 12, 1913, 1.
23. *Ibid.*
24. Reverend Haslip contacted me by mail when he learned that I was doing research about the *Wexford*. The location seems to indicate that the lifeboat probably floated free from the wreck when it finally settled to the bottom off the St. Joseph area. Undated letter, postmarked August 19, 2002.
25. *Ibid.*
26. Anne Talbot was interviewed by the author at the time of the report.

The life jacket was apparently burned in a bonfire along with other "trash" from the driving sheds as the farm was prepared for sale. It was not until after the *Wexford* wreck had been found that its value as an historic artifact was recognized.

27. Although it is tangential to the current paragraph, one needs to consider the chart datum at the time in 1913, to determine where the *Wexford* might have made its first traumatic contact with the bottom, in the troughs, between the huge waves. According to Patrick Donnelly, Coastal Resources Manager for the Lake Huron Centre for Coastal Conservation, "Water level data for Lake Huron goes back to 1918, when the level was 0.7 metres above chart datum (176.7 m IGLD). It appears to be on a downward trend after that until 1926, so it might have been slightly higher in 1913 (possibly by 0.2 or 0.3m). It is realistic that she would have bottomed out at Black's Point on one of the huge boulders that sit on the bottom in that area of the lakeshore south of Goderich."

28. The cooks had a real dilemma in stormy conditions on these old ships. During heavy weather they managed best as conditions would permit. They used racks on the galley stove to hold the cooking pans in place, used wet cloths on tables so dishware would not slide, resorted to canned goods instead of fresh-cooked food, offered cold plates, sandwiches, or whatever. The crew did not expect the everyday variety on the menu at these times. On older vessels, such as the *Wexford*, where the deck crew accommodations were near the bow, they had to go aft on a lifeline to reach the galley. This was by means of a cable rigged the length of the deck, between the forward and aft house, or forward and aft of cabins amidships. Sailors attached themselves with ropes spliced to rings that were free to run in both directions. Sometimes this safety harness was tied to the person, or they had the option of just holding on. During icy conditions and in gales, this was not always possible. From the 1920s, ships with a forward and an aft house had enclosed side tunnels below the main deck and the side tank tops on both sides of the ship. Ships today, with accommodations aft, make life much easier and the placement of accommodation near the galley resolves this problem.

29. It is interesting to note that her stack was removed for some unidentified reason during one of her winter storage periods at Collingwood Harbour. What repairs or modifications that were undertaken are not known. Was there some weakness that played a role in the presumed storm event? Captain Bud offered the following observations, August 22, 2009, in a note to me:

> Looking at the stack again and wire rigging arrangements: In Collingwood aerial view from aft, shrouds and stays appear a little slack. Could this explain the missing one [during winter lay-up] in the postcard view? Seems they had removed and replaced it with possibly a new one. Six in all: 4 shrouds and 2 stays. The two aft shrouds are leading forward and are fastened to the upper bridge deck. The forward two lead aft, and are possibly fastened to the spar deck. One stay leads forward, possibly fastened to the lower bridge deck, and the aft stay looks to be made fast to the after end bulkhead of her coal bunker.

A friend with a sound knowledge of physics, Mike Earle, completed the mathematical calculations to determine how much ice would be required to provide neutral buoyancy to a steel cylinder, similar in structure to a ship's funnel, of various dimensions. He calculated that a thickness of ice as little as two inches for a steel-wall thickness of 1/8 inch or a coating of just over five inches for a wall thickness of 3/8 inch could create neutral buoyancy on such a steel cylinder. Given the range of other circumstances that could cause a normally sinkable object to float, I believe that this possibility must at least be considered. For those readers who wish to see the detailed calculations, I invite them to contact the author at *shipwreck@eastlink.ca*, the email address for my website at *www.shipwreckwexford.ca*.

30. Efforts were made to do a detailed magnetometer survey to examine the beach and what metallic objects lay beneath the sand, to determine whether it is possible that any large metallic object remains,

buried there, to document these stories. In November 2000, Patrick Donnelly, of the Lake Huron Centre for Coastal Conservation, provided documentation to serve as a starting point for shoreline research near Naftel's Point to determine whether any wreckage remains might still be present to verify whether the vessel began to break up in this area, offshore, south of her Goderich destination. The documentation consisted of 1992 aerial photographs that had been analyzed stereoscopically, to assess starting points for magnetometer research. A walk from Black's Point to Naftel's Creek will reveal numerous cylinders of metal — flared on one end and pressed flat. Open, they might be 20–24 inches in diameter and in about 18-inch lengths. Would the inner core of the *Wexford* stack have been assembled of such pieces? The Naftel descendant who offered the original information was Keith Homan, a friend of the author.

31. For those who wish to explore the physics of flotation, water has a specific gravity (SG) or density of one gram per cubic centimetre. Anything with an SG of less than one (1) will float. Clear ice has an SG of around 0.8 to 0.9; white ice contains more air and measures around 0.6. Ice floats. Grains, including oats, barley, corn and wheat have SGs of about 0.5 to 0.8; they also float. Pine is about 0.5. Lignumvitae, the dense wood first used for lock hinges in the Erie Barge Canal, is greater than an SG of one, and sinks. The challenge is to determine how much ice, encrusted on a structure like a frigid metal smokestack, is required to neutralize the obviously enormous weight of such a structure. A physicist could calculate the requirements. The photographs of ice-shrouded vessels in the book will show you how ice can accumulate on decks and rigging. You will have to decide whether this is a harebrained theory, or whether such a phenomenon could, in fact, help to carry a normally sinkable object toward shore in the unusually heavy seas that occurred during the Great Storm event. Most of us have experienced the process of feeling heavy objects becoming much lighter when they are submerged in water. How much ice do you have to add to neutralize the buoyancy? In the relatively warm water of Lake Huron in November, how long could any ice encrustation survive? In its

unshipping, would the six metal shrouds that held the stack in place have torn loose pieces of wooden deck structure, such as the timber frame for the doors to the coal bunker, sufficient to drag this heavy metal object along as the flotsam was cast ashore?

You can decide for yourself. There has to be a reason behind the folklore about the mysterious stack found along the shore.

Another factor could well be how things move around underwater over time. In a note to the author, October 6, 2009, David Trotter offered: "One thing we all have seen is significant movement of shipwrecks and parts of ships due to extreme wave action. The *Regina*, one year, was found to have rolled significantly after one winter. I expect anything round can go some distance. We have found bottles, drums, etc, rolled up to the side of a shipwreck where they "stopped due to the ship.""

32. Telephone dialogue with the author, October 6, 2009.

33. *London Evening Free Press*, November 12, 1913, 1.

34. In dialogue with the author during the summer of 2002, as Phil was refining his search for the missing clock. Confirmed by email note, July 21, 2002.

35. The local histories for Hensall village and the census records for Hay Township do not seem to identify any medical doctor with the surname of Campbell. The records do include a Dr. Campbell who was called a veterinarian. A search of area cemetery records has not revealed the true identity and details about this coroner.

36. Normally, the cargo would have been insured separately, although I have not been able to document any amount for this trip. Insured values of cargo are listed for other vessels lost in the storm, but not for the *Wexford*.

Chapter 4: The Crew List, November 1913

1. Skip Gillham, of St. Catharines, has written hundreds of short articles on marine history that have appeared in weekly newspapers around the Great Lakes.

2. Other notes will confirm that the body of Captain Cameron was found at Kettle Point and taken to Thedford.

3. Bayfield Historical Society newsletter, September 2009, 1–2.

4. *The Saturday News*, Collingwood, November 15, 1913, 4.

5. Details provided later in the account.

6. *The Collingwood Bulletin*, November 13, 1913, 1.

7. *Globe and Mail*, November 11, 1913, 1.

8. Also see information above by Skip Gillham that suggests crew was left behind elsewhere.

9. *The Collingwood Bulletin* (November 20, 1913, 1), lists crew members Brooks, Scott, Gordon, Dodson & Peere as "found." Richard Lougheed, George and Mrs. Wilmott are simply shown as "missing."

10. Newspaper, *Collingwood Enterprise*, November 13, 1913, 1.

11. According to *The Collingwood Bulletin*, November 13, 1913, 1. No first name could be located.

12. Unsourced news report, November 12, 1913. No first name could be located. In the crew list there is still confusion about whether Rogers was in fact the Second Engineer or an Acting Second Mate in the absence of McCutcheon. I do not have an answer, but wonder if he might have been the Second Engineer. Because there was clearly a Second Mate, Rogers could also have been a second Second Engineer. There is also a possibility that Rogers could have been the missing "third passenger" said to be aboard, a sailor from another vessel returning to a port closer to home. There is no evidence to clarify any of these suppositions.

13. *The Saturday News*, Collingwood, November 15, 1913, 1.

14. *The Collingwood Bulletin*, November 13, 1913, 1.

15. *Ibid.*

16. *Ibid.* Having to cross the river by boat, or to divert and turn upriver to the highway bridge made the search more difficult to continue southward.

17. *Ibid.* Reported originally as "Orrin" in several different newspapers, but said to be "Orin" by Robert Orin Gordon of Whitby, Ontario (a descendant, a great nephew), as sent in an email note and subsequent letter to Captain Bud on June 25, 2002, and confirmed March 17, 2010.

18. *Ibid.*

19. *Collingwood Enterprise*, November 20, 1913, 3.

20. Donald McDonald is listed as a missing sailor in *The Signal* of November 13, 1913, in the lead story, "Awful Marine Disaster on the Great Lakes," along with the name of Murdoch (also Murdock) McDonald. A cousin, Roderick McDonald perished in 1916 on Lake Erie when the vessel *Merida* foundered in the so-called "Black Friday" storm. Spelling is as taken from cemetery tombstones.

It is next to impossible to sort out the MacDonald (McDonald) clans in the Goderich area. The 2009 telephone directory lists 17 "MacDonalds," one "Macdonald," two "Mcdonalds," and no less than 10 "McDonalds," not including the two restaurant listings. I have talked several times to descendants of the "old" Goderich families, but have not been able to define any clear delineation of the family lines. It is generally accepted that the "MacDonalds" are of Scottish descent, while the "McDonalds" are of Irish origin. While there are some family connections that have evolved in this community over the generations, there are clear distinctions among the clan lines, several of which were well-separated before their ancestors ever arrived in this country. There are at least two branches of the MacDonald clan that lived on the north side of the old Goderich harbour, and at least one more that lived on the south side, and yet another who worked in the Marlton Shipyards on Ship Island, in the early days when the town was located on the flats. Even descendants of the same family have mixed the spelling of the surname. I once tried to sort out the various clans — and gave up after reaching an impasse after separating out just five of the local family units connected to the waterfront. To compound the challenge, the mariners often were best known by nicknames. Simple ones like "Mac," "Reddy," "Spike," and "Skip" are easier to trace than monikers like "Johnny Buddy Anti" or "Johnny the Bud," or "Cuddy," or even "Johnnybuggerhell," the nickname for the nickname "Cutty Buddy Anti" — who was known as the "best corker (caulker) from the Marlton (ship) Yards whose services were in demand around the whole region for his skills." One "John A. MacDonald," an acquaintance, was describing for me the names for some of his own ancestors, including his grandfather, John Malcolm MacDonald, in a conversation as we prepared for events at one of the local marine heritage festivals back in 2003, and also confirmed these nicknames in recollections exchanged in August of 2009. It is also apparent that some current descendants of "McDonalds" now use the spelling "MacDonald" for their surname. Confusion abounds!

21. In a conversation with the author, August 20, 2009.

22. "Murdoch" is spelled *Murdock* on the tombstone, according to Reg Thompson, local Goderich librarian and genealogist. He stated, "I might add it is a chilling thing to look at, seven registrations in a row, all 'Sailor' and identical details about the *Wexford* and the storm, each carefully handwritten. There is not a precise death date given; it says 'Sometime between Nov 9 and Nov 11.'"

22. *The Signal*, November 20, 1913, 1.

23. *Ibid.*

24. Follow-up note to the author after a telephone discussion, April 18, 2001.

25. *The Collingwood Bulletin*, November 20, 1913, 5. The same edition reports that a "Mr. Walter Robinson, of Rydal Bank, near Bruce Mines, came to Town on Tuesday at noon, having received a message stating that the body of his cousin had been found ..." Apparently the Wilmotts had lived with Robinson for eight years at Rydal Bank. During a visit, "At the time they were speaking of the storms and Mrs. Wilmott said that she was very much frightened at them and that they always remained in the cabin." Mr. Robinson felt that they therefore had gone down with the ship and there would be very little hope of ever finding them. He might be easy to identify as he was "tattooed on different parts of the body."

This author has just completed the publication of a book called *Four Years on the Great Lakes: The Journal of Lt. David Wingfield, RN.* There is a small touch of irony in that Wilmott's father was resident at "37A Wingfield Road" in Walthamstow, London, England.

26. Boyer, Dwight, *True Tales of the Great Lakes.* Cleveland, OH: Freshwater Press Inc., 1971.

27. *The Collingwood Bulletin*, November 20, 1913, 5.

28. Reported in *The Signal*; date not shown. It has also been suggested

that Glen lived in Clinton, inland from Goderich.

29. Through a niece, Lorraine Shellenberger, in an unsolicited phone call to the author as news reports of the discovery of the wreckage made their way around the Great Lakes, July 24, 2001.
30. *The Saturday News*, Collingwood, November 15, 1913, 4.
31. *Ibid.*
32. *The Collingwood Bulletin*, November 20, 1913, 1.
33. News clipping; undated, unsourced.
34. *Ibid.*
35. *Detroit Free Press*, November 15, 1.
36. *Ibid.*
37. *Collingwood Enterprise*, November 20, 1913, 1.
38. Conversation with Walter McIlwain, July 10, 2006.
39. Dialogue with the author, July 23, 2009.
40. There are numerous reports and much folklore suggesting rewards in the amounts from $10 to $50. This amount of $25 seems to represent the accurate figure.

Chapter 5: A Memorial, November 16, 1913

1. *The Signal*, November 20, 1913, 1.
2. *Ibid.*, December 4, 1913, 8.
3. *Ibid.*
4. *Ibid.*
5. *The Signal*, November 27, 1913, 8.

Chapter 6: Weather Forecasting in 1913: Descriptions of the Storm

1. Warnings of an impending storm from the northwest.
2. William Ratigan, *Great Lakes Ship Wrecks and Survivals* (Grand Rapids, MI: Wm. B. Freedmans Publishing Company, 1960, revised 1977, 125–26). Reprinted 1989.
3. *Detroit Free Press*, November 10, 1913, 1.
4. This version is from the 1865 translation by Alexander Pope, Volume II, 69.

5. The 1913 *Annual Report* is cited numerous times in this book. I have a photocopy of the relevant portions of the document, the origins of which are unclear. (It was passed along, third-hand, from the Kingston Maritime Museum or the National Archives as it was called then.) However, it is noteworthy that the organization is American, in place for United States vessels and crew. The parallel organizations in Canada, specifically the Canadian Mercantile Marine Association and the Dominion Marine Association did not seem to be so highly organized and played a lesser role in the aftermath of the storm. They did not appear so prominently in the news reports following November 9, 1913, nor did they seem to play a major role in any of the inquests. They did, however, play a role in fundraising to support the widows and orphans of drowned sailors from Canadian vessels. Some data published by the Lake Carriers' Association may be suspect for the non-member, Canadian vessels listed in their reports. For example, I wonder if the basis for the persistent accounts of the *Wexford* carrying steel rails — when it is clear that she carried 96,000 bushels of grain — is from the Table of Losses published in 1914, when the intended vessel was actually the *Leafield*, similar in appearance, and also British-built, but which sank in Lake Superior in the same storm.

6. *Annual Report*, 1913, by the Lake Carriers' Association, 151.

7. Cited in an article called "Storms," circulated widely by email to the marine community by Robert B. Townsend, Carrying Place, Ontario, September 16, 2002, after the *Wexford* was found.

8. *Huron Historical Notes*, 1988, Vol. 24, 12–14.

9. *Hay Township Highlights*, 256.

10. Anna G. Young, *Off Watch: Today and Yesterday on the Great Lakes* (Toronto, ON: The Ryerson Press, 1957) 151–52.

11. For the full text, visit the website, *www.crh.noaa.gov/dtx/stm_1913.php*, accessed August 2009.

12. Note to the author, September 30, 2009.

13. The term "three sisters" is used to describe an event during a storm where three unusually large waves appear in succession, the second and third often larger and more devastating in impact than the first.

14. Note to the author, September 30, 2009.

15. Top-hamper is additional weight above the centre of gravity, which "hampers" balance.

16. The account can be found at *www.wmhs.org/html/storm.html*, as of August 2009.

17. The *Regina* was actually upbound.

18. *Annual Report*, 1913, Lake Carriers' Association, excerpts from pages 151–53.

19. As published in the electronic version on *www.sailnet.com*, my copy taken October 21, 2000.

20. Just how tall the waves could actually become on Lake Huron has been discussed elsewhere in this text.

21. *Annual Report*, 1913, Lake Carriers' Association, 151.

Chapter 7: The Carnage of the Storm

1. Dwight Boyer, *True Tales of the Great Lakes* (Cleveland, OH: Freshwater Press Inc., 1971), 282–83. Actually, the body of Donald McDonald was not recovered along with that of his cousin, Murdoch, at the Turnbull farm.

2. *The Collingwood Bulletin*, November 13, 1913, 1.

3. *The Port Huron Times-Herald*, Wednesday November 12, 1913, 1.

4. The spelling "Knyvet" is used in most news reports; the spelling "Knevitt" is shown in the inquest transcript on page 1.

5. *The Port Huron Times-Herald*, November 15, 1913, 3, reported:

> Sarnia, Ont., November 14. Three Sarnia Indians are on the list of drowned from the steamer *McGean*. The bodies of the three sailors were found washed ashore five miles below Goderich. They were lashed to a life raft lettered the steamer *John A. McGean*. The three bodies are those of George Smith, John Owen, and Thos. Stone. Capt. C[hauncey] R. Ney, in command of the *McGean*, resides some twelve miles below Sarnia at Sombra village. It is believed that he, too, has perished. Undertakers

Phippen and Simpson of this town have left for Goderich
to take charge of the bodies of the three Sarnia Natives.

6. According to George Parsons, well-known Goderich resident, son
of "G.L.," and the last remaining member of the Parsons family in
Goderich. Three generations of the Parsons lived in a large house
at the corner of West and Wellington streets, just above the harbour.
The first was the family of Captain James G. Parsons, father of the
"G.L." Parsons, the superintendent at the Goderich Elevators during
the storm. Benjamin Parsons, the great uncle of Captain James, was
the first mayor of Goderich in 1850. Details are reported in an article
in the *Huron Historical Notes*, 2001, Vol. 37, 14,15.
7. Goderich Inquest transcript, 2.

Chapter 8: The Aftermath: Consequences Abound

1. *The Signal*, November 20, 1913, 1.
2. First reported in *The Collingwood Bulletin*, November 20, 1913, 4.
3. *Annual Report* 1913, Lake Carriers' Association, 29.
4. *The Signal*, November 20, 1913, 2, under headline "Whitney to Blame."
5. *Ibid.*
6. The Bruce Peninsula, culminating essentially at Tobermory.
7. As noted elsewhere, several newspaper reports indicated that the
bodies were being pilfered by scavengers who were alleged to be
picking the pockets of the dead.
8. *Annual Report*, 1913, Lake Carriers' Association, excerpts from pages
28–30.
9. Official Report of the Debates of the House of Commons, Third
Session, Twelfth Parliament, Vol. 113, January 23, 1914, 136.
10. *Ibid.*, 136–37.
11. *Ibid.*, 136–38.
12. *The Star*, November 27, 1913, 1.
13. A report in the *Detroit Free Press*, November 1, 1906, page number
not given, shows that the importance of wireless was beginning to be
recognized well before the year of the Great Storm:

Are Studying Wireless: Chicago Nautical School — Has
One Woman Enrolled

Chicago, October 31 — Wireless telegraphy will this
winter form one of the courses taught at the nautical
school conducted by Lieut. W.J. Wilson in the Masonic
temple. At the first session last night, telegrams were sent
from one room to another by means of a small machine,
and the would-be captains were set at work figuring out
the intricacies of the Morse telegraph code. The school
now has forty-six students enrolled. One woman has
joined the class and several more will enter later.

Chapter 9: The Goderich Inquest

1. Peter Sturdy, *The Hole in the Wall: An Informal History of the Goderich Harbour and Other Things*, Goderich, ON: Dancam Press, 2003, 155.
2. Inquest transcript, 6.
3. Captain Reginald Bassett's testimony is found on pages 7–13 of transcript.
4. *Ibid.*
5. In reality, newspaper records show that watches stopped anywhere from around midnight on November 9 to near 2:00 a.m. *The Collingwood Bulletin*, for example, November 20, page 7, reports that watches stopped, as found on various bodies at 11:53, 1:15, 1:23, and 1:30 a.m. This information may verify the period during which the storm reached its greatest intensity.
6. Bassett's testimony.
7. Inquest transcript, 14–15.
8. *Ibid.*
9. Wind reports were given in *The Signal*, November 13, as offered by Robinson in the actual transcript (pages 16–22), for all quotations cited below. In summary, for ease in tracking the storm intensity: Winds abated overnight November 8 to become about 10 miles per hour at 9:00 a.m. November 9; 20 miles per hour at 2:00 p.m.; 40 miles per hour by 4:00 p.m.; and 60 miles per hour by 3:00 a.m., now the early morning of the November 10. Some casual reports suggest

that the wind was severe in Goderich by the time church started on Sunday morning. In his recollections about the role of his father, Lionel G. Parsons, the superintendent of the Goderich Elevator Company, son George reports two things that contradict the starting time for higher winds. He recalls that "Dad heard the *Wexford*'s distress whistle and bolted from the church … [he] tied down the steam whistle at the elevator, hoping the ship would 'home in' on the sound." He suggested: "While the gale force winds from the west would bring the *Wexford*'s whistle sounds ashore, they would prevent the elevator whistle reaching the *Wexford*, combined with the muffling effect of the blinding snow storm." Parsons also said, "My mother recalls that the winds were so strong from the West that on the way up Nelson Street to the church, the pram she was pushing was literally wrestled out of her hands and pushed ahead of her up the hill." Quotations from the *Huron Historical Notes*, Vol. 37, 2001, 14.

10. All of Robinson's testimony is found on pages 16–22 in the transcript.
11. *Ibid.*
12. Inquest transcript, 128–31.
13. In the transcript, the dialogue indicates that Captain Steven said that "she was going up" when he sighted her. That is surely an error in the record. He later confirmed that she was, in fact, headed down, and suggested that the *Wexford* should have reached Goderich Harbour by "about half past two in the afternoon." See page 135 of the transcript.
14. Inquest transcript, 139.
15. *Ibid.*, 151–56.
16. *Ibid.*, 159.
17. Captain Frank Scott was the brother of James A. Scott, the chief engineer on the *Wexford*.
18. *The Collingwood Bulletin*, November 20, 1913, 1.
19. Yet another wild estimate based on incomplete examination of the records!
20. The infamous "sucker hole," as mentioned in the prologue.
21. This vessel was surely the steamer *McKee*, under command of Captain Reginald Bassett Jr., who was called to testify at the hearing.

Actually, he stated that he was four or five miles offshore, not "several hours," and did not come into Goderich because he could not see the land. He turned and proceeded elsewhere. He could not make Sand Beach (now Harbor Beach) either, and had to seek refuge in the St. Clair River at Sarnia.

22. In *Lighthouse: Journal of the Canadian Hydrographic Association*, Edition 62, Fall/Winter 2002, 2.

23. I once saw a placemat illustrating these plans, apparently used at a banquet held at the local Sunset Hotel to host politicians and military officials visiting Goderich in the very early 1900s, as Goderich, particularly the Ridgewood Park site north of the Maitland River valley, was being touted as the best spot in Ontario to establish a military camp. The "new harbour plan" was offered as an additional incentive that might entice a naval installation in this same location.

24. Called an island in the days before the river was diverted to make the new harbour opening, when it was part of the "12-acre beach" adjacent to the southerly extension of Colborne Township on the north side of the river.

25. Original maps of the Maitland River entrance at Lake Huron show the presence of shallows and an offshore island that literature of the day would suggest was inconstant. The area was subject to many storm-induced changes. As soon as the Canada Company piers were constructed, *circa* 1828–30, it is clear that the shoreline began to change as the natural littoral drift of sand and silt, with the current running from north to south, was blocked. The shoreline to the north began to build up. Maps produced in the 1860s, when changes to the outer piers were being contemplated, show accretion to the shoreline was significant. The same phenomenon continued after the construction of the new piers in the 1870 period. Dredging challenges continued. Following the creation of the new outer harbour area in the late 1980s, the construction of the long stone wall has intensified the siltation problem. Officials at the Maitland Valley Conservation Authority would tell you that the sand starvation for the shoreline south of Goderich — all the way to Kettle Point — is now a significant problem, exacerbated by the stone wall that blocks the natural movement

of shoreline beach-building materials. The resultant problems, and the almost two century long controversy about it, continue. On the positive side, the need for dredging within the area protected by the outer breakwaters seems to have been reduced.

26. *The Goderich Signal*, August 30, 1928, 2, 7.

27. Bill Forrest was the "brawn" and Bill Bermingham was the "brains" behind a small dredging and marine construction company based out of Goderich Harbour for several decades after the beginning of the last century. They were successful in building the breakwaters after failed attempts by another out-of-town contractor. Bermingham went on to found Bermingham Construction, a major marine works contracting company in the Hamilton, Ontario, area, still in operation more than a hundred years later. Always innovative, and shifting well beyond marine works, Bermingham Construction brought the first diesel impact hammer to North America in the early 1950s and started developing their own line of foundation specialty equipment in the late 1960s. The Berminghammer trade name has become synonymous with leading-edge technology around the world.

"Big" Bill Forrest remained a resident on Ship Island, in the back end of Goderich Harbour, until he was booted out after a legal encounter with the province of Ontario, losing a land claim action that, according to legal precedent today, he would have won.

Chapter 10: Searching for the *Wexford*

1. Reported in the *Great Lakes Weekly*, August 29, 1918, and also recorded in *Ship Information and Data Record 87342* at the Milwaukee Public Library. The story also figured prominently in the pages of the local media, where the captain of the *Mariska* insisted that he passed within 20 feet of two spars, both at the approximate spacing of the *Wexford*. "Both of these were seen distinctly in the fall of the water between seas, one shorter than the other with the after spar slightly bent … this can be none other than the *Wexford*." The clipping in my file has neither date nor source information.

2. The closest shoal would be off Wright's Point, a few miles north of Goderich at Point Farms Provincial Park.

3. The claims by Murphy are documented in the final archaeological survey report submitted by Bob Carey to the Ontario Ministry of Culture and Recreation in 2003. Murphy's position is also summarized in notes written under date of May 31, 2001, posted and quoted on public message boards.

4. A partial text of the April 10, 1975, *The Goderich Signal-Star* story follows:

> The wreck of the *Wexford*, one of the eight ships lost in the Great Storm of November 9, 1913, has been located by Captain Robert Wilson of Sarnia and William Humphries of Mooretown. The location of the ship just north of Goderich Harbor was the culmination of three years of research by Wilson and Humphries which included numerous personal contacts, letters and telephone calls. They have received permission from the federal government under Section X of the Canada Shipping Act and hope to make their first dive as soon as the ice clears which Mr. Humphries optimistically suggested could be the middle of April.
>
> The team of divers on the salvage project are: Lawrence Brander, Mike Hughes, Jim MacDonald, and William Humphries, under the direction of Captain Robert Wilson. Once the boat has been marked they hope to begin the salvage operation in May. Artifacts from the ship will be going to the Moore Township Museum, the Huron County Pioneer Museum in Goderich and the Knox Presbyterian Church in Goderich.
>
> The *Wexford* has been resting on the bottom of Lake Huron for almost sixty-two years, and the diving team is hopeful that artifacts from the wreck will be on display in area museums early this summer.

5. Information from several conversations with the author while Jim

Bridle was the proprietor of a harbourfront restaurant in Goderich in the early 2000s.

6. At this time the Huron County Museum does hold at least three artifacts from the *Wexford*: a wine bottle, decanted; a crockery pot; and a piece of porcelain china. These items were illegally removed from the wreck site in the year 2000 and taken into the custody of Ontario marine archaeologist Peter Englebert while their removal was investigated. No charges were ever laid and the items were handed over to the museum for long-term safekeeping.

7. Now called Lake Valley Grove.

8. Also spelled "Hillsborough."

9. Undated letter, postmarked August 19, 2002.

10. Verbal report to the author, 2001.

Chapter 11: The Wreck Today

1. Author's Note: I wrote the following account shortly after my first trip to the *Wexford* wreck site on the survey tug *Danel Mac*. It was a visit seemingly pervaded by elements of the supernatural.

2. This term refers to the repetitive pattern of sweeping back and forth in successive rows across the surface of the water, using a GPS as a guide, in the same pattern as one would follow while cutting a lawn, to ensure that no gaps were left in the lake bottom surveyed.

3. Yes, there was only one! He was not replaced after his retirement in 2003 for a long period. Ontario's last marine archeologist was Erika Laanela. She was hired three years after Englebert left, stayed for two years, and then left to pursue further academic studies. Ontario now operates with some kind of regulation that seems to require that you have to be a "commercial" diver to dive for work in the province. There is no category for scientific diving, as there is at the federal level. Presently there is a marine heritage advisor in Ontario. There has been no active dialogue between that person and the diving community and groups like SOS, to my knowledge at this time (summer 2009). The Ministry of Culture research tug, the *Blue Fin*, still sits, almost derelict, on the hard at Maitland Valley Marina, Goderich, where she was last used to conduct initial underwater survey work

to search for the *Carruthers* in the deep water off Point Clark, north of Goderich, in 2002–03.

On a positive and perhaps helpful note, the Ministry of Culture has recently announced that Dr. Simon Q. Spooner has joined the Culture Services Unit, Programs and Services Branch, as marine heritage advisor. Simon, who has extensive field experience, holds a Ph.D. in maritime archaeology from the University of Bristol. Recently, he has been advising the governments of France and the Dominican Republic on the protection of historic shipwrecks. Prior to becoming involved in archaeology he worked in London (UK) as a chartered surveyor. He is co-founder and president of the Anglo-Danish Maritime Archaeological Team (ADMAT), a non-profit organization (based in Surrey, England and Monte Cristi, Dominican Republic) working on the investigation and preservation of historic shipwrecks in the Caribbean. He is also the president of ADMAT-FRANCE and vice-president of ADMAT USA. He holds a B.Sc. and is a member of the Royal Institution of Chartered Surveyors, as well as The Institute of Field Archaeologists. Dr. Spooner is also a member of the Nautical Archaeological Society. Perhaps Dr. Spooner will see fit to initiate further reviews of the Ontario Heritage Act. I will make it a point to draw the plunder of the *Wexford* shipwreck to his attention.

4. Other reports indicate that at least one blade is missing.
5. Ron Beaupre, in a telephone conversation with the author, October 5, 2009.
6. Dan Thomas of Stratford, Ontario, is certified by the National Association of Underwater Instructors (NAUI) as a Master Diver and has a strong interest in military and marine history. He has many childhood memories from his hometown of Goderich, of being in Lake Huron or the Maitland River with mask, fins, and snorkel, trying to determine what might be on the edge of visibility. He helped with the official *Wexford* survey, making meticulous notes and recording his observations in a number of detailed sketches.
7. See final paragraphs of About the Author section at the end of the book.
8. According to Peter Englebert, it was not likely that Cameron could have made his way to the stern belowdecks. By this time it would have

been pitch-black below, and passage to the stern was interrupted by the engine room, immediately aft of midships. If it were possible to get to either end of the ship, it would not have been easy, but might have been possible if the "tween" deck, the space between the main and spar decks, had been open. Email note from Englebert, April 18, 2001.

9. Such a plate might normally have been a form of builder's plate. Sometimes a special engine plate was placed in a conspicuous location. No one has yet offered a definitive answer to the question of what this bronze plate represents. Sketches made during the formal deck survey indicate that it is essentially a compass rose, about 13½ by 15 inches overall, its design in bronze having been completed with an inner and outer circle of diamonds, set in the cardinal and intermediate locations as on the points of a compass. It may have served as some reference for taking bearings while standing on deck, away from a ship's compass.

10. The Paul Schaus observations, sent for publication, were reported to me and to Bob Carey in a series of email correspondence to us, dated from October 15, 2000. These observations are also included in the final survey report, 2003, as submitted by Bob Carey.

11. *Ibid.*

12. Reference was made earlier to the anchor windlass probably being inoperable. It may have been impossible to reach the windlass area. If Cameron had any power or steerage he may have tried to beach her. In any attempt to approach the shore, such as the rocky shore at Black's Point which was strewn with large boulders, she could have incurred additional damage that indeed led to her foundering.

13. Email note from Paul Schaus to the author, October 15, 2000, as before.

14. *Ibid.*

Chapter 12: The Plunder of the *Wexford*

1. See discussion of legislation regarding underwater heritage sites and clarification of the position of SOS in Appendix 3.

2. This is Ian MacAdam of MacDonald Marine, Goderich Harbour, operator of the tug *Dover* that has run charters to the dive site and has assisted the local SOS and the local Marine Heritage Committee

with placement of marker buoys and other tasks related to minor wrecks along the Huron shore.

3. The *Hurd* was the Canadian Coast Guard cutter stationed at Goderich at the time.

4. A letter sent to the minister of culture for the province of Ontario. See Appendix B.

5. The *Atlantic* was an important shipwreck discovered in Lake Erie in 1948. Its ownership was disputed by Mike Fletcher, a diver from Port Dover who found her, and a California diving company that subsequently removed many artifacts from her. After prolonged court cases in both countries, her ownership has been vested in the province of Ontario, which continues, so far unsuccessfully, to retrieve several hundred artifacts illegally removed by the American firm.

6. These two deep-water wrecks (the *Hamilton* and the *Scourge*) on Lake Ontario, lost in a sudden squall in a battle during the War of 1812, are now legislated to be off limits to recreational divers. They are accessible only to licensed archaeologists, with special permits, and can be found in nearly 300 feet of water, 1,500 feet apart, a few miles offshore from St. Catharines, on the floor of Lake Ontario.

7. The following statement about ocean acidification was released by Randy Repass, Chairman, West Marine, U.S.A., in an email to all customers, asking for their direct political intervention, July 28, 2009:

> Ocean Acidification is primarily caused by the burning of fossil fuels. When carbon dioxide in the atmosphere ends up in the ocean it changes the pH, making the sea acidic and less hospitable to life. Over time, CO^2 reduces calcium carbonate, which prevents creatures from forming shells and building reefs. In fact, existing shells will start to dissolve. Oysters and mussels will not be able to build shells. Crabs and lobsters? Your great-grandchildren may wonder what they tasted like. Carbon dioxide concentrated in the oceans is making seawater acidic.
>
> Many of the zooplankton, small animals at the base of the food web, have skeletons that won't form in these

conditions, and sea life further up the food chain — fish, mammals and seabirds that rely on zooplankton for food will also perish. No food — no life. One billion people rely on seafood for their primary source of protein. Many scientific reports document that worldwide, humans are already consuming more food than is being produced. The implications are obvious. The issue of ocean acidification is causing irreversible loss to species and habitats, and acidification trends are happening up to ten times faster than projected. We want you to know what this means, how it affects all of us, and what we can do about it. Today, the atmospheric concentration of CO_2 is about 387 parts per million (ppm) and increasing at 2 ppm per year.

If left unaddressed, by 2040 it is projected to be over 450 ppm, and marine scientists believe the collapse of many ocean ecosystems will be irreversible. Acidification has other physiological effects on marine life as well, including changes in reproduction, growth rates, and even respiration in fish. Tropical and coldwater corals are among the oldest and largest living structures on earth; the richest in terms of biodiversity, they provide spawning areas, nursery habitat and feeding grounds for a quarter of all species in the sea. Coral reefs are at risk! As CO_2 concentrations increase, corals, shellfish and other species that make shells will not be able to build their skeletons and will likely become extinct.

I do not have current acid levels for the Great Lakes, but the same rationale seems to be applicable. Lake water acidification is a well-documented problem and concern. There are numerous studies; considerable debate about the topic continues.

Epilogue: Remembering the *Wexford*: November 11, 2000

1. In conversation with the author, September 14, 2009.

Appendix A: "Discovery of the *Wexford*" by David Bannister

1. In the tween deck space? On the builders' plan, the No.1 cargo hold is separated by a watertight bulkhead aft of the chain locker and the end of the space below crew accommodation. There should also be a watertight bulkhead ahead of this space, creating the forepeak tank, which normally would carry water ballast. The No. 2 cargo hold shows a watertight bulkhead between No. 1 and No. 2, with an after bulkhead separating this space from the coal bunker. The No. 3 hold is separated from the engine room by a bulkhead. An aft bulkhead sets off the crew space and galley above and aft from the after-peak tank. The bunker space aft of No. 2 cargo hold may have been used as cargo space on the Great Lakes, a bulkhead perhaps being removed.

Appendix C: Legislation Affecting Marine Archaeological Sites

1. *Changes to the Ontario Heritage Act: Discussion Guide*, Ontario Ministry of Culture, December 2002.
2. Ontario Heritage Act, R.S.O. 1990, Chapter O.18.
3. Note to Paul Carroll, July 27, 2009.

BIBLIOGRAPHY

Books

Andra-Warner, Elle. *Wreck of the Edmund Fitzgerald: The Legendary Great Lakes Disaster.* Part of the Amazing Stories series. Canmore, AB: Altitude Publishing Canada Ltd., 2006.

Bamford, Don. *Freshwater Heritage: A History of Sail on the Great Lakes, 1670–1918.* Toronto: Natural Heritage Books–Dundurn Press, 2007.

Barry, James P., *Wrecks and Rescues of the Great Lakes.* Holt, MI: Thunder Bay Press, 1994.

Bowen, Dana Thomas. *Lore of the Lakes.* Daytona Beach, FL: Dana Thomas Bowen, Publisher, 1940.

_____. *Shipwrecks of the Lakes.* Daytona Beach, FL: Dana Thomas Bowen, Publisher, as reprinted by Freshwater Press Inc., Cleveland, Ohio, 1995.

Bowyer, Dwight. *True Tales of the Great Lakes.* Cleveland, OH: Freshwater Press Inc., 1971.

Brown, David G. *White Hurricane: A Great Lakes Gale and Americas Deadliest Marine Disaster.* New York: Barnes & Noble Inc., by arrangement with the McGraw Hill Companies, 2007.

Carey, Bob. *Archaeological Site Survey for the* Wexford. St. Thomas, ON: Bob Carey, self-published, 2003.

Carroll, Paul, ed. *Huron Historical Notes,* Vol. 37. Goderich, ON: Huron County Historical Society, 2001.

_____, ed. *Huron Historical Notes,* Vol. 38. Goderich, ON: Huron County Historical Society, 2002.

Donahue, James L. *Steaming Through Smoke and Fire: True Stories of Shipwreck and Disaster on the Great Lakes.* Sandusky, MI: The Historical Society of Michigan, 1990.

Gibb, Alice, ed. *Hay Township Highlights: 150 Years of Diversified Progress.* Zurich, ON: Hay Township Book Committee, printed by *The Aylmer Express,* 1996.

Hemming, Robert J. *Ships Gone Missing: The Great Lakes Strom of 1913.* Chicago: Contemporary Books Inc., 1992.

Kinder, Gary. *Ship of Gold in the Deep Blue Sea.* New York: The Atlantic Monthly Press, 1998.

Kohl, Cris. *Shipwreck Tales of the Great Lakes.* (See *Dive Ontario Two* within.) West Chicago: Seawolf Communications, Inc., 2004.

_____. *The Great Lakes Diving Guide.* West Chicago: Seawolf Communications, Inc., 1998.

_____. *The 100 Best Great Lakes Shipwrecks: Volume 1.* West Chicago: Seawolf Communications, Inc., 1998.

Landon, Fred. *The American Lakes Series: Lake Huron.* Indianapolis and New York: The Bobbs-Merrill Company, 1944.

Lundbladh, Janne, ed. *The Lore of Ships.* Gothenburg, Sweden: A.B. Nordbok, 1975.

Oleszewski, Wes. *True Tales of Ghosts and Gales: Mysterious Great Lakes Shipwrecks.* Gwinn, MI: Avery Color Studios Inc., 2003.

Paulsen, Gary. *Caught by the Sea: My Life on Boats.* New York: Delacorte Press, 2001.

Prothero, Frank and Nancy. *Tales of the North Shore.* Port Stanley, ON: Nan-Sea Publications, 1987.

Ratigan, William. *Great Lakes Ship Wrecks and Survivals.* Grand Rapids, MI: Wm. B. Freedmans Publishing Company, 1960, revised 1977; reprinted 1989.

Salen, Rick. *The Tobermory Shipwrecks.* Owen Sound, ON: The Mariner Chart Shop, Tobermory, 1975.

Scott, James. *The Settlement of Huron County.* Toronto: The Ryerson Press, 1966.

Shelton, Napier. *Huron: The Seasons of a Great Lake.* Detroit, MI: Wayne State University Press, 1999.

Smith, J.W. "Blue Peter" and T.S. Holden. *Where Ships are Born: Sunderland 1346–1946: A History of Shipbuilding on the River Wear.* Sunderland, UK: Thomas Reed and Company Limited, 1953.

Stonehouse, Frederick. *A Short Guide to the Shipwrecks of Thunder Bay.* Alpena, MI: B&L Watery World, 1986.

Sturdy, Peter. *The Hole in the Wall: An Informal History of the Goderich Harbour and Other Things.* Goderich, ON: Dancam Press, 2003.

Volgenau, Gerry. *Shipwreck Hunter: Deep, Dark and Deadly in the Great Lakes.* Ann Arbor, MI: Ann Arbor Media Group, 2007.

Wachter, Mike and Georgann. *Erie Wrecks West.* Avon Lake, OH: Corporate Impact, 2001; reprinted 2006 and 2009.

Wachter, Mike and Georgann. *Erie Wrecks East.* Avon Lake, OH: Corporate Impact, 2003; reprinted 2007.

Wachter, Mike and Georgann. *Erie Wrecks and Lights.* Avon Lake, OH: Corporate Impact, 2007.

Wallace, Dorothy, et al. *Memories of Goderich: The Prettiest Town in Canada.* Goderich, ON: The Town of Goderich, 1977.

Young, Anna G. *Off Watch: Today and Yesterday on the Great Lakes.* Toronto: The Ryerson Press, 1957.

Videography and Electronic Media

Edmund Fitzgerald: Interactive Explorer, The. Negaunee, MI: CD by International Software Engineering, 1999.

Mixter, Ric. *Final Run: Storms of the Century.* Saginaw, MI: Airworthy Productions, 2003.

_____. *Great Lakes in Depth: Wexford. McGreevy Show 26*, MMI Airworthy Productions, 2001.

_____. *Lake Fury. Storms of the Century.* Saginaw, MI: Airworthy Productions, 2002.

Partners in Motion. *Disasters of the Century, Episode 16: Eye of the Storm.* History Television, 2002.

Robinson, Captain C. "Bud." *Ships On Canvas: marineimages.50megs.com.*

Spears, Mike. *What's Going to Happen to Baby Jane?* A 22-minute training video circulated by Save Ontario Shipwrecks: Mike Spears Films, 2000.

Stayer, Jim and Pat. *Wexford: Victim of the Great Storm of 1913.* Lexington, MI: Out of the Blue Productions. 2001.

Trotter, David L., *Collision! Calling All Vessels!* Canton, MI: Undersea Research Associates, 2000.

TV Ontario. *Discovery of the Wexford.* Toronto: TV Ontario Studio 2, January 30, 2001.

Wachter, Mike. *Diving the Wexford.* Avon Lake, OH: Corporate Impact, 2001.

Marine Heritage Websites

Bowling Green State University: Historical Collections of the Great Lakes: *www.bgsu.edu/colleges/library/cac/page39984.html.*

Brendon Baillod: *www.ship-wrecks.net/shipwreck/index.jsp.*

Huron County Museum and Historic Gaol. Virtual Museum website: *www. virtualmuseum.ca.* This Community Memories exhibit combines text, photographs, and audio records of artifacts recovered after the storm, as well as other marine-related items and models to tell the story of the Great Storm of 1913.

Lewis, Walter, Maritime History of the Great Lakes: *www.maritimehistoryofthegreatlakes.ca.*

Save Ontario Shipwrecks: *www.saveontarioshipwrecks.on.ca.*

Swayze, David. David Swayze Shipwreck Data Base: *www.greatlakeshistory.homestead.com/home.html.*

Wachter, Mike and Georgann: *www.eriewrecks.com.*

Wisconsin Marine Historical Society: *www.wmhs.org/html/links.html.*

INDEX

Agreement and Account of
  Crew, 64, 65, 105, 282
All Saints Cemetery
  (Collingwood), 113
All Saints Church
  (Collingwood), 110
Allin, Jeremy, 24
Alpena, Michigan, 55, 72, 86,
  104, 146
Alpena Public Library, 24
Amherstburg, Ontario, 263
Anderson, Debra, 24
Andrews, George, 189
Andrews, Robert, 189
Argentina, 61, 281
Arklow, Ireland, 60
Ashtabula, Ohio, 86
Askew, Peter, 226
Association of Great Lakes
  History, 232
Atfield, Larry, 196
Azores, 65, 66, 105

Bailey, Samuel J., 108
Baillod, Brendon, 25, 262
Bamford, Brent, 24, 46–51,
  209, 214, 215, 221, 230,
  247, 278
Bamford, Don, 27, 29, 324
Bannister, David, 26, 243, 307
Barlow, Audrey and Bill, 25
Bassett, Captain Reginald,
  179, 180, 182, 183, 298
Bassett, Captain (and
  managing director)
  William J., 57, 63–67,
  70, 78, 86, 90, 94, 97,
  100, 104, 114, 155, 163,
  173, 182, 227, 277, 297
Bayfield, Ontario, 49, 91, 93,
  98, 100, 107, 109, 155,

160, 162, 163, 201, 204,
  215, 228, 230, 245, 247,
  263, 264, 266
Bayfield Archives, 107
Bayfield Historical Society,
  28, 107
Beaupre, Ron, 24
Begarnie, Les, 27, 205
Belle Isle, Detroit, 232
Bentley, H.G., 64
Bermingham, Bill "Spike,"
  199, 200, 300
Bermingham Construction
  Company, 200, 300
Black's Point, 40, 89, 92, 95,
  97, 162, 202, 205, 206,
  209, 212, 286, 288, 304
Black's Point Road, 17, 114
Blackman, Albert E.J., 103,
  104
Blake, Ontario, 99, 107
Blake Inquest, 99, 107, 159,
  176
Bluewater Beach (Lake
  Huron), 264
Bone Yard (Goderich
  Harbour), 18, 264
Borden, Honourable Robert
  Laird, 17
Boston, Massachusetts, 98
Bowen, C.E., 170
Bowling Green, Ohio, 89, 92,
  283, 312
Bowling Green State
  University, 89, 92, 156,
  161, 283
Boyer, Dwight, 112, 153
Brander, Lawrence, 27, 205,
  301
Breede, Claus, 233, 253
Bridle, Jim, 205, 302

Britannia Road (Goderich),
  194
British Admiralty, 268
British Board of Trade, 63
Broad, Marlo, 24
Brophey Bros. Funeral
  Home (Goderich), 119,
  155, 156, 204, 240
Brown, David G., 276
Bruce County Museum
  and Cultural Centre
  (Southampton), 233,
  263
Bruce, County of, 114, 233
Bruce Mines, Ontario, 292
Bruce Peninsula, 167, 296
Buffalo and Lake Huron
  Railway, 197

Cameron, Captain and
  Master Mariner Alex
  Campbell, 73, 107
Cameron, Captain Frank
  Bruce, 73, 107, 108
Camp Petawawa, 194
Campbell, Dr. A.B., 99, 107,
  113, 159, 289
Campbell, Mr. ___, 185
Canada Company, 197, 198,
  262, 299
  Huron Tract, 197, 262
Canada Shipping Act, 204,
  301
Canadian Coast Guard, 19,
  34, 35, 125, 131, 305
Canadian Hydrographic
  Services, 43, 299
Canadian Mercantile Marine
  Association, 166, 177,
  294
Cape Hurd, 134

Carey, Barb, 48
Carey, Bob, 13, 17, 24, 27, 45–51, 111, 202, 207, 209, 214, 217, 221, 227, 230, 231, 232, 235, 246, 247, 277, 278, 301, 304
Carmichael, W.J., 282
Carrying Place, Ontario, 294
Carver, Alf, 114
Chalmers, Donald "Don," 26, 40, 46–48, 50, 51, 209, 211, 221, 226, 227, 232, 246, 248, 261, 278
Chicago, Illinois, 132, 157, 297
Chisholm, Clark, 99
Clarey, Jim, 27
Clark, ___ (coroner), 77
Clary, J., 208
Clerke, Dr. H.S., 100
Cleve, Paul, 162
Cleveland, Ohio, 131, 132, 137, 157, 167, 275
Cleveland Steamship Co., 157
Cleveland Viaduct, 137
Cobourg, Ontario, 74
Cobourg Street, Goderich, 237
Colborne, S., 64
Colborne Township (Huron County), 133, 299
Collingwood, Ontario, 66, 67, 70–73, 90, 99, 100, 107–10, 112–14, 128, 137, 155, 180, 181, 287
Collingwood Harbour, 28, 67, 68, 88, 127, 181, 287
Collingwood Museum, 13, 24, 49
Collingwood Opera House, 167
Collingwood Shipbuilders (hockey), 74
Collingwood Shipbuilding & Engine Company Limited, 13, 57, 59, 68, 69
Collingwood Shipbuilding Yards, 28, 67, 68, 72, 146
Coppermine, Ontario, 137
Cork, Ireland, 60

Corunna Steamship Company (Fort William), 55
Courtney, Robert, 25
Craigie Cottages (Goderich), 193
Cromwell, Oliver, 60
Crosby Steam Gage and Valve Company, 98
Cumming, Tim, 45, 278
Cunha, Walter, 226
Cussler, Dr. Clive, 21, 275
Cut Line Road, 98, 162

Davis, Thomas, 159
Dawson Museum (Detroit), 232
De Tour (also Detour), Michigan, 79, 85, 179
De Tour Passage, 85, 149
Deal, William, 62, 100, 281
Deedler, William R., 25, 140
Deep 3 Scuba (London), 27
Delve, Owen, 25
Department of Public Works (DPW), 199
Detroit, Michigan, 46, 108, 113, 132, 141, 157, 266
Detroit Marine Historical Society, 26
Detroit River, 132
Doherty, Ann, 241
Doherty, John, 241
Dominion Marine Association, 134, 166, 167, 173, 294
Donnelly, Patrick, 286, 288
Doolin, Ralph, 151
Doxford & Sons Company, see also William Doxford & Sons Shipyards, 45, 53, 57, 58, 61, 67, 244, 278
Dubuisson, Monsieur, 62
Duck Island, 73
Duluth (Minnesota), 139
Dunkirk, Dunquerque (France), 29, 57, 62, 64, 65, 105, 282
Durand, Joe, 230, 266

Earle, Mike, 28, 287

Ebel, Captain Harold, 266
Ecorse, Michigan, 55
Edwards, Clayton, 237
Englebert, Peter, 302
Erie, Lake, 19, 27, 34, 35, 86, 112, 128, 132, 133, 173, 188, 207, 240, 248, 291, 305
Erie Barge Canal, 288
Erie Shoal, 34
Erie Wrecks, 27, 207, 311
Erwin, Alfie, 107
Erwin, Harry, 107

Father Point (Ste-Anne-de-la-Pointe-au-Père), 66, 282
Feltner, Dr. Chuck, 19
Ferguson, T.A., 170
Finland, 64, 105
Folkes, Patrick, 25, 114
Foote, Captain James B., 72, 136
Foote, Captain N., 137
Forbes, Kim, 24
Ford Motor Company, 51
Ford, Reverend James E. (Victoria Street Methodist Church), 106
Forrest, "Big" Bill, 195, 199, 200, 300
Fort William (Thunder Bay), Ontario, 45, 55, 57, 63, 67, 69, 72, 86, 105, 108, 111, 139, 146, 159, 172, 284
Fotheringham, Reverend James Boath (later Archdeacon of Huron), 106, 117, 118
France, 62, 64, 65, 105, 303
Friends of the Wexford, 12, 26, 233, 243
Fulford, Captain Laird, 28

Gardiner, Glen I., 13, 25, 241
Gaunt, Murray, 237
Geddes, Captain William Alfred, 136
Gemeinhardt, Phil, 28, 91, 98, 99, 162
Georgia–Florida line, 126

Index

Georgian Bay, 66, 69–71, 73, 128, 169, 199, 205

Germany, 64, 105

Gildersleeve, Mr. H.H., 167

Gillham, Skip, 105, 289, 290

Gillians, Ralph, 107

Gilpin, Mayor ___, 108, 113

Glazier, Sharilyn, 176

Goderich, Ontario, 11–13, 17, 25, 30, 31, 39, 40, 46, 48–51, 56, 66, 67, 69–73, 76, 80, 81, 84, 85, 87–90, 92–94, 97, 99, 104–07, 110–14, 118–20, 122, 124, 128, 130, 133, 134, 137, 155, 160, 162, 166–68, 170, 172, 173, 175–200, 202, 205–09, 212, 213, 223, 228, 237, 238, 241, 243, 245–48, 264–66, 271, 272, 277, 280, 284, 286, 288, 291, 292, 295, 296, 298, 299, 301–03

Goderich, Township of (Huron County), 158

Goderich Bone Yard, 264

Goderich Coroner's Inquest, 71

Goderich Elevator(s), Elevator and Transit Company, 13, 49, 87, 159, 166, 185, 188, 296, 298

Goderich Harbour, 18, 31, 36, 70, 71, 84, 86, 88, 94, 110, 112, 128, 129, 171, 173, 177, 179, 189, 191–93, 196–200, 204, 205, 262, 264, 265, 269, 276, 298, 300, 301, 304, 305

Goderich Inquest, 24, 44, 70, 86, 93, 107, 126, 156, 173, 175–200, 277, 280, 285

Goderich Marine Heritage Committee, 17, 23, 24, 40, 45, 50, 193, 202, 212, 265

Goderich Marine Heritage Festival, 27

Goderich Port Management Corporation, 196

Gozzard, Ted and Jan, 263

GPS (Global Positioning System), 19, 85, 174, 193, 212, 214, 246, 302

Graham, Doug, 28, 110

Grand Bend, Ontario, 12, 26, 40, 45–47, 49, 100, 106, 107, 109, 155, 160, 162, 201, 204, 213, 228, 232–34, 246, 261, 263, 192

Grand Bend Cemetery, 107, 155

Gray, William, 267, 268

Great Lakes, 12, 13, 19, 20, 25, 26, 31, 37, 39, 40, 46, 49, 51, 55, 60, 63, 68, 73, 101, 105, 106, 116, 117, 128, 131, 132, 135, 136, 141, 142, 171, 181, 190, 205, 213, 229, 236, 239, 243–47, 250, 251, 262, 276, 281, 306, 307

Great Lakes Engineering Works (Ecorse), 55

Great Lakes Historical Society, 204

Great Lakes Shipwreck Research Group, 232

Great Lakes Towing Co., 71

Great Storm of 1913, 12, 13, 19, 28, 39, 42, 45, 46, 54, 63, 84, 107, 111, 114, 116, 118, 120, 122, 123, 125, 127, 130, 142, 144, 146, 177, 204, 212, 223, 229, 233, 236–39, 243, 251, 262, 272, 276, 282, 285, 288, 301, 312

Great War (First World War), 31

Greenwood, John O., 57

Grindstone City, Michigan, 275

Hager, Reverend William K. (North Street Methodist Church, Goderich), 106

Hall, Phil, 278

Hamilton, Ontario, 57, 63, 77, 266, 300

Hamilton, Patricia, 24

Harbor Beach, *see also* Sand Beach, Michigan, 87, 137, 144, 147, 166, 183, 299

Harty, Peter, 185

Haslip, Reverend Edward C., 90, 92, 155, 163, 206, 207, 285

Hawley, Jan, 17, 24, 50, 51, 193, 202, 209, 212

Hay Lake (Lake Nicolet), 73, 79, 85, 284

Hendrick, Elgin, 106

Hensall, Ontario, 99, 107, 159, 289

Hicks, "Farmer," 98

Hicks, Leonard, 99, 162

Hicks, Maurice, 163

Hicks, Maurice Sr., 99

Hicks' Farm, 98, 99, 162

Hillsboro (Hillsborough) Beach, 206

Holland, 64, 105

Homan, Jo-Anne, 11

Homan, Keith, 11, 25, 51, 214, 221, 288

Homan Beach, 265

Homan Inlet Marina (Goderich), 215

Hotel Bedford (Goderich), 134

Hudson, R.M., 67

Hughes, Mike, 27, 206, 301

Humphries, Bill, 27, 204–06, 301

Hunt, Ray, 226

Hunter, Dr. Archibald Cross (Coroner), 126, 156, 158, 176–78, 183, 189

Hunter, James "Jim," 128

Hunter, J.B., 119

Huron, County of, 30, 133, 136, 237, 251, 252, 261, 262

Huron, Lake, 11, 17, 18, 31, 37, 40, 45, 46, 48, 50, 66, 69–71, 76, 78, 85, 91, 93, 101, 109, 118, 124, 128, 129, 132, 133,

135–37, 141, 142, 146, 149, 151, 155, 160, 161, 163, 165, 169–71, 173, 182, 190–93, 200, 204, 217, 219, 225, 232, 237, 239, 243, 245, 246, 248, 261, 262, 265, 271, 272, 285, 286, 288, 299, 301, 305
Huron County Courthouse, 175
Huron County Crown Office, 176
Huron County Historical Society, 30, 50, 131
Huron County Museum and Historic Gaol (Goderich), 24, 76, 205, 206, 223, 230, 233, 237, 250–53, 283, 302
Huron County Pioneer Museum (Goderich), 301
Huron Institute Collection (Collingwood Museum), 28, 49
Huron Tract, see Canada Company
Hywel-Jones, Merilyn, 29

Iliad of Homer, The, 127
Imperial Measurement, 43
Interlake Line (Toronto), 76
Interlake Steamship Company (Cleveland), 157, 275
Irish-American Fenian Raids, 56
Irish Rebellion, 1798, 61
Irish Tour, 1649–50, 60

Jamieson, Gordon, 87, 284
Jennings, William T., 189
Jewell, Duncan and Linda, 12
Johnston, Chris, 189
Johnston, Percy, 114
Johnstone, Captain Frank, 173, 188

Kanaby, Ed, 87
Kelly, John D., 178, 179

Kettle Point, 90, 92, 99, 100, 107, 110, 134, 154, 160, 206, 289, 299
Killoran, Mr. J.L., 177
Kincardine, Ontario, 90, 106, 134, 202, 261, 263, 265, 266, 278, 285
Kingsbridge, Ontario, 263
Kingston, Ontario, 24, 76, 160, 227
Kingston Marine Museum, see Marine Museum of the Great Lakes
Knox, Loftus Lin (Town Clerk), 185
Knox Presbyterian Church (Goderich), 111, 115, 118, 122, 128, 205, 241, 301
Kohl, Cris, 25
Kovacevic, Terry, 233

La Salle, Sieur de René-Robert Cavelier, 20
Laanela, Erika, 302
Labour Day Wreck, 17, 265
Lake Carriers' Association, 84, 86, 103, 114, 128, 130, 134, 143, 149, 151, 157, 167, 168, 170, 177, 277, 281, 283, 294–96
Lake Huron Centre for Coastal Conservation, 286, 288
Lake Nicolet, see Hay Lake
Lake Valley Grove, 302
Lakes Disaster Fund of Canada, 117, 118, 167
Lambton, County of, 176
Lambton Heritage Museum, 206, 233
Landon, Fred, 39, 276
L'Anse-St-Jean, Quebec, 266
Laviolette, Ralph, 107
LCD (liquid crystal display), 85
Leamington, Ontario, 90
Lee, Ron, 27
Legate, Tim, 234
Leonard, Albert "Ab," 196, 239
Leonard, Captain William, 11

Lewis, Edward, Norman "E.N." (MP), 114, 170, 171, 173, 194
Lewis, Walter, 25, 26, 262
Lexington, Michigan, 208, 228, 231, 232
Lime Island, 71, 78, 137, 182, 282
Limerick, Ireland, 60
Liverpool, England, 29, 57, 281
Lloyd's Register, 13, 57, 63, 269
London, England, 13, 29, 57, 62, 63, 65, 98, 105, 292, 303
London, Ontario, 27, 46, 111, 134, 207, 232, 260
Long Point, 137, 222
Loran C [lo(ng-)ra(nge) n(avigation)], 19
Lougheed, Mr. A.H., 109
Lyons, Captain Stephen A., 144–47

MacAdam, Ian, 231, 304
MacDonald, Allan, 266
MacDonald, Bert, 266
MacDonald, Bruce, 266
MacDonald, Donald, 112
Macdonald, Jim, 205, 301
MacDonald, John A., 291
MacDonald, John Malcolm, 291
Macdonald, Judy, 111
MacDonald (McDonald), Malcolm, 111, 112
MacDonald, Reddy, 31
Macdonald, Ronald "Roddy," 111
MacDonald Marine (Goderich), 196, 304
Mackley, Howard, 132
Magnetic and Meteorological Observatory (Toronto), 124
Maitland Cemetery (Goderich), 105, 106, 111, 119, 238, 239
Maitland Inlet Marina, 209
Maitland River, 195, 198, 262, 265, 299, 303

Index

Maitland Valley Conservation Authority, 299

Maitland Valley Marina, 209, 302

Manore, Christopher Columbus "Cub," 47

Manore, John, 47

Manual of Seamanship, 268

Marine Museum of the Great Lakes (Kingston), 111, 115, 118, 122, 128, 205, 241, 301

Marlton Shipyard (Goderich), 195, 266, 291

Marquette, Michigan, 138

Maxwell, Harold, 113

Maxwell, Mary Jane Scott, 113

McCarthy, Captain Patrick D., *also seen as* D. Patrick McCarthy, 188

McConkey:
Amanda, 76–77
Amy, *see* Amy McConkey McKerman
Bert, 76
Captain Edward, 75, 76, 283

McDonald:
Angus, 111, 112
Annie (Mrs. Norman Sr.), 111
Daniel, 111, 112
Lorne "Husky," 111, 112
Malcolm, 111, 112
Murdock, 110, 111, 154, 291, 295
Norman Jr., 111, 112
Norman Sr., 111, 112
Pearly, 112
Roy "Plug," 111, 112

McDonald, Captain ___, 266

McDonald, John, 111

McDonald, Captain Malcolm, 88, 110

McDonald, Roderick, 110, 291, 291

McDonald, Ronald, 110

McGraw, Robert, 205

McGreevy, Robert "Bob," 11, 12, 25, 26, 321

McIlwain, Walter, 114, 293

McInnes, Mr. A.M., 183, 184

McInnes, Walter, 77

McIntosh, Arz, 131

McKernan, Amy McConkey, 76, 283

McLean, Fran, 241

McLellan, Stan, 25

McLeod, Dan, 178

McLeod, Ken, 23, 282

McLlwain, Robert, 189

McNaughton, Honourable Charles, 237

Merchants Mutual Line (Toronto), 157, 283

Michigan, Lake, 128, 133, 142, 240, 266

Michigan, State of, 46, 55, 87, 111, 132, 138, 141, 143, 157, 208, 228, 232, 266, 275

Michigan Department of Natural Resources, 232

Michipicoten Island, 137

Millar, Dr. Peter McLean, 27

Mills, Dr. Frank, 237

Ministry of Citizenship, Culture and Recreation (Ontario), 23, 49, 217, 223, 233, 248, 249, 301–03, 307

Mixter, Ric, 284

Mogelstine, Captain Knox, 62

Montreal, Quebec, 13, 57, 63, 65, 66, 281

Moore, Blanche, 74

Moore, Harry, 137, 138

Mooretown, Ontario, 204, 301

Mooretown Township Museum, 205, 206

Munday, Captain Albert Roy, 25, 31, 32, 42, 99, 142, 162

Munday, Bertram Roy, 31

Munnings, Benjamin C., 193

Murphy, Patrick "Pat," 204, 225, 301

Naftel, Charles James Slocombe, 89

Naftel, Knyvet (Knevitt), 89, 95, 97, 158

National Association of Underwater Instructors (NAUI), 303

Newcastle-On-Tyne, England, 63

Newspapers/journals/ magazines:
Collingwood Enterprise, 71, 72
Detroit Post and Tribune, 67
Great Lakes Weekly, 300
Huron Signal (Goderich), 198, 265
Inland Seas (Vermillion, Ohio), 204
Lake Log Chips (Center for Archival Collections, Bowling Green State University, Ohio), 207
Namesakes (Freshwater Press, Cleveland), 57
Saturday Evening News (Collingwood), 72
Smith's Canada, 197
The Collingwood Bulletin, 57, 63, 66, 94, 116, 154, 167, 290, 292, 297
The Detroit Free Press, 108, 165, 296
The Detroit News, 85
The Globe and Mail (Toronto), 103
The Goderich Signal-Star, 45, 204, 301
The London Evening Free Press, 209
The London Free Press, 88, 89, 99, 104, 105, 136, 284
The Owen Sound Sun Times, 108, 282
The Owen Sound Times, 128
The Port Huron Times-Herald, 155, 276, 295
The Saturday News (Collingwood), 108
The Sault Ste. Marie

Evening News, 156, 282
The Signal (Goderich),
  105, 115, 175, 189, 291,
  292, 297
The Star (Goderich),
  175
Village Squire
  (Brussels), 131
Ney, Captain C.R., 295
Nieuwland, William, 12, 26,
  321
Niven, William, 87, 88
Normans, 60
Northcastle Marine
  Boatyards (Goderich),
  263
Norway, 64, 105
NUMA (National
  Underwater and Marine
  Agency), 21, 275

Ontario, Lake, 305
Ontario Heritage Act, 255,
  256, 258, 259, 303
Ontario Hockey Association,
  74
Ontario Provincial Police,
  257
Owen, John, 295

Padfield, John, 226
Padfield, Dr. Paul, 27, 215,
  223, 224, 226, 231, 233
Panghorn, Michigan, 266
Parliamentary Load Line
  Committee, 267
Parsons, Benjamin, 296
Parsons, George, 185, 296,
  298
Parsons, Captain James G.,
  296
Parsons, Lionel George
  "G.L.," 159, 166, 185,
  188, 296, 298
Peever, Dick, 18
Pemberton, Chris, 25
Pennington, Lenna, 160, 241
Pennington, Ron, 160, 240,
Pie Island, 33, 275
Playter, Captain George, 72,
  78, 128, 180, 182
Plimsoll, Samuel, 267

Plimsoll Marks, 267, 269
Plymouth, England, 62
Point Aux Barques, 266
Point Clark, 49, 73, 80, 87, 93,
  154, 162, 187, 202, 261,
  263, 265, 266, 277, 303
Point Edward, Ontario, 90,
  92, 97, 154, 155, 160,
  162, 163, 206
Pope, Alexander, 293
Port Albert, Ontario, 263, 265
Port Arthur (Thunder Bay),
  138
Port Austin, Michigan, 144,
  145
Port Austin Reef, 275, 285
Port Colborne, Ontario, 34
Port Dalhousie, 77
Port Dover, Ontario, 305
Port Dover Harbour
  Museum, 252
Port Franks, Ontario, 39,
  155, 160, 201, 245, 263
Port Huron, Michigan, 85,
  131, 132, 144, 165, 166,
  168, 228, 284
Port of Goderich, 69, 87, 171
Port Sanilac, Michigan, 228
Postill, Garth, 264
Potter, James B., 121
Poulter, Jay, 27, 47
Prince, Brian, 27, 255, 259
Propeller Club, *see*
  Southampton Propeller
  Club

Qua, Mrs. Alex (Bassett), 90

R.M. Hudson & Company
  (Sunderland, England),
  13, 279
Radiotelephone equipment,
  126
Repass, Randy, 305
Richardson, Captain
  William, 61
Richardson & Co.
  (Cleveland), 157
Rimouski County, Quebec,
  282
River Slaney, 60
River Tyne, 55

River Wear, 53, 55, 58, 242,
  244
Robinson, Captain C.E.
  "Bud," 2, 11–13, 26, 29,
  142, 276, 279, 321
Robinson, Dean, 131, 142
Robinson, Captain Edward,
  173, 188
Robinson, Jeanette, 26
Robinson, Walter, 292
Robinson, Captain William,
  89, 178, 184–86, 188,
  297, 298
Root, F.D., 71
Ross, Reverend George E.,
  106, 111, 117, 120
Rowell, Newton Wesley, 168
Royal Canadian Navy, 31,
  142
Ruffle, William, 87, 88
Rydal Bank, Ontario, 292

Salkeld, Harry, 189
Salkeld, Isaac, 189
Salkeld, John W., 189
Sallows, Reuben R., 12
Sand Beach, Michigan, *see
  also* Harbor Beach, 87,
  183, 299
Sarnia, Ontario, 70, 114,
  134, 139, 154, 166, 183,
  204, 205, 228, 295, 296,
  299, 301
Sarnia Reserve, Chippewas
  of Sarnia First Nation,
  159
Sault River, 137, 138
Sault Ste. Marie, Michigan,
  111, 143, 156, 282
Sault Ste. Marie, Ontario, 72,
  108, 157
Sault Ste. Marie Museum, 24
Save Ontario Shipwrecks
  (SOS), 27, 171, 209,
  230, 233, 234, 255, 259,
  302, 304
  Huron Shores SOS, 46,
  50, 233, 265
Schaus, Paul, 27, 51, 58, 213,
  214, 221, 304
Schelken, Dave, 233
Scotch boilers, 55, 57, 69

Index

Scott, Captain Frank, 109,
188, 298
Scott, Professor James "Jim,"
237
Scott, Mike, 27
Seager, Charles A., 177,
183–87
Shark Marine, 262
Shaw, Melissa, 24
Shellenberger, Lorraine, 393
Ship Island, 195, 199, 291,
300
Ships:
Abercorn (propeller,
wood), 264
Annamac (tug), 264,
266
Anne (schooner), 265
Argus (steamer), 25, 40,
90, 111, 157, 239, 266,
275, 278, 285
Arthur Orr (steamer),
127
Atlantic (side-wheel
steamer), 235, 248, 252,
305
Azov (schooner), 266
Blue Fin (research tug),
302
C.C. Ryan (steamer),
266
Canadian Navigator
(bulk cargo), 269
Charles S. Price
(steamer), 106, 131, 132,
155, 157, 239
Chelmsford (barque),
100
Cherub (gunboat), 56
City of Midland
(steamer), 85
City of Ottawa
(steamer), 136
Clinton (steamer), 265
Collingwood (steamer),
109, 188
Corunna (steamer), 55
D. Ferguson (schooner
barge), 266
Danel Mac (tug), 18,
213
Dover (tug), 304

Dredge #1, 266
Dundee (steamer), 12
Edmund Fitzgerald
(bulk freighter), 33, 42,
93, 146, 259, 275
Elise (steamer, packet
freighter), see also
Wexford, 29, 49, 57, 62
Empress (of Fort
William) (steamer), 159
Evening Star (schooner),
265
Fairmount (propeller),
138, 186
Fannie Campbell
(schooner), 266
Fashion (side-wheel
steamer), 266
General Hunter (brig,
RN), 263
G.C. Crawford
(steamer), 285
G.R. Crowe (steamer),
173, 188
Germanic (passenger
steamer), 72
Gilly (cargo freighter),
266
Griffon (barque), 20,
261
H.B. Hawgood
(steamer), 73, 87
H.B. Smith (steamer),
138, 149, 157, 239
H.M. Hanna Jr.
(steamer), 144, 157
Halifax (steamer), 279
Hamilton (schooner),
235, 259, 305
Hamonic (steamer), 136,
139
Horton (tug), 89, 91, 97,
134
Hurd (Coast Guard
cutter), 231, 305
Huronic (steamer), 122,
138
Hydrus (steamer), 40,
149, 157, 239, 266, 275,
285
I.L. Quiney (unknown),
265

India (steamer), 265
Isaac M. Scott
(steamer), 157, 239
J.A. McKee (steamer),
12, 63
J.F. Durston (steamer),
133
J.H. Sheadle (steamer),
144, 146
J.S. Minor (schooner),
266
J.T. Wing (lumber
schooner), 31, 32
John A. McGean, 97, 157,
158, 162, 184, 186, 239
James Carruthers
(steamer), 25, 33, 40,
49, 90, 129, 142, 145,
146, 149, 157, 162, 186,
239, 262, 265, 266, 277,
303
Kaministiquia (steamer)
(also Kaministiqua), 73,
80, 87, 130, 172, 187,
191
L.C. Waldo (steamer),
157
Lambton (revenue
cutter), 134
Leafield (steamer), 109,
113, 149, 157, 239, 268,
294
Lewis Hotchkiss (barge),
266
Lightship No. 82, 157,
240
Lynda (also Linda)
Hyndman (tug), 263,
264
Louisiana (steamer),
157
Lurline (steamer), 265
Malta (schooner), 263
Marine City
(schooner), 265
Mariska (steamer), 202,
300
Mary Watson
(schooner), 265
Matoa (steamer), 157,
138
Merida (steamer), 291

Midland King (steamer), 138

Minnedosa (schooner), 46

Nashua (lumber hooker), 266

Neeping (steamer), 12

Nemesis (schooner), 266

Olga (schooner), 264

Ottawa (naval destroyer), 31

Paipoonge (steamer), 137

Paliki (steamer), 12

Phenix (steamer), 266

Phillips (tug), 264

Plymouth (barge), 157, 239

Price (steamer), 155

Rathbun, 264

Regina (steamer), 75, 77, 92, 149, 155, 157, 163, 239, 283, 289, 295

Rockaway (schooner), 265

Rumrunner (motor yacht), 213–15

S.N. Parent (steamer), 173, 188

Saguenay (steamer), 279

Scotia (wood propeller), 264

Scourge (schooner), 235, 259, 305

Sheadle, 146

Superior (tug), 266

Sweepstakes (schooner), 234

Tecumseth (also *Tecumseh*) (schooner), 264

Turret Cape (steamer), 12, 188

Turret Chief (steamer), 12, 13, 84, 111, 157

Victoria K. (fishing tug), 72

W.L. Forrest (tug), 12, 264

Wales (tug), 266

Wexford (steamer), 2, 11–13, 17, 18, 20, 23–29,

32, 39–42, 45–51, 53–74, 85–88, 90–101, 103–14, 127–31, 142, 144, 146, 149, 154, 155, 157, 159, 162, 163, 166, 172, 179–87, 189, 191, 193, 201–09, 211–39, 243–48, 251, 252, 256, 261, 265, 267, 268, 277–79, 281, 282, 284–86, 288, 289, 292, 294, 298, 300–03

Willis King (steamer), 85

Winona (steamer), 138

Shulman of Buffalo, 158

Siddal, Ed, 205, 264

Sloggett, Captain James, 62, 281

Smith, Geo. L., 158

Smith, George, 295

Smith, Jeremy, 20

Smith, Milton, 131

Smith, Brigadier Morgan, 264

Snug Harbour (Goderich Harbour), 194, 199

Sombra, Ontario, 76, 295

Soo, *see* Sault Ste. Marie

Soo Locks, 125

SOS, *see* Save Ontario Shipwrecks

South America, 61, 62

Southampton, Ontario, 114, 123, 124, 199, 263

Southampton Propeller Club, 123, 124, 141

Spar deck, 55, 57–61, 63, 70, 94, 95, 227, 268, 279, 280, 287, 304

Spears, Mike, 25, 311

St. Clair River, 84, 92, 132, 138, 183, 188, 205, 299

St. Clair Shores Library, 232

St. George's Anglican Church (Goderich), 117

St. Joseph, Ontario, 90, 93, 97, 99, 106, 107–09, 111, 113, 154, 162, 163, 201, 204, 209, 217, 225, 237, 263, 285

St. Joseph Island, 282

St. Lawrence River, 282

St. Mary's River, 132, 155, 180, 282

Stayer, Jim, 27, 208, 231

Stayer, Pat, 27, 231

Ste-Anne-de-la-Pointe-au-Père, Quebec, 282

Stephen, Captain ___, 87, 191, 284

Stone, Thomas, 158, 159, 189, 191, 295

Storm signals, 12, 124, 125, 128, 191

Stowe, Henry, 159, 178

Straits of Mackinac, 132

Sturdy, Harry, 167

Sturdy, Karen, 24, 156

Sturdy, Peter, 25, 177, 297

Sullivan, Dan, 25

Sunderland, England, 24, 29, 45, 49, 53, 55, 57, 58, 61, 66, 67, 84, 162, 242–44

Superior, Lake, 13, 33, 69, 79, 84, 85, 113, 114, 122, 125, 128, 131–33, 139, 140, 142, 149, 151, 180, 239, 243, 275, 294

Swan, Hunter & Richardson (Co.), 63

Swayze, David, 25, 261, 262

Talbot, Anne, 93, 285

Talbot, Edward Leonard, 93, 163

Talbot, Harry, 93, 163

Taleski, Doug, 27, 260

Taylor, John W., 186, 187

Taylor's Grove, 97

Thedford, Ontario, 90, 100, 107, 134, 176, 289

35th Regiment Bugle Band, 110

Thomas, Dan, 27, 218–21, 303

Thomas, Captain George, 63, 66

Thompson, James, 12

Thompson, Reg, 24, 292

Thompson Steamship Company (Cleveland), 157

Three Sisters, 142, 151, 182, 294

Thunder Bay, 69, 78

Thunder Bay Harbour, 139

Index

Thunder Bay Island, 146

Thunder Cape, 139

Tobermory, Ontario, 26, 114, 142, 167, 234, 296

Top-hamper, 35, 143, 295

Toronto, Ontario, 63, 72, 76, 77, 121, 124, 157, 167, 172, 191, 243, 249

Townsend, Robert B., 294

Trotter, David L., 21, 25, 40, 41, 46–48, 202, 208, 209, 212, 213, 221, 232, 262, 264, 275, 277, 289

Trotter, Mickey, 51

Turnbull, Robert, 90, 99, 106, 135, 153, 154, 227, 285

Turner, Harold, 237

Tween deck, 56, 61, 70, 97, 220, 227, 280, 304, 307

Tyne & Wear Archives, 58, 278

Undersea Research Associates, 21, 25, 40, 46, 208, 212, 232, 262

University of Western Ontario, 24, 39

Upper Canada Tract Society's Mission to Sailors, 122, 123

Upper Lakes, 66, 67, 135, 172, 188, 192

Vikings, 60

Wachter, Mike and Georgann, 25, 27, 207, 312

Walker, Captain Thomas, 61

Wallace, Dorothy, 311

Walthamstow, England, 292

Waterford, Ireland, 60

Watters, Dr. William "Bill" N., 2

Watts, Captain James B., 133

Weichel, John, 25

Welland Canal, 54, 186

Western Canada Flour Mills (Goderich), 186

Western Steamship Co. Ltd., 57, 58, 63–67, 70, 71–72, 105, 157, 227, 243, 277, 280

Westlake Mortuary (Zurich), 90

Wexford, see Ships

Wexford Crew

Allan, Gordon (crew), 113

Berwin, Walter (crew), 113

Brooks, Archibald (Second Mate/Acting First Mate), 108, 154, 290

Caesar "Cesare," Solliere (deckhand), 80, 113

Cameron, Frank Bruce (Captain), 43, 73–75, 77, 85, 87, 90, 92, 94, 95, 97, 99, 100, 105–108, 110, 146, 154, 155, 182, 220, 277, 282, 283, 289, 303, 304

Dodson, Allan (watchman), 109, 154, 290

Ferguson, ___ (Acting Second Mate), 108

Flynn, James (crew), 113

Glen(n), James (crew), 112, 113, 153, 154, 293

Gordon, Orin (wheelsman), 109, 290

Lougheed, Richard "Victor" (Second Engineer), 100, 109, 154, 290

Maxwell, Jim (crew), 113

McCutcheon, James (First Mate), 108, 290

McDonald, Donald (crew), 88, 106, 110, 154, 291, 295

McDonald, Murdoch (Murdock) (passenger), 110, 111, 154, 291, 295

Peere, George (crew), 113, 290

Peters, Charles (crew), 113

Rogers, ___ (Second Officer, as listed

in undated news clipping), 108, 290

Scott, James "Jimmie" George (Chief Engineer), 109, 154, 290, 298

Spiers (Speers), Thomas (crew), 113

Wilmot(t), George (cook), 79, 94, 112, 154, 290, 292

Wilmot(t), Mrs. George (stewardess), 112, 290, 292

Wexford Town, England, 60, 81

Whitefish Bay, 140

Whitefish Point, 122, 137, 138

Whitehouse, Daisy May, 31

Whitney, Captain Edward Orsen, 84, 86, 170, 177, 283

Whitney, Sir James P., 168, 296

Wicklow, Ireland, 60

Wiener, F.E., 170

Wilke, Steve, 27

William Doxford & Sons Boatyards, 45, 53, 57, 58, 61, 67, 84, 244, 278

Wilson, Mel, 29

Wilson, Captain Robert, 204, 205, 301

Wilson, Robin, 27, 51, 213

Wilson, Lieutenant W.J., 297

Wingfield, Jocelyn, 29

Winsor, Hank, 25, 88

Wisconsin Marine Historical Society, 25, 144, 312

Woodhall Funeral Home (Thedford), 134

Young, Anna G., 136, 139, 294, 311

Young, Hugh "Father" (Purser), 139

Zurich, Ontario, 90, 99, 100, 107, 154

ABOUT THE ARTISTS

Captain C. "Bud" Robinson. Robinson's cover painting of the *Wexford, The Last Sighting,* is but one of his hundreds of sketches, gray scale renditions, and dramatic oil paintings of historic lakers that have plied the Great Lakes. His collection includes schooners and older vessels of historic significance. Bud's work is well-known in maritime circles across North America. He is a Canadian artist, now residing near Tobermory, Ontario, and hails from a family of marine artists, all of whom conducted their craft while piloting these great ships as masters. Bud's great-grandfather was the lightkeeper at the time of the Great Storm of 1913. You can see Bud's work at *marineimages.50megs.com.*

Robert McGreevy. A well-known American marine artist from Michigan, McGreevy's dramatic paintings *Wexford Under Sail* and *Wexford As She Sits Today* represent but two of his fine marine artworks. In all, McGreevy has completed more than 300 paintings of Great Lakes ships, encompassing all periods of ship design and development. For the past three years, Bob has worked almost exclusively in oils, using this medium to produce a new series of paintings under the title *Lost Legends of the Lakes.* His wonderful work can be found at *www.mcgreevy.com.*

William Nieuwland. Another Canadian artist, Nieuwland, from the Grand Bend area, is a well-known Ontario painter who has won accolades for his work. Born in 1944 in a small rural town in Holland, Bill remembers drawing clouds reflected in shimmering waters as early as age seven. With a photographer's eye for realism, he excels in depicting unexpected detail in his paintings. He is most often the winner of "viewers' choice" awards at public art exhibitions. His work is meticulous and conveys images of the waterfront environment in a surrealistic style. His dramatic painting of the *Wexford* in her final moments was completed right after the long missing wreck was found in 2000. Bill's work can be found at *www.theartistbill.com.*

Paul Carroll with a Wexford *lifeboat oar.*
Photo by Mary Carroll.

Paul Carroll grew up as a "wharf rat." He had the privilege of gamming with the last of the "old salts" from Goderich Harbour. His first part-time job was working on the fishing tug *Larry John*, for Ab and Florence Leonard. He ventured by rowboat, with his childhood friend and fellow fishing chum, the late Larry Atfield, to explore Ship Island, at the back end of Goderich Harbour — the home of shipyards and ship chandlers for more than a hundred years. He and his buddy scrambled through the tangled vines and sumac that hid the harbour-side graveyard for derelict schooners and tugs, relics from the heyday of sail and steam.

His interest in the waterfront has persisted. As a member of council and reeve for the town of Goderich in the early 1970s, he brought forward the first comprehensive Waterfront Development Plan for the long-term evolution of the shoreline — an underutilized resource. He has edited a set of notes to outline our marine heritage for the Huron County Historical Society and assisted in the placing of plaques for a marine heritage walkway along the Goderich waterfront. Paul was involved in the side-scan sonar search for the long-missing shipwreck, the *Wexford*, and he continues the ongoing search for the *James Carruthers* as time permits. He has acted as collaborator and co-author/editor with fellow sailor and marine historian Don Bamford for two marine books: *Freshwater Heritage: A History of Sailing on the Great Lakes, 1670–1918* and *Four Years on the Great Lakes: The Journal of Lieutenant David Wingfield, RN.*

Paul's first contact with a shipwreck was in the 1950s, on a primitive electromechanical depth sounder on the fish tug *Larry John*, while setting the nets somewhere southwest of Goderich. The location was not clear. An almost perfect silhouette presented itself in the roll of graph paper streaming out of the machine. "I still remember it clearly," says Paul.

For commercial fishermen, these images were places to avoid — but what difference would it make then to a 10-year-old? After all, if Ab Leonard said it was a place to avoid, then it was most obviously a place to avoid! Ab travelled long distances when the fishing was poor and he needed to find the catch. He even risked setting his nets in some deeper water, found just over the invisible border, on the American side.

Only the memory of that graven shipwreck image — not the location — was burned into Paul's mind.

Is it possible that early passage over a shipwreck was his first encounter with the *Wexford*?

Also by Paul Carroll

Four Years on the Great Lakes, 1813–1816
*The Journal of Lieutenant David Wingfield,
Royal Navy*
Don Bamford and Paul Carroll
978-1-55488-393-6 $28.99 £16.99

David Wingfield joined the Royal Navy at age
fourteen and his service took him to the Great
Lakes during the War of 1812. This account of
the war, as seen through the eyes of a young
seaman, provides a fascinating snapshot of
people and places during this turning point in
the history of the Great Lakes.

Of Related Interest

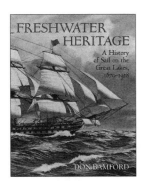

Freshwater Heritage
A History of Sail on the Great Lakes, 1670–1918
Don Bamford
978-1-89704-520-6 $34.95 £17.99

Freshwater Heritage represents the culmination
of a lifelong passion for sailing and for the
history of sail as it applies to Canada. Author,
sailor, and boat builder Don Bamford takes
us deep into the psyche of sailing as it applies
to historical events on the Great Lakes and to
stories of the people and places of the time.

Lake Erie Stories
Struggle and Survival on a Freshwater Ocean
Chad Fraser
978-1-55002-782-2 $24.99 £13.00

Lake Erie is the shallowest and second smallest
of the Great Lakes, but it is also mysterious,
unpredictable, and known by mariners for its
sudden violent weather and dangerous shoals.
The lake has been the stage for some of the
most dramatic events ever to occur on the
North American continent. This fascinating
book takes the reader inside the remarkable
personalities and harrowing events that have
shaped the lake and the towns and cities that
surround it.

Available at your favourite bookseller.

DUNDURN PRESS
www.dundurn.com

What did you think of this book?
Visit www.dundurn.com for reviews, videos, updates, and more!